The Internet of Things

Ulrich Sendler
Editor

The Internet of Things

Industrie 4.0 Unleashed

Springer Vieweg

Editor
Ulrich Sendler
München, Germany

Translated by Connect-Sprachenservice GmbH – Zweigniederlassung Regensburg, 93047 Regensburg, Germany

ISBN 978-3-662-54903-2 ISBN 978-3-662-54904-9 (eBook)
https://doi.org/10.1007/978-3-662-54904-9

Library of Congress Control Number: 2017958713

Translated from the German language edition: *Industrie 4.0 grenzenlos,* © Springer-Verlag Berlin Heidelberg 2016.
Springer Vieweg

Printed on acid-free paper

This Springer Vieweg imprint is published by Springer Nature
The registered company is Springer-Verlag GmbH Germany
The registered company address is: Heidelberger Platz 3, 14197 Berlin, Germany

Preface

You are looking at a very special book. It is not a new edition of my first book on Industrie 4.0. It not only expands upon the information on the phenomenon known both domestically as well as in several other countries as the fourth industrial revolution; it also examines an abundance of questions having less to do with technology than with the consequences of technological development for humans, society and, yes, even nature. In a certain sense, it is also a political book about the industry of the future. And it ventures a glance back at the history of the industrial revolution(s), because knowing where we have come from is the best way for us to understand where we might be heading.

It is also a special book because it is certainly unique in having an official Chinese organization such as Xinhuanet contribute Chap. 7, which illuminates the Industrie 4.0 initiative from a Chinese perspective, compares it to the program "Made in China 2025" and illustrates not only the current development status but also China's strategic goals in pursuing that program. I would like to especially thank the CEO of Xinhuanet in Beijing, Tian Shubin, for his contribution. As is the case with the other authors' chapters, you will find a great variety of opinions, perspectives and assessments with regard to the industry of the future which do not necessarily represent the opinion of the editor. However, taken together, they paint an insightful picture.

The title of this book, "The Internet of Things – Industrie 4.0 Unleashed" may seem rather flagrant, as if to say: Everything is turning Industrie 4.0 and everything will be fine!" Yet that would be a complete misunderstanding. True, the title is purposefully ambiguous, but the notion that the book has been generated as a marketing ploy is off the mark. On the contrary, it is precisely the boastful marketing slogans and comparable marketing events that are the object of critical observation. In the opinion of this editor, less pageantry would be better for everyone involved.

The first book on Industrie 4.0 which I edited was released in the German language in 2013, and in Chinese in 2014. This book, too, has been published in German and Chinese, and subsequently in English. Thus, the topic has truly been "unleashed" in every sense of the word, including breaking national boundaries.

The fourth industrial revolution, to which Industrie 4.0 refers, is seen around the world as the next step of industrialization. There are several similar initiatives in a number of countries, with an animated exchange of information between some, and even close cooperation between others. To be able to assess this global development and investigate its interconnections is one of the motives behind this book and its title.

Globalization, too, will play a new role in this technological transformation. When products all around the world are connected via the internet, when product data is generated, collected and processed on a global scale, new channels are created along which industry and business can communicate with one another. What is more, new services are evolving which can redefine the global role of individual suppliers. This change also means that companies can emerge internationally with ideas for new products and services that may pose a threat to established, long-standing local heroes once those new ideas start competing with the existing offerings.

Figuratively, Industrie 4.0 is "unleashed" because there are only very few sectors and areas of industry—if any—that are not affected. Digitalization has no borders, now encompassing all of industry. Much of what we are used to will be turned inside out, or, to be more precise, turned data-side out. We must understand this great change and accept the related challenges. This, too, is a focus of the book.

The topic has also been "unleashed" because industry now serves as one of the central players on the internet stage. Specifically, industrial products and associated services are becoming part of the global network, which extends even beyond the scope of long-since globalized trade and, by the way, will also drastically change it.

If you believe that Industrie 4.0 only concerns industry, you are seeing borders that do not exist; not only because almost everything that we use in daily life has been industrially developed and produced, but also because the digitalization of products and production has effects on areas of society and life which seem to have nothing at all to do with industry: health care and insurance, city administration and traffic, supply and demand—to name just a random few.

If, however, industrial development has such effects on virtually everything, then it seems logical that the environment, climate and the use of natural resources will also show effects. So, should we really view this topic as purely technical? Wouldn't it make more sense to influence at an early stage what shape it will take and what concrete effects should ideally result and not to wait around, only to set up borders in retrospect? So far, it has not proven practical to merely react to technical and technological innovations instead of taking part in their design. With the Internet of Things and Industrie 4.0, this would be downright dangerous: Development has picked up such a pace that even now it seems irresponsible just how late and how slowly we are getting into the discussion about its consequences.

Thus, it is completely justified to include the word "unleashed" in the title of this book. And its readers? Exactly who will read this book? To whom is it directed? Are its readers also "unleashed," uninhibited by borders (which, naturally, from the perspective of the editor and publisher, would be the best-case scenario, albeit a rarely achieved one)? Of course not.

Primarily, this book is intended for those playing the most active roles—for the people in charge of industry itself: management, product managers, leaders in research and development and technical directors. They all should become familiar with this topic inside and out, as they will need to deal with it in the coming years and perhaps decades; they should have a book on hand in which they can find serious proposals and answers to all important questions in this realm. At the very least, however, they should find in it the questions that will be raised and that they must inevitably ask themselves.

This book is also written for those who are involved with Industrie 4.0 out of political, professional, social or other reasons. They should be able to find a neutral place where no attempt is made to sell them anything else except for the offer to seriously focus on the topic.

In the realm of research and development as well as in education at public, private or business institutions, this book addresses readers on both sides: educators and researchers as well as learners and those involved in research projects. A good deal of written material already exists, but unfortunately still too little to be useful as learning material, regarding both factual and technical resources.

The various languages leave no doubt that this book also has an international readership in mind. Because the topic is being discussed around the world, there is a need for clarification of content on all continents. In China, interest is especially great for several reasons, which will be discussed in detail. This is not only evident in the impressive print run volume of the Chinese edition; it is also reflected in an examination of the initiatives in Germany and China, from two perspectives: the German and the Chinese point of view.

In the USA and other countries, interest levels are also high. Even though various approaches have been chosen, there is a great deal of consensus in the basic assessment regarding what will change and what needs to change in industry. This book will also contribute to that international debate.

While writing my own chapter and incorporating the contributions of authors from very different areas, I attached great importance to making the book easily accessible for all target groups mentioned: Even those readers who are not professionals in the area, who are neither engineers nor computer scientists nor production managers dealing with the digitalization of industry on a daily basis should understand what is on the experts' minds.

Quite simply, this book intends to meet relatively high expectations. Not only have the many authors helped this editor in aiming for those expectations with their contributions, without which several subareas could not have been covered. There are also a few important people whose assistance considerably contributed to the book's completion. As it turns out, in addition to freelance work as a technology analyst, technical author, speaker and consultant, producing the manuscript for such a tome is actually no easy task. My sister Jutta Sendler and my friends

Hartmut Streppel and Reiner Schönrock stood by my side consistently, reading, commenting and correcting. Their support was especially important to me regarding the question of whether the text was truly readable and comprehensible. I wish to express my heartfelt thanks for their efforts. I would also like to thank Anton Sebastian Huber who, although still working full-time as the CEO of Siemens Division Digital Factory until the end of May 2016, repeatedly helped me to connect the theoretical side with the necessary and possible elements of the practical side; not to mention that he also contributed a chapter of his own this time, too (Chap. 14).

What is the point of this book? To explain interconnections and clarify significant questions of industrial development, but also to spark interest and curiosity: Because Industrie 4.0 is far from being the purely technical topic it is thought to be in many circles. And it sheds light on many opportunities for industrial society which cannot be valued highly enough or followed intensively enough.

Munich
May 2016

Ulrich Sendler

Contents

List of Contributors

Prof. Dr.-Ing. Reiner Anderl, Born in 1955, he received his doctorate at the Technical University of Karlsruhe in 1984, worked in midsize companies (plant engineering) and was promoted to professor at the University of Karlsruhe in 1991. Since 1993, he has worked as a professor for data processing in construction in the mechanical engineering department of the Technical University of Darmstadt. From 1999–2001, he served as the dean of the Mechanical Engineering Department, and from 2001–2003 as the vice dean. From 2001 until the end of 2004, he was a spokesman for Special Research Area 392, "Development of Environmentally Sound Products." In May of 2005, he was appointed to the post of adjunct professor at the Virginia Polytechnic and State University, and in October of 2006, received a guest professorship at the Universidade Metodista (UNIMEP), Piracicaba, Brazil. From January 2005 to December 2010, he served as the vice president of the Technical University of Darmstadt. As of November 2009, he has been a member of the Academy of Sciences and Literature in Mainz, and since 2009, served as a member of the German Academy for Technical Sciences (acatech). He has been the vice president of the Academy of Sciences and Literature in Mainz since 2011. In June of 2013, he was elected as the spokesman for the scientific board of the *Plattform Industrie 4.0*, and re-elected in December of 2015.

Oleg Anokhin, Darmstadt, Germany.

Alexander Arndt, Darmstadt, Germany.

Thomas Damerau, Division Virtual Product Creation, Fraunhofer-Institute Production Systems and Design Technology, Berlin, Germany.

Dr.-Ing. Roman Dumitrescu, has been the CEO of "it's OWL Clustermanagement" since 2012, and as of 2016, the Director of the Fraunhofer Institute for Mechatronics Systems Design in Paderborn. After completing studies in mechatronics at the Friedrich Alexander University of Erlangen-Nuremberg, he served as a scientific assistant in the Department of Product Development at the Heinz Nixdorf Institute of the University of Paderborn. Under the direction of Professor Jürgen Gausemeier, he received his doctorate in the area of "Development Methods for Advanced Mechatronic Systems." From March of 2011 to December 2015, he initially served as the departmental manager of the Fraunhofer project group Mechatronics System Design in Paderborn.

Prof. Dr.-Ing., Martin Eigner, founded EIGNER + PARTNER GmbH in 1985, for which, ultimately in the form of an AG, he served as the chairman of the board of directors. From July 2001 to August 2003, he was the chairman of the supervisory board and CTO of EIGNER Inc. in Waltham, Massachusetts, the new headquarters. In 2003, the company was fused with Agile and sold to ORACLE in 2007. Mr. Eigner founded the consulting company ENGINEERING CONSULT in 2001, of which he has been the managing director since its inception.

After receiving his doctorate in 1980 at the Technical University of Karlsruhe, he served as the manager of the Technical Data Processing and Organization Division of the Robert Bosch GmbH. His focus lay in the realms of the technical data center, electronics predevelopment and microprocessor applications, rationalization, product clearance and product modification.

As of October 1, 2004, Dr. Eigner has held a chair in virtual product development at the Technical University of Kaiserslautern.

Since 1984, Dr. Martin Eigner has served as a guest lecturer in Karlsruhe, Sofia and Izmir. He volunteers in several industrial and professional associations. In 1985, he was awarded the honorary ring of the Association of German Engineers (VDI), in 1994 he was named honorary professor of the State of Baden-Württemberg, Germany, and in 1999 named an honorary professor of the University of Karlsruhe.

Dr. Christopher Ganz, Group Vice President Service R&D, ABB Technology Ltd., is responsible at ABB for supporting service aspects in research and development. After studying electrical engineering at the ETH Technical University in Zurich and receiving his doctorate in control engineering, he held various positions in research and development in the area of power plant control technology at ABB. Subsequently, he was responsible for the corporate research program Control and Optimization. In his current role at ABB headquarters in Zurich, Christopher Ganz manages corporate-wide projects in the realm of service technologies, including remote maintenance and IoT technologies.

Anton S. Huber, Chief Executive Officer of the Siemens AG, Digital Factory Division, born on January 6, 1951, in Mühldorf am Inn, Germany.

Anton S. Huber began his career at Siemens in 1979, in the Components Division. After holding various positions in business and technical areas, he had a leading role in the 1989 acquisition of Bendix Electronics in the USA and its subsequent integration into Siemens Automotive LP. In 1991, he became the president and CEO of Siemens Automotive LP in Detroit, Michigan.

In 1998, Anton S. Huber managed the integration of the Westinghouse business, acquired by Siemens and including conventional power plants, into the Power Generation Division. As of October 1, 1999, Huber was named as a member of the board of the A&D Division. He was responsible for product development and manufacture, as well as for business development in the region of Asia and the Pacific. In January of 2008, he became the CEO of the Siemens Industry Automation Division. As of October 2014, Mr. Huber has served as the CEO of the Digital Factory Division.

Kai Lindow, Division Virtual Product Creation, Fraunhofer-Institute Production Systems and Design Technology, Berlin, Germany.

Dr.-Ing., Jan Stefan Michels, is the manager of Standards and Technology Development of the Weidmüller Group, responsible for the areas of technology development for electronics, technical standards and process development. In cooperation with his team, he develops new technologies in industrial connectivity and automation for future applications, covering a spectrum stretching from transmission technology to industrial analytics. In addition, his tasks include actualizing and implementing standards for product functions and processes. Mr. Michels is a member of the Plattform Industrie 4.0 and Task Force 2, Research and Innovation, of the ZVEI (German Electrical and Electronic Manufacturers' Association) Steering Committee Industrie 4.0, and is also active in other relevant work groups in the environment of intelligent technical systems. Before his employment at Weidmüller, he was a scientific assistant at the Heinz Nixdorf Institute of the University of Paderborn, Germany, working in the realm of technology and innovation management.

Dr. Tanja Rückert, Responsible for the Digital Assets & Internet of Things (IoT) line of business at SAP SE, Dr. Rückert promotes digital transformation through the development of intelligent and highly-networked SAP software. Dr. Rückert has the overall responsibility for all SAP solutions in the realms of production, supply chain management, asset management, IoT and Industrie 4.0. As the executive vice president in the Products & Innovation Division, she reports directly to development chairman Bernd Leukert.

Directly after joining SAP in 1997, Dr. Rückert became involved in a variety of customer implementation projects, later taking on responsibility for quality assurance within the context of developing SAP corporate software. As the COO, she managed day-to-day business in Human Resources and subsequently for the entire product development department.

Dr. Rückert holds a doctorate in chemistry from the University of Würzburg and the University of Regensburg. She divides her time between Silicon Valley and SAP headquarters in Walldorf, near Heidelberg, and is the mother of two children.

Ulrich Sendler, born in 1951, completed secondary school at the Ernst Moritz Arndt Classical Secondary School in Krefeld. Before studying precision engineering at the Heilbronn University of Applied Sciences, for which he received a degree in 1985, he was a toolmaker and NC programmer. Subsequently, he was employed in the CAD System Development Department at Kolbenschmidt, followed by a position as an editor at CAD-CAM Report, Heidelberg.

Since 1989, he has worked as an independent journalist, author and technology analyst in the realm of industrial software. In 2009, the Springer Verlag publishers printed the *PLM Kompendium*, of which he served as the editor. In 2013, Ulrich Sendler was the initiator and organizer of the industry summit "System Leadership 2030" in Feldafing, Germany. His book *Industrie 4.0—Beherrschung der industriellen Komplexität mit SysLM* ("Industrie 4.0—Controlling industrial Complexity with SysLM") became a bestseller in China. As of 1995, he has been head of the sendler\ circle, a special interest group of software and service providers for industry. This book is the eleventh which he has edited.

Tian Shubin, CEO and president of Xinhuanet GmbH, vice president of the Chinese Internet Society and perpetual board member of the Chinese Journalist Association. Previously, he served as the office manager of the Xinhua news agency in Ningxia, Chongqing, Yunnan and Jiangsu. He is the author of several professional articles about industry and business. For an extended period, Tian Shubin has concerned himself with the realm of industrialization development in the age of globalization.

Prof. Dr.-Ing., Rainer Stark, born in 1964, studied mechanical engineering at the Ruhr University of Bochum as well as at Texas A & M University. From 1989 to 1994, he worked as a scientific assistant to the chair of construction design in the Technical Department of the University of Saarland, Germany. Upon achieving the degree Dr.-Ing. (Dr. of Engineering), he transferred to the Ford AG, where he last held the position of technical manager of "Virtual Product Creation and Methods" at the Ford Motor Company Europe. As of February 2008, he has been the head of the Industrial Information Technology Department at the TU Berlin and the director of the virtual product creation business segment at the Fraunhofer Institute for Production Facilities and Construction Design.

Pan Zhi, is the general director of Xinhuanet Europe, a subsidiary of Xinhuanet GmbH in Europe. In 1999, he began working for the Xinhua news agency. From 2001 to 2004, he worked as a correspondent in the area of business and technology for the Xinhua office in Berlin. In 2008, as a scholarship holder, he participated in the media messenger program of the Robert Bosch Foundation, completing a three-month training program in Hamburg. From 2010 to 2014, he worked as a chief correspondent in the Den Haag office of the Xinhua news agency. Pan Zhi has made a name for himself with several professional articles. In 2015, he transferred to Xinhuanet.

Part I

The Basics

Introduction

1

Ulrich Sendler

Abstract

Some speak of industrial revolution and mean the transition from an agricultural economy to an industrial society. Others speak of a fourth industrial revolution and mean a new stage of technological progress. Others still think that it is nonsense to speak of revolution, and that industry is simply continuing to develop in an evolutionary manner. A brief look at the history of industrial revolution thus seems fitting.

Germany as an industrial location is playing a central role in the Industrie 4.0 initiative (*Initiative Industrie 4.0*). Will a research initiative grow into something very practical for Germany? And just what does Industrie 4.0 have to do with the major issue of digitalization, which is now monopolizing all media? Just because the name "Industrie 4.0" unfortunately smacks of it, does not mean that the initiative necessarily only benefits industry. Yet those of us who wish to investigate the topic naturally want to know who will actually profit. This introductory chapter seeks to illuminate these questions.

1.1 The History of Industrial Revolution(s)

Originally, the term "industrial revolution" referred to the transition from an agricultural economy to an industrial society. In general, the spark is seen to be the steam engine: a thermal power engine which generates steam in a boiler through combustion and converts the heat, or more specifically, the pressure produced by the steam, into mechanical work. It is not possible to define an exact timeframe,

U. Sendler (✉)
Mauerkircherstraße 30, 81679 Munich, Germany
E-Mail: ulrich.sendler@ulrichsendler.de

U. Sendler (ed.), *The Internet of Things*,
https://doi.org/10.1007/978-3-662-54904-9_1

because it took a while for the steam engine to be viable economically, before even ultimately possessing the power to fundamentally change society and its form of doing business.

Over millennia, humankind has used renewable energies, primarily water and wind, to achieve higher productivity for certain tasks than was possible with manpower alone. And even long after the steam engine began its triumphal procession, water power managed to retain its superiority over the new technology in large parts of Europe.

The first economically serviceable steam engine was invented in 1712 by Thomas Newcomen in England. Its degree of efficiency was 0.5%, referring to the energy expended for the performance achieved. In comparison, a modern combustion engine has a degree of efficiency of between 30 and 50%. It was only in 1769 that James Watt was able to improve the steam engine to the extent that it ultimately achieved a degree of efficiency of 3%. Watt also coined the phrase horsepower (HP), which was subsequently used as a unit of power for several centuries.

Widespread use of the steam engine dates to the mid-19th century, when, in Germany alone, its numbers increased within the course of a few decades to almost 10,000 engines. After employing the steam engine in mines for drainage, inventions appeared which, along with the spinning machine and loom, formed the cornerstone of the textile industry, yet also led to machine tools, railroads and ships. The mass availability of coal and steel, made possible by the development of efficient mining and processing methods, changed the world.

Everyone today who thinks that China and other Asian countries are attempting to cover their backlog demand for industrialization by deceptively copying modern machines and products of leading industrial nations will appreciate a historical side note from the Industrial Revolution in Germany, which can be found, among other sources, in a book about James Watt by Hans L. Sittauer [1]: The first steam engine employed in German mining in the late 18th century was built according to Watt's design and purchased in England. The engine, as well as studies conducted by German engineers and scientists at Watt's company in England, were subsequently used to generate the sketches with which the German reproductions were built, against the wishes of the inventor. The industrial spies came on order of Prussian King Frederick II, Baron von Stein and others, some having been pursued in England with arrest warrants and escaping apprehension by fleeing. By the way, with regard to the first steam engines built in Prussia, it was reported that susceptibility to failure of those copies of the original was the source of much ridicule. (We will examine in more detail the very serious intentions of China and its industry to not only catch up to the Western state of the art but considerably pass us in the coming decades. It would certainly not be possible by copying according to the Prussian example.)

Coal became a source of energy, steam power increased human productivity to previously unknown levels, and the steam engine enabled not only the industrial production of goods but, with the steam locomotive and steamship, provided a completely new type of transportation. In addition, the steam-powered cylinder printing press, paper machines, stereotype and rotary printing brought on a veritable printing revolution, setting the foundation for just the type of innovative, quick and mass communication that industry needed. The modern industrial society was born.

Best-selling author Jeremy Rifkin, whose book "The Zero Marginal Cost Society" was published in 2014 [2], proposed the theory that every time transportation, communication and energy are redesigned simultaneously, a new economic system is born. At any rate, capitalism was the child of the Industrial Revolution. The basis for communication, transportation and energy was formed by the steam engine and the resulting possibility for the industrial use of coal.

With the discovery of crude oil and its economic uses, with the invention of the combustion engine, with electricity and the conveyor belt for the mass production of goods, including the automobile, and with the telephone as a new means of communication, the start of the 20th century is seen as the beginning of a second industrial revolution. The division of labor and mass production not only led to a jump in productivity, but also to the crystallization of a consumer society. People no longer only bought what they needed to live on; more and more people were able to afford a multitude of consumer goods and thus a rising standard of living. While the first industrial revolution began in England, spread to France and Germany before reaching the USA and other countries with a slight delay, it was American industry which led the way in the second revolution right from the start. Yet, even if the telephone, combustion engine and crude oil repositioned communication, transport and energy, it did not create a new economic system—unless we consider the creation of the communist economic order in parts of the world to be a new economic system. However, neither Russia nor China were significant elements in the second industrial revolution—and in the industrial core countries of Europe and the USA, communism just could not take hold.

Then, in the mid-twentieth century, the computer came on the scene. Math departments generated computer science departments. Electrically-controlled machines and systems that could be switched on and off became programmable systems. Stored program control (SPC) systems, hitting the market at the end of the sixties of the preceding century, are seen as the catalyst for the third industrial revolution. Automation and robots altered the face of industry again, because more and more production could be carried out by machines and robots, while humans shifted to the function of monitoring those steps.

However, we have to remember that this third industrial revolution was only defined after the fourth one was posited by the German initiative *Industrie 4.0*. In the USA, the current change through the appearance of the Internet of Things on the industrial stage is only now considered to be the third revolution. The third phase, which above all was the stage in which production was permeated by automation and robotic assembly lines, became a great period of success for German industry. Just when all other industrial nations were concentrating on services and outsourcing production to so-called low-wage countries, when the ratio of industry to gross value added of those countries was diminishing, Germany as a production location placed its bets on precisely those strengths—its strengths—driving production automation ever further toward the optimum.

At the same time—and this is usually forgotten or ignored as something insignificant in the debate about the third industrial revolution—at the same time, digitalization of the entire value creation process was setting in: computer-controlled lathes and milling machines (NC tool machines) in production; computer-assisted drawing, and later, 3D modeling (CAD); computer-assisted modeling in all technical disciplines of engineering, product development and production; the use of models for visualization and simulation have made it possible to digitally try out and test product design, even for cars and airplanes, and construct entire systems in the manufacturing industry without even having to cast one expensive prototype as hardware. Today, there is hardly one step left in the value creation chain that has not somehow been supported by some kind of software.

Yet what happened in the USA? There, too, computers and information technology were drivers for innovation; however, not as much in traditional goods manufacturing as in the absolute focus on computer technology itself. It was IBM computers that brought digitalization to companies around the world. It was primarily Unix producers such as Sun Microsystems and Hewlett Packard in the USA that facilitated engineering. It was the company Microsoft which made the utilization of computers a matter of course on a massive scale. The internet was also born in the USA, and to date, the rapid development of new enterprises making larger sums of money with data on the internet than any other company before them with any kind of product is unbroken.

Thus, while the third industrial revolution in Germany catapulted several branches of the manufacturing and processing industries to the forefront, always accompanied by the German global corporation Siemens, who brought programmable logic control units into the world, the economy in the USA was dealing with the IT revolution, triggered by computer hardware and software. One could say that industry split into one part that was more focused on hardware with Germany as the leading site and into another part whose business models were to be increasingly found in software, then the internet and ultimately in data, with the USA as the leading site.

By the way: Even though software encompassed all areas of society, even though transportation, communication and power generation became increasingly reliant on software in order to function at all, this basic change also did not lead to a new economic system.

So now, the fourth industrial revolution has been hailed in Germany, and the third in the USA. A barely perceptible innovation has been identified as a catalyst: the possibility of connecting virtually every product with the internet or other wireless networks, making it a data storage medium, not unlike a smartphone or tablet. With the aid of software and digital components, data can be generated, collected, transferred and analyzed. With this data, in turn, services never seen before can be offered in connection with products, much like text message services, which did not exist before the advent of cell phones. After the digitalization of processes and the programming of automation comes the digitalization and networking of products. For a while now, the term "Internet of Things" has existed for this phenomenon—especially in Anglo-Saxon countries—and we will examine it in more detail later. What is more, visionaries already envision machines and production systems controlling themselves.

However, with a view to the splitting of industry into the hardware industry, primarily in Germany, and the software industry, mainly in the USA, we can naturally ask the question: Who will be a step ahead in this new phase? Will the hardware world champions be able to prevail with their products, even on the internet? Or will the data world champions close the deal, including products from Germany?

There are a few remarkable aspects about this short history of industrial revolution(s):

Every one of the drastic changes, which were always characterized by human activity being replaced by machine operation, was accompanied by the great and widespread fear that it would rob humans of work opportunities. All industrial revolutions have, in fact, led to the loss of jobs. And yet, at the same time, new types and more numerous jobs were also repeatedly created; because despite the existing worldwide population growth, which has graced us with more than seven million people, the majority is in fact increasingly in a better position to earn their livelihood through their own work. It makes no sense that the current transformation to digital networking should deprive a larger number of people from jobs and thus livelihoods than the number of new jobs and earning opportunities arising as a result.

However, the first two industrial revolutions had the effect of also leading to various revolutions of the newly created working class and ultimately to communist economic systems. And where capitalism established itself, the exploitation to a monstrous degree of children and teenagers, lawlessness and social insecurity all led to social movements and finally to a social market economy as we know it today. Whether or not the new industrial revolution, the digitalization of economy and society and the networking of all people and devices will once again lead to drastic changes, remains to be seen. What appears certain is the fact that society needs regulations to prevent people from falling into social insignificance because they cannot keep up with the pace of rapid technological developments.

The triumph of industry began with the exploitation of fossil resources. Up to about the third industrial revolution in the second half of the last century, not only were raw materials consumed and destroyed to a previously unknown extent, but at the same time, industrial production led to so much environmental and air pollution that, in the meanwhile, nobody can deny that the dramatic climate change, which has been taking place for an extended period of time, can only be countered with a radical change in the way we live and work.

For a long time, this only seemed like a topic for the ecological Green parties, but is now also spreading to industry on a large scale. Entrepreneurs in the German state of Baden-Württemberg openly campaigned for the Greens in the state parliamentary elections of 2016; the Rockefeller family, who became billionaires by exploiting crude oil, announced in March of 2016 that they were withdrawing from the oil business for ecological and ethical reasons and selling their shares to Exxon-Mobil; in as early as 2011, the motto of the largest industrial trade show in the world, the Hanover Fair, was "Greentelligence". And signs indicate that, with the fourth industrial revolution, the technological foundation has been established to also use our natural resources and the environment in a "smart" way.

The previous history of industry additionally shows us that the uninterrupted increase in pace at which innovations enter the market with economic success is inherent. It took more than 50 years for the steam engine to mature to the point of stimulating the first Industrial Revolution. The first phase took almost 150 years, until the early 20th century. Mass production and Taylorism dominated the second phase for almost 70 years. The third industrial revolution, with software-controlled automation, only took 40 years. The historical cycles from one fundamental industrial innovation to the next are becoming ever shorter. To believe that the fourth phase would lead to a slowdown and take considerably longer than the previous one would be naïve. On the contrary: In only a few years, just the beginnings of the internet economy alone have led to such a crucial change in the rankings of the most successful international companies that it seems more logical to assume that the Internet of Things (a detailed explanation of this term can be found in Sect. 2.1 ff.) will alter industry even more rapidly than ever before.

Finally, there is another aspect worth considering: The first three industrial revolutions primarily involved a change in manufacturing methods and the related energy needed. They began with the most important step in industrial value creation: with production. The internet, on the other hand, initially took on and reshaped advertising, services and trade, that is, the final links in the value creation chain, once the products had already been produced. Now, it encompasses service and maintenance, and products are becoming "smart", with the ability to become the medium for new services. It is only in the last step that, this time, those parts of the value creation chain are reached which directly affect product development and production. The relationship between industry and its customers is also turning around (see Fig. 1.1).

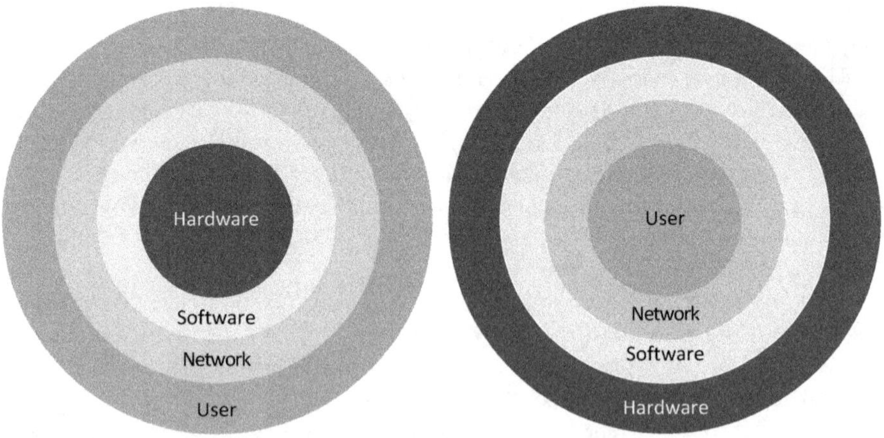

Fig. 1.1 This graph is based on an image by Zühlke Engineering, and shows how the relationship between product and user has completely turned around. On the Internet of Things, the user is the focus. (Sendler)

Customers and the market now play the primary role. In future, enterprises must cater to customer wishes as early as in the planning, development and production stages. That is the only way products in the future will be able to be sold.

Whether the current revolution, which was termed Industrie 4.0 in Germany, is an industrial revolution or simply a continuation of evolutionary development, is a question which has repeatedly surfaced in the debates of recent years. There are even voices saying that it is not a fundamental change at all, because now, the decisive basis of industrial manufacturing is still the use of microelectronics. This whole debate is pointless. Those who do not see the profound changes most likely do not want to see them. It is much too obvious that we are neither talking about temporary hype nor that the situation is not simply a continuation of familiar forms of producing and doing business. The more pertinent question is whether Jeremy Rifkin was right in his assumption that digitalization and interconnection via the internet will change the basis for communication, transportation and energy so profoundly that a new economic system will arise.

He believes that the future belongs to the share economy, and that capitalism will gradually recede, because, in one business sector after another, products and services for which a great deal of capital was previously necessary can be created with little or almost no capital. His hypotheses are surely worth a closer look, and there are references in a few other chapters in this book that could support those hypotheses.

1.2 Germany's Leadership Role

It is often claimed that German engineers have good ideas and develop innovative technologies, but that the resulting products are more likely to conquer the world's markets originating from the USA or Asia. Especially marketing is said to be less successful in Germany than elsewhere. That may be true, and there are a few such cases, for instance the compressed MP3 audio format. Yet there are also several examples of how not only a particular technology was developed in Germany but also successful marketing made the respective products successes: streetcars, the dynamo, the printing machine, and the automobile, just to name a few.

With Industrie 4.0, it has even been possible to first develop the marketing strategy and then the product. The German initiative was the first in the world to lay claim to naming the fourth industrial revolution, and that at a time when even in Germany hardly anyone understood what it meant. Incredibly, this marketing strategy has been decidedly successful. Within five years, there have been more than a dozen European initiatives having the same topic—some of them with an explicit connection to Industrie 4.0. Even the clever move of keeping the German spelling, *Industrie 4.0*, and not adopting the English "Industry" is having an effect: Occasionally, you will find the German spelling even in Asia and the USA.

That may seem unusual to some observers, but it is not surprising. Several German companies are market leaders in their respective sectors. This not only applies to large corporations in the automotive and automation industries, but also, and especially, for the so-called hidden champions, the incredible wealth of small and midsize companies producing machine tools, electrical components, drive systems, control systems and countless other products. Usually, it is not even common knowledge that these products are global market leaders.

Thus, it is no coincidence that the Industrie 4.0 initiative was developed and started in Germany and has had a great impact on the world from its native land. In the past 40 years, German industry has taken the optimization of automation to the extreme, while a number of formerly leading industrial nations have looked for salvation in a concentration on services and in outsourcing production. In Germany, digitalization of the industrial process and the use of IT systems in all areas of value creation has been achieved to a much broader extent than in many other countries. Today, many producers of such information technology consider the German market to be one of the most important, if not the most important, in the world. Occasionally ridiculed as perfectionists and standards fanatics, there are plenty of companies in Germany who have already made remarkable progress toward developing their digital twin, even if a degree of consistency vital to Industrie 4.0 is still missing, a point which will be discussed subsequently in this book.

Another aspect which has contributed to Germany's favorable position as an industrial location: In recent decades, research and development proved to be a steadily growing investment target, especially on the part of companies. Furthermore, together with specialists in the companies, researchers at technical research institutes have contributed to numerous innovations. At the beginning of this century, acatech, the German National Academy of Science and Engineering, was founded. What other countries such as the USA, Great Britain and Sweden had long since established was now also available in Germany. And a few German national associations of engineers and production engineers, especially the Scientific Society for Product Development (WiGeP), are the largest of their kind worldwide.

Industrie 4.0 was initially the name of a team of scientists and representatives of industry at acatech. The group's result report was the starting signal for the national initiative. The mission statement and guidelines of acatech explain:

> One significant goal of acatech – the German National Academy of Science and Engineering – is to provide technical advice to the realms of politics and science on scientific and political questions regarding the future [3].

Based on the advice of acatech, Industrie 4.0 and the digitalization of industry became a core concern of the federal administration's digital agenda. Thus, a research subject was able to be turned into a successful international initiative, based on broadly developed, automated production in several industries and on methods of developing advanced mechatronic products. Now the trick is to prevent initial successes from going to the heads of the parties involved. You see, the entire world has come to realize that the Internet of Things has also brought digitalization and networking to industry. There is already competition and there will be even more, which is a good thing: because competition stimulates business. Especially the international reaction proves to doubters in Germany that Industrie 4.0 is not just a pipe dream, but signifies an international trend that was only first put into words in Germany.

World market leadership is no longer certain in the foreseeable future based on traditional products. The usage, collection, storage and evaluation of data will come to the fore in future products. Several enterprises in Germany have already utilized the initiative in recent years to prepare themselves, perform research in that direction and organize pilot projects. Those who still believe they have plenty of time can orient themselves toward that trend. Yet many more need to take action than have done to date. Advancement achieved through an early initiative has put Germany as an industrial location into pole position. Everyone knows that the race has not yet been won.

1.3 Digitalization as a Megatrend

In the five years since its start, quite a bit has happened, and not only in the initiative itself. National as well as international discussion about the future of society has discovered digitalization as a central theme. Regarding the technical advancements of humans, today the term digitalization has a high priority, if not the highest. Considerable hopes are being placed in the concept, yet digitalization is also the source of enormous fear about the future.

It would be worth it to conduct a study on why this term has only now become the focus of all debates concerning technology, industry, the economy and society. Why did it not start ten years ago? Why wasn't the significance of digitalization the catalyst for the establishment of *Industrie 4.0*?

In the group's 116-page final report, which was submitted to representatives of the German federal government in October of 2012 with the title "Germany's Future as a Production Location – Recommendations for Implementation of the Future Project Industrie 4.0" (*Deutschlands Zukunft als Produktionsstandort sichern—Umsetzungsempfehlungen für das Zukunftsprojekt Industrie 4.0*), the word "digitalization" only appears one single time: on p. 71, Chap. 6, regarding the international comparison. Those who remember initial discussions about the initiative in the early part of the last decade can confirm that Industrie 4.0 was not considered a part of general digitalization, but rather almost exclusively as the next step in the evolution of industry, or, as its next revolution.

Since the end of 2015, the German state of Bavaria has been home to a digitalization center (ZdB), under the direction of a long-time representative and driver of information technology, Prof. Manfred Broy. When the state of Baden-Württemberg was putting together its new administration, the topic of digitizing the economy and the role of Baden-Württemberg in this procedure was a primary focus. In March of 2016, the *Süddeutsche Zeitung*—most probably along with several other newspapers—included an insert from the Federal Ministry for Economic Affairs and Energy (BMWi) with a title that translates as "Digitalization and You – How our Lives are Changing." It was the print form of the "Digital Strategy 2025", published online at www.de.digital on March 14 by the same ministry.

Is it a coincidence that this strategy is oriented toward the same year as the campaign of the Chinese State Council, who adopted the first ten-year plan to modernize industry under the name "Made in China 2025"? At any rate, it shows that the Ministry for Economic Affairs is thinking beyond its own legislative period in planning this strategy. Yet if you study the Digital Strategy, you realize that Industrie 4.0 is mentioned in a few spots and great importance is put on industry for the digitalization of Germany; the corresponding chapter was written by Prof. Siegfried Russwurm, a member of the board of directors of Siemens AG and one of the leading industrial representatives in the *Plattform Industrie 4.0*. But in total, the publication gives the impression that the larger the topic becomes and the greater the possible radius of operation, the more unclear the significance of the term becomes.

For instance, the Digital Strategy, in the last of its "Ten Steps into the Future," states that a "control center for the Digital Strategy 2025" in the form of a "digital agency" is being established. On the one hand, it is intended to function as a "think tank to prepare politics" for the issue, and on the other, as a service center to stand by the federal government in implementing the strategy "in a competent, neutral and lasting manner." The author of the description of this digital agency is Prof. Dieter Gorny, an agent for the Creative and Digital Economics of the BMWi and chairman of the Federal Association of the German Music Industry (BVMI). Does this mean that the Ministry for Economic Affairs sees the digitalization of the music industry as exemplary? Or is an effect similar to that of the digitalization of the music industry expected for the digitalization on the manufacturing industry? Why can someone representing the music industry best advise society, consumers, manufacturers, business and the government when the issue is digitalization on the whole?

The topics touched upon in the Digital Strategy concern a number of ministries besides Economic Affairs and Energy. Education cannot orient itself toward digitalization without the German Federal Ministry of Education and Research (BMBF), and the BMBF is represented in the management board of the *Plattform Industrie 4.0*. The digital infrastructure is the responsibility of the Ministry of Transport. The legal framework and questions of cybersecurity are assigned to the areas of the Ministry of the Interior and the Ministry of Justice. The future of employment under the conditions of digitalization is an issue for the Ministry of Labor and Social Affairs—and yet, the Federal Ministry for Economic Affairs and Energy (BMWi) is the only editor cited for the digital agenda.

It is true that digitalization has included all areas of society and will quickly permeate it even further. Thus, it is no coincidence that four spheres of operation of the "old" ministries are affected. But isn't it necessary to encounter this comprehensive change of society and life, trade and the economy with more of a comprehensive change of political structures than only a digital agency under the direction of a representative of the music industry? Doesn't Germany need a ministry for digitalization? Aren't changes to state administrations necessary, for instance regarding education and training, data protection and the police force?

With regard to Industrie 4.0, it is high time to clearly outline the role of this initiative in the new, widespread debate on digitalization. In any case, it is necessary to think about its borders, because, in fact, Industrie 4.0 primarily affects that part of digitizing society which includes industry and not, for example, service areas that have nothing to do with industrial products and production. Services which have been newly added to the offerings of industry because of the Internet of Things and Industrie 4.0 are not all necessarily comparable with services in other areas—such as the music industry or the insurance and banking sectors. Data as a new source of value creation in industry, especially in its business-to-business activity, is completely different from that of the consumer goods business. To group all of these areas together will not result in clarity, but more likely in confusion.

1.4 Who Will Benefit from Industrie 4.0?

In discussions about the initiative, I repeatedly encounter people who do not know any specifics about it, yet still have an opinion as to who will benefit and who will suffer. "Industry" wants it so that they can sell more of their products. In the interest of industry, "we" should finally become transparent citizens, whose needs are so well known that "industry" can force all of the supposedly necessary products on us before we even ask for them and without asking us. So, it benefits "industry" and harms "us".

This opinion is not as rare as you might think. People supporting it think of consumer goods manufacturers when they think of industry, because normal citizens have nothing to do with the other manufacturers. And they think of the routes along which consumer goods reach their end users. Two demarcations are needed here: between various types of consumer goods and between manufacturers of consumer goods and those producing investment goods.

The opinion stated in simplified form above includes another aspect worth considering: It assumes that Industrie 4.0 is primarily a continuation and expansion of what U.S. internet companies do with our personal data without asking us. As a trade-off, they simply supply us with cheap or free services via apps. But does Industrie 4.0 have anything to do with personal data? And if so, where is this the case, what types of products are involved and in what industries? What is the difference between industry data from machines, robots, production lines and chemical plants on the one hand and personal data on the other? And how must manufacturers and customers deal with various types of data? Answers to such questions can be found in Chap. 2.

A further related question, which is somewhat more difficult to answer is: If Industrie 4.0 is not primarily about personal data, if anything is more likely to change for investment goods rather than consumer goods, does that even have anything to do with me, if I am not employed in industry? And if so, what? Just as it is becoming ever more difficult to understand what is happening in the background of the digitalization process because software is invisible, so, too, will it become even harder to understand what is going on in industry. It will become even harder because, up to now, the work of engineers and the procedures in industrial operations have only been understood by people directly involved in them. Yet since Industrie 4.0 and the digitalization of industry also have far-reaching effects on the lives of all people in the country (and beyond), it is becoming even more important to address the matter.

Those who understand that we are actually dealing with a fundamental transformation in production methods which, with its value creation processes, will also change everything that we have been used to up to now, will soon ponder whether autonomous machines and robots will finally render humans superfluous and thus unemployed. Even the business leaders in Davos posed this question to themselves in early 2016. They also put numbers into the world which only intensified such fears, because they give the impression that they were determined in a scientific manner. Seven million jobs would be lost in the wake of digitalization in the coming years, while only two million new jobs would be created. According to this calculation, a loss of five million jobs would be the side effect of digitalization. Even if it is not quite reliable to use an opinion survey of managers to make conclusions about the actual future of the job market, everyone taking this topic seriously must address these questions.

What is certain is that Industrie 4.0 will change the way we work in industry, and to an extent which cannot be mastered with the previous knowledge gained in schools or universities or with the skills and abilities acquired in vocational training. New courses of study will be necessary, and new structures for training and education, because the existing departments and courses of study were intended for "old" industry and oriented toward it. Are people capable of learning what they need quickly enough for this development? Who will help them in this venture? What must be changed in public education as well as vocational training to be successful? And how can the necessary changes be achieved beyond the previous borders between states? Those are also justified questions whose answers depend on whether Industrie 4.0 itself will be a success or not.

References

1. Sittauer, H. L. (1981). *James Watt. Biographien hervorragender Naturwissenschaftler, Techniker und Mediziner*, Vol. 53 (p. 76). Wiesbaden: Springer (ISBN 978-3-322-00696-7, ISBN 978-3-663-12183-1 (eBook)).
2. Rifkin, J. (2014). *Die Null-Grenzkosten-Gesellschaft—Das Internet der Dinge, Kollaboratives Gemeingut und der Rückzug des Kapitalismus*. (*The zero marginal cost society: The internet of things, the collaborative commons, and the eclipse of capitalism*, German translation). Frankfurt: Campus (ISBN 978–3-593-39917-1).
3. http://www.acatech.de/de/ueber-uns/leitbild-und-leitlinien/leitlinien-politikberatung.html. Accessed May 12 2016.

The Basics

2

Ulrich Sendler

Abstract

Even five years after the official start of the initiative, most people are not familiar with the term "Industrie 4.0". Those who have addressed the topic even have trouble producing a relatively plausible explanation for it. Thus, this chapter deals with the basics: the official definition of Industrie 4.0, its position in the larger context of digitalization, the terms "smart product" and "smart product development," as well as with the platform and the ecological system. Finally, the initiative's explosive force on society will be analyzed.

2.1 What Is Industrie 4.0?

When this editor's first book was published, there was no official definition. The German *Plattform Industrie 4.0*—at the time still led by three industrial associations, Bitkom, VDMA (the German Mechanical Engineering Industry Association) and ZVEI (the German Electrical and Electronic Manufacturers' Association)—then supplied such an official definition. This definition can be found in the implementation strategy submitted to the platform in April of 2015, whose leadership was taken over by the German federal administration. Its core message states:

> The term Industrie 4.0 stands for the fourth industrial revolution, a new level of organization and control of the entire value creation chain during the life cycle of products. This cycle is oriented toward increasingly individualized customer demands and stretches from the concept, to the order, to development and manufacture, to the delivery of a product to the end user, right up to the recycling process, including the associated services [1].

U. Sendler (✉)
Mauerkircherstraße 30, 81679 Munich, Germany
E-Mail: ulrich.sendler@ulrichsendler.de

U. Sendler (ed.), *The Internet of Things*,
https://doi.org/10.1007/978-3-662-54904-9_2

The fourth industrial revolution thus indicates a new level in the "organization and control of the entire value creation chain." So as to leave no doubts about just what is included, this value creation chain is specifically and comprehensively defined, from its inception to the services connected with the products. This makes clear that we are dealing with a fundamental transformation in industrial production methods, and not simply a change of any single part of those methods.

Nevertheless, ever since the initial debates, including the discussions of the team having founded the Initiative, composed of acatech (the German National Academy of Science and Engineering) and a research union, pivotal links in the value creation chain have been repeatedly pushed aside or completely negated, as if they were not so important. Mostly, the debate concentrates on changes in production, that is, in manufacturing products. Neither the path from idea to product nor its development, design, or engineering, seem important. In addition, even services and new business models based on them, as well as new value creation paths, all too often fall by the wayside.

For instance, on the homepage of acatech itself under "Dossier on the Future of Industrial Sites," it reads: "With the entrance of the Internet of Things, Data and Services onto the production scene, a fourth industrial age has dawned" [2]. After this statement, there is a picture and a quote from both German Chancellor Dr. Angela Merkel and from the president of acatech, Prof. Henning Kagermann. According to that statement, the Internet of Things, Data and Services is only "entering the production scene," but not that of industry and its overall value creation.

Such statements—of which, unfortunately, there are plenty—represent an inadmissible simplification and reduction of the definition, with broad consequences. You see, those who have nothing to do with industrial manufacturing can relax and move on to other topics; if it only involves production, it is none of their business.

This narrow view limited to production has several causes, and one can presume that those individuals who use such arguments do not do so consciously, and certainly do not mean it in a malevolent way. Let us not forget that all previous phases of industrial development primarily affected production. The fact that this is no longer the case is one of the great peculiarities, and it is time we understood this phenomenon with all of its facets. Secondly, production is that link in the industrial value creation chain that costs the most money. That is why, in past centuries, a primary objective was to optimize, rationalize and save, especially in the realm of production. Thirdly, Industrie 4.0 really does affect production, and it will lead to another boost in productivity which will make a difference. To the extent to which it is possible to bestow components of machines and systems, drives, connection assemblies, and conveyor belts with so much "intelligence" that they can act increasingly autonomously, it is not only the case that human labor will be reduced and other routine jobs made redundant; completely new partnerships and networks are possible, out of which the familiar factory can be turned into a factory network. The effects of Industrie 4.0 on production are indeed tremendous.

If, however, the limitation to production were true, the significance of the overall initiative would hardly be so extensive as to require the attention of greater parts of society. It would be fairly similar to the third industrial revolution, which of course was only called that in retrospect. When programmable logic control was used for IT-supported automation, nobody but manufacturing firms cared. And, except for specialized media, hardly anyone noticed. Yet what is so special about the fourth industrial revolution is that it is actually calling into question and altering production methods on the whole—prompting consequences extending far beyond manufacturing companies.

Industrie 4.0 is changing our industry overall—starting with the concept itself, because it no longer exclusively and predominantly stems from the brain of an inventive engineer, but via the internet from the market, from customers, partners, the competition, from all around the world; through product development, design and programming, via tests and the simulation of digital product models, up to virtual commissioning, because data from manufacturing can be used with data from engineering to accelerate and optimize these process steps. It is also changing services, which no longer only refer to customer service, repair and replacement parts delivery, but rather a number of new services, from preventive maintenance to optimized operation, for instance involving hourly billing.

What serves as the basis for this? The second sentence of the official definition answers the question in the respective section of the implementation strategy:

> The basis is the availability of all relevant information in real time through the networking of all instances taking part in the value creation chain as well as the ability to use the data at any time to derive the optimal value creation flow. By connecting people, objects and systems, dynamic, real-time optimized, self-organized and cross-corporate value creation networks are created, which can be optimized according to various criteria, such as costs, availability and resource consumption [1].

This is difficult for non-specialists to follow. What does "all relevant information" mean? How is it made available in real time? What is so different about the networking and connection of people, objects and systems that alters the entire value creation flow?—Because all machines and systems were already interconnected for automation; people were already able to obtain all relevant information from the devices, rapidly in the moment such information was needed.

There are three main factors which have changed in recent years:

1. Digital components such as sensors, actuators, cameras and microphones nowadays are so small and can be produced so inexpensively that we can use them to teach things to see, hear and feel. By the way, several German producers are leaders in the world market for such products.
2. Since the 2010s, an internationally applicable protocol, IPv6, has existed which enables almost everything to be supplied with its own internet address. This enables a device to establish contact to other devices and people as well as send and receive data.
3. Finally, information science as an engineering discipline has matured and is on the way to become the most important discipline of all. It is used to help networked, sensitive things to act in a sensible and increasingly autonomous manner.

These factors now make the step that separates the third from the fourth revolution possible. It is a bit like the difference between a smartphone and the first generation of mobile telephones. A mobile phone allowed people to connect, send and receive text messages, and communicate with anyone. With a smartphone, you can access the internet, and via the smartphone, services such as GPS navigation and updates are offered without having to be actively queried about or request such services. In industry, the difference is that, until now, devices were programmed, connected via an intranet or directly to one another and controlled by a program to perform certain steps, and existing data could be retrieved. In the future, devices can make data available via the internet, trigger actions using their data, or perform an operation themselves based on data, without the need of involving humans.

That is precisely what is meant by the Internet of Things, which we will subsequently examine in more detail. All things can become nodes and terminals on the internet, even machines and systems, but also washing machines, central heating systems, air conditioners, cars, bicycles, watches and eyeglasses.

The great task posed to industry is the development and production of such internet-capable, communicating products, which can be turned into data storage devices, such as smartphones or tablets; and beyond this, developing services and business models that allow additional value creation with these novel products. And ultimately, industry itself must utilize the new opportunities via the internet and the data of things which then gradually become available, in order to optimize its own processes and adjust to new technologies.

Let us use an example with which everyone is familiar: the printer. In recent years, a generation of devices has appeared on the market that serves not only as just a printer, fax machine and scanner. These devices can also connect to the internet with their own IP addresses. If an ink cartridge is running low on ink, the device warns the user and recommends a new cartridge, from the printer's manufacturer, of course. With a click of a mouse, the cartridge is ordered and soon delivered before the installed cartridge is completely empty. None of the printer manufacturers makes any noteworthy profit from selling printers themselves. Printer manufacture is typically undertaken by suppliers, is reduced to an absolute minimum of work and other expenses and costs are brought down as much as possible. The printer providers, who are no longer genuine printer manufacturers, make their actual turnover with the accessories that the customer needs: especially ink cartridges, paper, photo paper, and specialty papers. A connection to the internet enables an increased access to the customer and thus a closer customer connectivity than is possible via a normal retail store.

To be able to offer such printers, these devices must thus be "intelligent." They must be networked and possess the capability of not only measuring the existing volume of ink in the individual cartridges and displaying a respective warning at the right moment, but they also have to automatically offer a suitable replacement and trigger the purchasing process. It is most likely these features harbored in the software of such devices that make the difference between competitors on the market today. Perhaps these features represent the most important components of the products that former printer manufacturers can still develop themselves. And the bigger the customer and corresponding number of printers in use, the larger the profit that is generated by these services, and the greater the advantage is to corporations, for instance, based on the smooth operation of all printers in all departments. The printer production itself—and here we come back to the previously mentioned unjustified limitation of the topic of Industrie 4.0 to manufacturing—the production itself has become a secondary element for printer providers.

If you can understand Industrie 4.0 in this way, you will immediately realize that the fourth industrial revolution is not only changing production methods and industrial processes, but also the products of daily life and the way we use them: in short, our lives and work.

Thus, Industrie 4.0 is not only about what digitalization is doing to industry and is not just of interest to industry. Industrie 4.0 is part of the digitalization of the entire human society, which will trigger even greater changes in our daily lives than the smartphone, because it is being increasingly incorporated into all objects of our lives.

2.2 A Short History of Digitalization

Although the term "digitalization" has been around for a while, and although it has been advancing for more than half a century, it has only been in recent years, after the start of Industrie 4.0, that public debate about it has begun which has reached and interested broader levels of society. We are still at the beginning of the clarification process of what digitalization means for society and its economy, for humans and their lives and work; yet meanwhile there is no doubt, that it will change all of life on this planet.

On Wikipedia, you can find the assumption that in 2002, for the first time, humankind was capable of storing more information digitally than using analog means, such as on hard drives instead of in file folders. Wikipedia estimates that the global technological information capacity in the year 1993 was only 3% digital, but in 2007, just 14 years later, it had reached 94%. These assumptions are based on a publication by Martin Hilbert and Priscila López in Science Magazine in 2011 [3]. The beginning of the so-called digital age is often dated to the end of the 20th century.

However, the digitalization of information did not begin until shortly before the mid-20th century. In Germany, Konrad Zuse built the first functional, fully automatic and freely-programmable computer in the world, the Z3, in 1941. As early as the last years of the Second World War, the first freely-programmable computers also appeared in England and the USA.

The goal of these machines was to calculate. In the 1980s, a professor of electrotechnology in Heilbronn used to refer to computers in his lectures as "high-speed idiots." Nobody—not even an autistic person—can solve mathematical problems as quickly as a calculating machine. The only thing the computer needs is for information to be reduced to 0 or 1, black or white. That is all that compilers, or translation programs, do: They convert a program written in a higher programming language, the source code, into a bunch of zeroes and ones, the machine code.

The purpose of higher programming languages is for people to be able to abstract from concrete details and describe tasks in a more general form. The science that teaches this process is known as informatics, or information science. It was created in the late 1960s. Its early years generally took the form of courses of study which crystallized from departments of mathematics. The first course of study in information science in Germany was offered at the Technical University of Munich in 1967.

Whereas early computers were large mechanical machines driven by giant electron tubes, Zuse was able to create the first fully electronic computer with his Z3. Texas Instruments and Intel, among others, put the first commercial microprocessors with integrated circuits on the market in 1970/1971. The incredible tempo at which the progressive miniaturization, especially of electronics, then took place was the prerequisite for mainframe computers to be replaced initially by midrange computers, then PCs. Today, every smartphone boasts a performance capability and storage capacities (some, depending on the respective contract with a telecommunications provider, even at no extra charge) which, in the 1980s, corporations could hardly finance for their computers. A computer at a machine builder company in Neckarsulm, Germany, on which an internally-programmed CAD system ran in 1980, cost almost one million Deutschmark and had a main memory of three megabytes. Moore's law, named after Gordon Moore in 1970 and still repeatedly proven true today, predicts that the complexity of integrated circuits, having minimal component costs, will double every one to two years. The smaller and more powerful the necessary hardware was, the more it could calculate and the faster practical fields of application and programming developed.

It is, of course, no coincidence that hard-wired machine control was able to be replaced by programmable logic controllers (PLCs) at that time as well. In fact, the success of the PLC and automation is seen as a main characteristic of the third industrial revolution. Just as was the case in production facilities, the microprocessor and the free programming of all types of machines prevailed. NC and subsequently CNC machine tools, lathes and milling machines, as well as freely-programmable robots conquered manufacturing plants.

While programs initially were integral parts of computers, at the end of the 1960s, the term "software" appeared to denote them. In the 1970s, the US administration ordered the manufacturer IBM to differentiate between hardware and software on its invoices. In the mid-1980s, Microsoft was responsible for the next big step, the millions of users of the personal computer, the PC. With this step, for the first time on a large scale, hardware was displaced by software, because Microsoft did not offer PCs, but rather the operating system, on the one hand, that is, the software which allowed the computer to process programs, and on the other hand, application software such as the Office programs. The computer itself was sold by partners, who initially only served Microsoft as suppliers. In the computer business, software displaced hardware. IBM experienced a profound crisis in the years to follow, which almost ended in the complete destruction of the company. Luckily, it was able to surmount the transition to doing business with software.

In one fell swoop, companies and entire industries were then exclusively focusing their business on developing and distributing software. In Germany, the firm SAP was established, and internationally, the software industry turned into one of the most important sectors, itself divided into sub-sectors.

IT for information technology and ICT for information and communications technology have become abbreviations that now almost everyone knows. The Center for Office and Information Technology in Germany, called CeBIT, was, from the time starting in 1986 and spanning about two decades, the most important international trade fair focusing on ICT. For several years, it was considerably more important than the Hanover Trade Fair, the world's largest industrial trade show, out of which it developed.

IT quickly came into use for all calculable tasks and work steps in industry. It was used for the digitalization of accounting and order processing, for programming machines and systems and for calculating the durability of products. In construction, computer-aided design (CAD) was responsible for the disappearance of drafting boards; computer-aided manufacturing (CAM) saw the automation of NC programming as derivation of CAD models; 3D modeling enabled the design of product surfaces, such as for automobiles, which was also visual evidence that, in decisive parts of processes, industry was no longer dependent upon handicraft.

The internet enabled software-controlled communication, which would soon connect people around the world in real time via mobile end devices. In addition to the internet and mobile computers, from notebooks to smartphones to tablets, it was miniaturization and the availability of inexpensive components that once again made new business models possible: because using a global positioning system (GPS) and the IP address of very end device, personal and user data of their users could be collected and evaluated, such as preferences for certain locations, shops or products.

The business models of the leading internet companies currently topping the list of internationally successful firms are simple: The company offers certain services, such as internet searches or electronic commerce free of charge or at a very low cost, and in return, consumer goods providers can purchase the respective service as advertising space, with which they offer their products to internet users. Never before have enterprises become such rich companies in such a short time where each individual firm has more financial power than some nations.

There is a significant change which has taken place in the process: Business deals are no longer made by selling software to users, but by selling personal user data to consumer goods manufacturers. To do so, user permission is obtained—if at all—by a single mouse click under endlessly long and rarely read "agreements".

Digitalization first made computer producers such as IBM great. Then, they passed the baton on to software producers such as Microsoft, and information technology hardware makers became suppliers or also switched over to providing software. Ultimately, the suppliers of user data triumphed over hardware and software producers. This not only led to the downfall of most mobile telephone manufacturers. In February 2016, the Google parent company Alphabet, which had been created in the meantime, for the first time was able to topple Apple as the first on the list of the most expensive corporations. In addition to the business model shared by internet enterprises dealing in user data, Apple still offers hardware and software, but Google does not. And Google is the area that finances all other areas of the Alphabet corporation.

It is the way in which internet enterprises have changed consumption, trade and, in fact, a large part of most people's lives with their services, supplied in several free apps, which has only now turned the topic of digitalization into a core topic of society, and on a worldwide basis, no less. Let me repeat very clearly: The foundation of this phenomenon is the internet and the networking of mobile end devices with the internet.

The networking of devices with the internet is also the foundation of Industrie 4.0. As such, the fourth industrial revolution is a part of general digitalization. After software conquered the realm of automation, in industry, too, data and its use via the internet has become a hot topic.

The Internet of Things initially only recognized smartphones and computers as networked things. Now, it is increasingly encompassing all industrially produced things. Just as with the smartphone, these things can become data storage devices with whose data business can be conducted. Just as with the smartphone, it could be the services connected to the respective device that represent the heart of such business transactions.

Digitalization first replaced hardware with software. Hardware became an add-on for the software. Then, the software was enhanced by the internet. Software made access to service offers possible. Today, in many sectors, product and service user data has already become the "material" from which value is created. Software, like hardware before it, has frequently been downgraded to add-on status, partially being offered free of charge, in order to do business with the data.

Considering Industrie 4.0 as a component of the digitalization of our society explains, to some extent, what is meant by the term. But this thought is also frightening, because much of general digitalization, much of what internet companies have innovated, is not only garnering praise, especially in Germany, but certainly also in other parts of Europe and the world. To that extent, it is worth more closely examining where the differences are, and what the digitalization of industry specifically entails.

2.3 Smart Products

At the beginning of the debate about Industrie 4.0, there was great confusion. Was it something other than the Internet of Things or only a synonym for it? Then, in 2014, the Industrial Internet Consortium was established in the USA, and lots of people thought that the Industrial Internet was a better name than the Internet of Things, and much better than Industrie 4.0. After the explanation of digitalization in the previous chapter, we can now try to differentiate them more precisely.

Even if, in the past ten years, The Internet of Things meant nothing more than the internet of mobile computer things, especially with regard to smartphones and tablets, to a certain extent it is the roof under which all other digitalization takes place. Because ever more things can be networked with the internet, ever more things are going to be on the internet. Just as the smartphone, these items, too, are potential data storage media. The term "Internet of Things and Services," which appeared at about the same time as the Internet of Things, additionally alludes to the fact that the networking of things is not an end in itself. Rather, it is the foundation for services that previously did not exist; services that enable new kinds of business—the most frequent reason for something becoming extremely popular on a large scale.

The internet has remained the same, but its end products, users and to what it interconnects have changed—because now, it is not only people connected to the internet, but also things. According to estimations, we will have nine billion people on Earth in a few years, most of whom will use the internet, but, in fewer than two decades, around 500 billion devices will be networked.

What does this have to do with industry? It is the source of all products, things and devices that are networked and can become the object of services. In order for them to be designed this way and capable of this new role, in order for them to be—and here is another relatively new word—cyber-physical systems, they must be developed and manufactured accordingly. That is the first connection between the Internet of Things and Industrie 4.0. Only things that can be conceived and constructed as interconnectable data storage media can be a part of the Internet of Things. Only if industry manufactures such things can the internet be used with those things. That is quite obviously not an insignificant role. The basis for a functioning Internet of Things is formed by the internet-capable things that industry first must supply.

The prerequisite for the development of the business of internet enterprises was the development of smartphones and tablets. If we are to believe the people in charge at Google, however, neither the development of these devices nor the development of the extremely successful business models based upon them were influenced by any kind of strategy or any plan of any kind. The devices were there, and their interconnectivity made it possible to develop the corresponding business models. In the process, you could say that the users of the devices were taken by surprise. Without being asked, they were given services and functions that brought them advantages. And they only discovered quite a bit later, if at all, just how business was being conducted with their data. Even then, most users didn't and still don't care. The internet, made available in return (almost) free of charge, with its virtually limitless access to knowledge and information and which makes life easier with countless helpful apps—this network was and continues to be so important to people that they barely even want to know about the business underlying it. Nor do they want to know about any abuse being committed with their data, nor about the monitoring possibilities to which their data is susceptible, for intelligence services as well as international corporations.

If the Internet of Things can be theoretically expanded to include all things because industry can design them accordingly with Industrie 4.0, it is no longer comparable to the initial attempts at the Internet of Things via mobile end devices. The basic purpose of networking mobile units was for people to be able to access the internet. This basic purpose does not exist for the other kinds of devices. A device itself is not motivated to use the internet and network. This time, the manufacturers and the customers are the ones who need to understand their own needs and wishes: Who can accomplish what tasks with which device in a different or better way, and who benefits from a particular device connecting to the internet? An additional question of special interest to manufacturers is: Who may be in the position to come between me and my customers with what kind of offer once the device is connected to the internet or could be connected?

The relationships are also quite different regarding the data itself. Basically, we are talking about device data. Whether a personal connection can be derived from that data cannot be answered universally. It depends on the device and its functions. Generally, however, it can be said that the device data is considerably more complex than personal consumer data. Device data can pertain to everything that is related to the usage of a device: its operating data, the purpose of its use, the location of its operation, the ambient conditions, resource consumption, service life and its current "state of health," as well as many other aspects.

Finally, the Internet of Things, conversely, is the technological basis with which industry can use digitalization for its value creation processes. In this way, the cloud, which we will discuss separately, can also become a source of new ideas for products and services, just as internet-based services are used for the optimization of industrial processes.

What exactly Industrie 4.0 means as a component of the Internet of Things (and Services) can only be clarified if we make a more specific differentiation: regarding the business segments and the products. In principle, Industrie 4.0 means something completely different to investment goods manufacturers than to consumer goods manufacturers. Ultimately, every company must decide what it wishes to accomplish within the context of Industrie 4.0 in the course of digitalization for every specific product and every individual service. Of course, it is not possible for us to examine all types of products and companies. But it is worthwhile to have a look at a few examples familiar to most readers.

Let us look at smart products. The association College International Pour La Recherche En Productique (CIRP), the International Academy for Production Technology, at its 23rd CIRP Design Conference in March of 2013, adopted an official definition. The formulation, by Prof. Michael Abramovici from the Ruhr University of Bochum, can be found at SpringerReference:

> Smart products are cyber-physical products/systems (CPS) which additionally use and integrate internet-based services in order to perform a required functionality. CPS are defined as "intelligent" mechatronic products/systems capable of communicating and interacting with other CPS by using different communication channels, i. e., the internet or wireless LAN (Lee 2010; Rajkumar et al. 2010) [4].

Smart products are thus cyber-physical products or systems with integrated, internet-based services. It is not enough that they are mechatronic and "intelligent" or possess a connection to the internet. They also have to have an integrated service that works via the internet or other wireless networks.

Let us first examine what that means in the consumer goods industry, because their products are closer to smartphones than machines or factories, and the effects of Industrie 4.0 in relation to such products are palpable for all people, not only for employees or managers of industry.

Consumer goods are products intended for consumption. Among them, a differentiation is made between short-term or immediately consumed goods, such as food, toothbrushes or shoe laces, and goods that are used for longer periods of time, meaning years or even decades. These include so-called white goods, such as refrigerators and washing machines or household or garden furniture and other furnishings, as well as a large part of clothing and other textile goods. We will leave out automobiles, because they are going to be examined separately.

Often, there is a direct connection between the two categories of short-term and longer-term consumer goods. A coffee machine is used for several years, and in addition to power and water, the consumer also needs ground coffee to make the beverage with the machine, and from time to time, some cleanser and perhaps a replacement part or two.

With such products, associated services can emerge, such as measuring the consumption of ground coffee or the period of machine use. This can result in the ability to make offers for new ground coffee, cleanser and even replacement parts, which either the manufacturer or a business partner has in stock. Especially if we are not simply dealing with a single machine in a single household, but rather hundreds of machines in a corporation or hotel chain, such offers will pile up. This is already happening today. We see it with the aforementioned printers, which signal the user when new cartridges are required and the paper needs to be refilled. Depending on the configuration when installed, this message can also be coupled with an order via the internet and using the fastest delivery method. In such cases, the printer manufacturer has an influence on the selection of supplier and product, and perhaps customers willingly pay more for coffee or ink cartridges, thus financing the additional services offered.

For this kind of product, several scenarios are possible: Example a: The customer does not use the service offered, but continues to purchase the goods in a shop; Example b: The customer—for instance, a large corporation—connects the machines with their own system, which evaluates the device's messages and connects to another supplier; Example c: The service is only used by so few customers that the development of that service is not worth it for the manufacturer.

This is the category which also includes the much-discussed networking of household devices or components of furnishings and buildings themselves, such as heating systems or doors, to the extent that, for example, they can be remotely switched on and off and regulated using a smartphone. This idea has been around for years. Before the Internet of Things became a reality, they were not achievable, or at least not economically successful. Whether they will be a success remains to be seen. At any rate, it is improbable that customers will voluntarily make their private and operational user data available just for related services, such as they do with smartphones. Services must be developed which are worth it. That is the great challenge for consumer goods manufacturers. The risk for the manufacturers, on the other hand, includes conceivable or even unpredictable service offers from third parties, which may become more important to consumers than the product itself.

In contrast to consumer goods manufacturers, a company in the investment goods industry does not produce for the end customer. Its customer is another industrial enterprise. Under certain circumstances, this customer sells consumer goods, and might be a manufacturer of industrial goods. A seller of electronic motors, for instance, delivers his products to a robot manufacturer, who uses the motors to drive the robotic arms. The robots, in turn, go to a manufacturer of large machines that uses the them for production. In this environment, the smart products are machines of all kinds, robots, manufacturing plants or process industry plants, but also components, assemblies and parts needed for those products. In such situations, possible services need to have a very different character. The most important fields in which examples are known to date involve customer service and logistics.

By connecting industrial products to the internet, their operational data, including ambient data and data exchange with connected devices, can be collected and evaluated on a large scale. Because, in contrast to a household appliance malfunctioning, the failure of a drive can lead to downtime for a plant and thus enormous losses on the part of the operator, the issue of service plays a very different role here. Based on the evaluation of as much data as possible from the respective device and its environment, malfunctions can be more easily predicted. Machine failures or downtimes can be reduced and, in many cases, even prevented. The more devices a manufacturer has on hand to evaluate, the better his analysis and the more reliable are his services. Nevertheless, industrial customers are generally only willing to take advantage of such services under very clearly outlined conditions and based on specific agreements—because, at the same time, data may, under certain circumstances, provide information on the processes that are controlled by the devices, which, in turn, could reveal precisely those competitive advantages that account for a company's lead in the world market.

In logistics, Industrie 4.0 plays a role because connecting transportation systems and the products to be transported to the internet can enable the delivery to be effected with utmost precision. Unnecessary waiting times and detours and excessively early or late deliveries can be avoided; search and retrieval can be automated to a much greater extent than was previously the case. However, despite these immense advantages, here too, such services can only be developed and executed based upon an agreement and explicit order.

Finally, one function rumored to be the primary objective of Industrie 4.0 could actually be conceivable for the distant future: the smart factory, in which a workpiece communicates via the internet with machines, right down to having a machine switch on a drill to supply itself with a threaded hole.

Yet no matter what type of smart product one wants to investigate in the investment goods industry, the questions of real-time capability and security play a very different role than is the case for consumer goods. Here, broadband availability is not a question of convenience, but of survival. The reliability of services has nothing to do with access to a search engine. Either the machine or system does its job or it will be very expensive for all involved parties. A malfunction or a service performed at the wrong time may even cost human lives. To that extent, developing the broadband infrastructure is not only about telecommunications and internet availability for the end user. Without a suitable infrastructure, industrial enterprises have no chance to achieve the necessary transformation.

Even if Industrie 4.0 is an integral part of general digitalization: This part is in no way comparable to the dimensions of what we have previously seen in the world of consumerism; it cannot be compared to the digitalization of music and language, nor the digitalization of communication, nor trade.

A special case among smart products is the automobile. In the past one hundred years, it was the core of private mobility. According to the German Federal Ministry for Economic Affairs and Energy (BMWi), in 2015, the automotive industry, including its large chain of suppliers, was the largest branch of the manufacturing trade in Germany and, based on turnover, the most significant branch of industry in Germany by far. Enterprises in this industry generate a turnover of more than 404 billion euros and directly employ more than 790,000 people. Around the world, the German automotive industry led the pack with its products in almost all product divisions. What role does Industrie 4.0 play in this industry and product? The answer is somewhat complicated.

The automotive industry set the pace for the second industrial revolution with its mass production and division of labor, as well as for the third revolution, with its software-controlled automation. Its production plants are among the most advanced and complex currently in existence. In them, a high degree of individual product variations is manufactured at conditions and prices previously only possible for the series production of identical products. Approximately 150,000 different vehicles roll off the conveyor belts before being followed by one that is virtually identical to a previous vehicle. Now the question is: How is this industry transforming its production to conform to the Internet of Things? How is it achieving the fourth industrial revolution?

If there were a qualifying examination, the automotive industry would not pass the test. Several studies prove that it is lagging behind with regard to digitalization. In November 2015, the BMWi, in collaboration with the ZEW (Centre for European Economic Research) in Mannheim and TNS Infratest, published a study of the German digital economy and degree of digitalization of the German economic sector—with the automotive industry exhibiting an especially poor performance. According to the *Monitoring-Report Wirtschaft Digital 2015* ("Monitoring Report, Economy Digital 2015") [5], automobile manufacturing, with an index value of 37, together with the health industry and other manufacturing trades (both at 36) are situated in the lowest category of the "deeply below-average digitized" sectors.

Regarding the digitalization of production, the automotive industry is thus facing an extremely large challenge. This is surprising, especially considering that this industry was one of the leaders in the 1990s. Nowhere else was the use of IT in processes as strongly anchored, and nowhere else was the use of modern technologies as advanced as in the automotive sector. Evidently, without anyone noticing, it then fell behind.

And what is the scoop on the automobile as a smart product? It is a consumer good of a special kind. Is it a mechatronic system? For sure. It is a highly complex mechatronic system of mechatronic systems. About one hundred software-controlled systems, from the door lock to the parking assistant, are not unusual for a car. Is this system of systems connected to the internet? For newer vehicles, the answer is also yes. Hardly a vehicle leaves the factory anymore without its own IP address, and the driver can use it to access certain services. Yet precisely at that point, with the integrated, internet-based services that make a smart product what it is: That is where it becomes difficult for the automotive industry.

Which services should be offered by the automotive companies themselves, and which by partners? Where is it reasonable and beneficial to the business end to take advantage of and integrate services provided by internet enterprises? A quick jump was made to Google and Apple, for instance, in integrating their navigation assistance systems. But in 2015, Audi, BMW and Daimler, in a concerted action, took over the Nokia mapping service Here, in order to free themselves from the products of the large internet firms. It seems that the automobile is a product based on which big league companies are becoming competitors on the internet.

The reason for this is simple: Just as is the case for a smartphone, a car can also use the internet to provide information pertaining to preferred places and other driver preferences, and using the GPS system, it can even be directed to offers of advertisers in a more targeted manner than just with a smartphone. The dilemma of the manufacturers is that their customers are paying a lot of money for the car and its "intelligent" accessories. It is not automatic that they will accept all of their movement data being evaluated for any business idea without question, as is often the case with smartphones. It is even less certain that they will want to opt for services which depend on the manufacturer or dealer of their vehicle that they can otherwise access via a smartphone while driving.

However, even without this dilemma, the automotive industry would still have problems. As an example, there was an Audi A5, built in 2013, for which an update of the GPS system in 2016 cost about 350 euros, according to a dealer. Such an update is wise at least once a year. But the owner has to go to the trouble of finding out if there is an update. The manufacturer does not provide the information, and even the dealer will only inform the owner when asked. On the other hand, a GPS program on a smartphone costs nothing and is kept up to date automatically. Why should anyone use the system integrated in the vehicle? In 2016, automobile manufacturers had not yet realized that a GPS system is not a component like an outside mirror that only needs to be available as a replacement part if damaged, or that a GPS system is a service for which customers require up-to-date data.

And yet the automotive industry will also be faced with additional challenges. The development and marketing of electric cars has stalled, and the combustion engine, whether diesel or gasoline, is becoming less popular, even without such catastrophic mistakes as the software-supported exhaust deception scandal at Volkswagen and, evidently, other auto makers as well. The significance of the automobile as a guarantor of mobility is fading fast. In cities, it is becoming old-fashioned to still be getting around by car. And people are becoming tired of the car as an object of prestige. Nowhere in the world are there more registered users of car-sharing schemes than in Germany. It is true that the automotive industry is active and a driving force in the car-sharing business, but this service probably will not be able to make up for the expected drop in sales for the medium term.

The automotive industry is important for Germany as an industrial location. And it is especially challenged by Industrie 4.0 and the Internet of Things. It will be exciting to observe how it will confront this challenge.

2.4 Smart Engineering

Engineering, the realms of design and product development, of testing and safeguarding, preparation and planning production and its necessary facilities—it has always been one of the most important areas of industry. A widely-known calculation states that, in engineering, about 80% of all production costs are determined by the selection of the materials, processing methods, tools and machines with which the product is manufactured, and by all decisions made in this area. Yet only 20% of production costs are incurred in engineering, because it has the fewest employees and the cost of its own tools are not comparable to the production facilities and materials.

This is an old and well-known calculation. Nevertheless, engineering is consistently disregarded where too much concentration is placed on cutting engineering expenses and not enough on the manufacturing costs, which could be kept lower through engineering. With Industrie 4.0, a whole different level of importance is placed on engineering. The fourth industrial revolution will change engineering earlier and more thoroughly than it will change production.

The truth is: the smart products mentioned above also require smart engineering. Mechatronic devices with integrated, internet-based services cannot be developed in the same way as mechanical or simple mechatronic products. Just as we have seen with the automobile, such mechatronic devices are highly-complex systems of systems. Such systems cannot be developed in the traditional side-by-side and consecutive way in which mechatronics, electronics and information technology were developed. They require systems engineering (SE).

For decades, systems engineering was the domain of aerospace, created out of the compulsion to master complex, large-scale projects with a very large number of participants spanning nations and continents. A new discipline was actually born from that industry: systems engineering.

Today, systems engineering is an issue in the automotive industry and, increasingly, also in mechanical and plant engineering. It no longer matters whether thousands of people are involved in a development project and the project has the dimensions of a space station or passenger airplane. Every machine tool, every processing center, even every drive motor can reach a level of complexity that cannot be handled without methods of systems engineering.

These methods no longer first deal with the individual elements of a new product which are then assembled and tried out. Instead, the entire system is always in focus. Initially, the requirements are determined and defined, then the corresponding system architecture designed. The next step is determining which functions are to be performed by which discipline.

All disciplines—which represent a best-case situation and the goal of systems engineering—work in parallel to implement the requirements to functionality and to develop the logic according to which the system will function. In the reality of modern industry, all disciplines work largely separated from each other, with difficulties in coordinating their results, because all specialized IT systems speak their own language, which is not understood outside of that special area, making data exchange or a common visualization, if not impossible, then only possible with a very large degree of effort.

While electrical, electronic, mechanical and IT specialists work with models, visually depict their development results and perform tests on digital models, that is, are able to simulate the target functions, this is not the case for multi-disciplinary systems. Model-based systems engineering is thus an extremely important topic for scientific and in-factory research and development, which will be examined in more detail in the chapters regarding research. Experts do not yet agree whether it is desirable or even necessary to strive toward a multi-disciplinary model of the overall system, or whether it is a better idea to enable the linkage of specialized models, which would then allow co-simulation.

When systems move their mechanical parts using software, which in turn is stimulated by electronic components, then it should be possible to test the model as if it were connected to the internet and already in operation. The tester would have to virtually give a command or be able to simulate data entry using another device, leading to the system performing the desired function. Only if industry is capable of running such tests in an early development stage can it reach a pace comparable to that of the software and internet industries. To do so, the prerequisites must be achieved via standards or system integration, and IT companies are currently working on that goal.

The other challenge posed to smart engineering looms at least as large: Because the division of labor has been taken to ever further extremes in the past hundred years and longer, and because, today, a specialist is so skilled in his or her area of specialty that there is hardly any more room for improvement, there is a lack of generalists. When mechanics and IT specialists receive a joint project, they often lack a project manager who understands both sides well enough to manage them competently.

The collaboration of the disciplines, which must work together for a modern system to be successful, is also lacking for other reasons. Specialization has led to competition between disciplines. Over several decades, certain power structures have developed in enterprises and between the disciplines which have now begun to falter. It is no longer a matter of course that the mechanical engineers dictate how a machine should be built. In some companies whose development teams ten or fifteen years ago were composed of more than 90% mechanical engineers now have teams with a higher number of electronic technicians and IT specialists. Some companies that dominated the world markets as electronics enterprises are software companies today. This is the case for IBM, as well as for Siemens, to name two of the most well-known examples. Around 20,000 employees at Siemens spend one hundred percent of their working time developing software. This shift in the significance of the disciplines is accompanied by fears of job loss, which are about as difficult to overcome as the media discontinuity between the involved IT systems. (We will not even get into the purely human barriers: A new method to make a task faster and especially more transparent for others may not even be desirable to those who are intended to use it; they may not want to have to be faster).

Yet that is just what industry has to achieve now if Industrie 4.0 is to be a success: The disciplines of engineering must come together and work on a common system model in order to compete with the smart people in the internet companies regarding innovation and speed of development.

2.5 Platforms and Ecosystems

New business models are on the horizon. Intelligently developed products connected in the internet will serve as data storage media to offer new services with the aid of the data. Just as can be done with smartphones today, in the future, apps will be made available through a variety of devices offering integrated, internet-based services. Along the way, there are already signs that the methods of doing business and trade are also changing. Where there previously were simple relationships between manufacturers and customers, this aspect, too, is now becoming more complicated.

Up to now, a manufacturer developed and produced a product, which was then sold on the market by that manufacturer or a retailer. During the development and production phases, business partners of the manufacturer generally supplied parts, components or services, but the basic principle was: The manufacturers sell their products to customers. The more products turn into smart products, the less this basic principle can be upheld.

In the publications and events surrounding Industrie 4.0 and the Internet of Things, two expressions are popping up more and more frequently which seem familiar to us but now stand for something else than they once did. These expressions are the terms "platform" and "ecosystem".

We already know several types of platforms: those in the automobile industry which enable manufacturers to develop various engines and components for one vehicle platform whose reusability has, however, been secured because they were developed for certain platforms and not for one particular vehicle model; the operating system of a PC is the platform on which the software of various producers can be used; of course, political or social groups also rely on platforms that define commonalities; there are drilling platforms and landing platforms, and the expression has several other meanings. When we speak of platforms in connection with Industrie 4.0, the best comparison is that of a computer operating system.

Just as an operating system on a smartphone can serve as a platform for millions of applications, new platforms are now being developed through which industrial services can be offered. It is not very promising for every product or every product line to program special apps that will only work with that product. It seems much more logical to develop apps for a particular type of industrial service, which then can be integrated with certain products or product types, regardless of who exactly manufactured the product. Such a service could, for example, be the search for and ordering of replacement parts, for products ranging from household appliances to cars. Most likely, platforms will develop on which such apps can run. At this point, it is hard to tell who the suppliers and who the operators will be. It could be leading industrial enterprises, cooperation between branches of industry, associations, ITC suppliers or even entirely new players specialized in this type of business.

Just as it is important for industrial enterprises to find out with which business models they wish to turn a profit relating to their future smart products, so, too, will it be important to identify the correct platform with which to do so.

The description of newly-forming platforms alone sheds light on the second expression that has acquired a new meaning: the ecosystem. To date, many people—especially in Germany—have understood it to signify an ecological system; a system that describes how people, nature and technology can interact to the benefit of the ecology. And internationally, many have understood the English term ecosystem as being the economic system of a country, region or the world. Now the term is surfacing in a new variation. It means the special system which in future will be used for the development, manufacture, distribution and use of smart products on the Internet of Things.

Because in addition to manufacturers of products and their suppliers and dealers, there are now also manufacturers and suppliers of platforms, apps and services, cloud technology and software. The number of participants may not be as large as in an ecosystem of computers and smartphones, but this number will grow considerably and become less well-defined than we have known from traditional industry. There will surely be more ecosystems than those in the environment of the smartphone, because the number of possible types of services extends well beyond what is achievable with smartphones. And everyone who transforms his or her enterprise to orient toward Industrie 4.0 also has to consider what role that enterprise will play in which ecosystem—because it is also clear that the decision will not be in favor of a single ecosystem, but rather most likely several simultaneously. The example of the internet of automobiles as described in Sect. 6.2 could be a typical case. Automobile manufacturers will soon have to network their vehicles in the ecosystem of China as well as in at least one in the western world.

2.6 Social Magnitude

What is the goal of Industrie 4.0? On the homepage of acatech, under the heading *Dossier Zukunft des Industriestandortes* ("Dossier for the Future of the Industrial Location"), in the introduction, which has been quoted elsewhere in this book, there is also the following assessment:

> Germany has the potential to become an international lead market and lead supplier in Industrie 4.0 and the services connected to it. From this transition, a new "Made in Germany" economic miracle can emerge, and value creation and jobs can be generated [2].

Industrie 4.0 is seen by its initiators and the Federal Republic of Germany, which it is pursuing as part of its high-tech strategy, as significant for the future of Germany as an industrial location. Germany could become a lead market and lead supplier, which could lead to a new economic miracle.

Faith is being placed on German industry to play a predominant role in the fourth industrial revolution. A lead market means that the German market would be at the forefront for smart products and related services. A lead supplier means that German industry would be the global leading supplier of products and services based on Industrie 4.0.

After having taken a close look at what type of products and services are involved, it is now clear: The decisive factor is the use of the internet for industrial value creation processes as well as for the use of products and services. With Industrie 4.0, Germany as an industrial site has signaled its demand to play a leading role on the internet in the future. After the beginnings of the internet economy, which focused exclusively on the networking of people with the aid of mobile computing end devices and the exploitation of the resulting personal data, the manufacturing industry has now taken the stage.

We are not talking about a simple expansion of previous economic activity to include data on the internet. We are talking about completely different, industrial and device-related data. And to use this data, suppliers require more than smartphones and operating systems. They need deep knowledge of industrial value creation, software-controlled processes, safe machines and their effective utilization. Internet companies cannot simply purchase this know-how and acquire it in just a few years. However, they may be able to dictate to producers the rules that will be used to do business with industrial data on the internet.

In several branches, German industry has forfeited its leading position. Whether it be the textile industry, consumer electronics, computers and their peripheral devices—this list of industrial branches lost to competitors in the USA and especially Asia is long. On the other hand, significant industries, such as mechanical and plant engineering, automation suppliers and manufacturers of sensors and actuators, the automotive industry and agricultural machines, manufacturers of household appliances and other sectors of the consumer goods industry, have succeeded in leading their global markets with regard to the quality of the mechatronic products. Their goods are so highly valued due to their "Made in Germany" label that even higher prices than competitor products cannot shake their top spot in those markets.

Besides production, Germany as an industrial location also has bred a few leading suppliers, such as SAP, Siemens or Telekom, which directly provide parts of the technology required for Industrie 4.0. Digital support of the value creation processes and cloud platforms top the list. In recent years, several smaller and mid-sized enterprises have begun to expand their IT and internet expertise and rise to join the circle of technology suppliers.

Thus, this claim that Germany as an industrial location has taken a leading role is justified. While this does not apply to all industries, it certainly applies to those which are pertinent to Germany's current global market position.

Whether this will lead to a new economic miracle remains to be seen. It is still unclear just how exactly the business model with an industrial internet will look. Of course, the broad global debate about the fourth industrial revolution is spurring lively competition. It has not yet been determined who will lead the race, and it will differ from one industry to the next.

Should Industrie 4.0 prove successful, "Made in Germany" will have a different significance in the future than has been the case. It will no longer be a stamp on a device indicating that the product was manufactured in Germany. In the future, it will be about the technologies that were employed for the development of a system and its integrated services; it will be about the methods of development, testing, manufacture and service. "Made in Germany" will then include smart engineering, smart products and smart services. Ideally, we would need another slogan than the brand "Made in Germany," since the old brand primarily refers to manufacture, evident in the "Made." Now, it is more about the "How" of the overall processes.

If Industrie 4.0 is successful, not only products and services will find customers around the world. Enterprises and nations will also want to shop at German companies, especially for technology and expertise regarding how this innovative industry works and how to make money with it.

Hopes are high that it will be a success. Germany as an industrial location could be just as important for the global internet economy in this next phase as the USA was in the first phase and still is today. The other possibility, that Germany would primarily produce the hardware while others shape the economy of the future, will not be explored further in this book.

Industrie 4.0 has a significance for industry and Germany as an industrial site that cannot be valued enough. Its success depends on a wealth of jobs—not so much those jobs than can be protected with Industrie 4.0 as the undoubtedly even higher number of jobs that can only be created for and through it. The job situation itself is one of the most important criteria for the prosperity of a society, the financial strength of a nation, and the weal and woe of everyone, including those who work neither in nor for industry. Yet the social magnitude of Industrie 4.0 does not end there.

The new products and opportunities of integrated services offer an incredible amount of possibilities to change our lives. Now that software and device networking offers virtually unlimited technical possibilities, the question is, what will society do with these possibilities? Should insurance companies use personal data for their business? Should the health status of accident patients already be available to hospitals when they are admitted? Which data should be free of charge and which should not? What rights does a person have toward a digitally-controlled, autonomous device? And vice versa? On the other hand: Should machines in the future be so intelligent that they can operate on a minimum of regenerative energy? Should industry use its smart products to contribute greatly to not only halting environmental damage but even enabling the environment to recover?

If anything is technically possible, society has to take on an influential role. What is done with Industrie 4.0 cannot be left to the free market to decide. The risks would be too great that the wrong things will be done, and the chance to achieve great things is far too important. At the same time, a new openness must emerge, in comparison to the past. Start-ups must be fostered, investments must be made easier, barriers to new technologies and services broken down. This is a balancing act that all of humankind must now master. If Germany is to play a leading role as an industrial location, it will have to be a leader in this type of influence as well.

In recent years, the awareness of entrepreneurs and enterprises has grown to recognize that the Earth and nature are not resources that industry can exploit at will. Humans have already damaged the natural environment with their industry such that complete recovery is no longer possible. It is no longer nature, with its millions of years of natural laws, that determines the climate and quality of the environment, but humans. In doing so, however, they have also taken on the responsibility to care for the future development of the natural environment.

A few years ago, just before the topic of Industrie 4.0 became the dominating theme of the Hanover Trade Fair, its motto had been "Greentelligence." It would be catastrophic if Industrie 4.0 led to a decline in the efforts of industry to pursue environmentally sustainable processes and products. The opposite must be the goal. The incredible opportunities of new technologies must be employed to make industry so "intelligent" that it can virtually autonomously lead to greater resource efficiency and sustainability, lower emissions and less environmental pollution.

From this perspective, the targeted leadership role of Industrie 4.0 in the world is almost more important than from an economic aspect: Only if the further industrialization of the world is done according to the principles of Greentelligence can the world's billions of people achieve a desired level of prosperity without simultaneously making ill or killing millions with smog and environmental destruction.

Industrie 4.0 has the right stuff to also promote a significant transformation in that sense as well; one that will unleash its effects far beyond industry. High hopes are also held for this aspect of success.

References

1. Umsetzungsstrategie Industrie 4.0, result report of the platform Industrie 4.0, editorial board of BITKOM e. V., VDMA e. V., ZVEI e. V., April 2015, p. 8.
2. http://www.acatech.de/de/aktuelles-presse/dossiers/dossier-zukunft-des-industriestandorts.html. Accessed 12 May 2016.
3. Hilbert, M., & López, P. (2011). The world's technological capacity to store, communicate, and compute information. *Science, 332,* 60 (print ISSN 0036-8075, online ISSN 1095-9203).
4. http://www.springerreference.com/docs/html/chapterdbid/409978.html. Accessed 12 May 2016.
5. Monitoring-Report Wirtschaft Digital. (2015). German federal ministry for economic affairs and energy, report on public relations. publikationen@bundesregierung.de.

3 Important Technologies

Ulrich Sendler

Abstract
Industrie 4.0 is based on the technical possibility of connecting products of all sorts to the internet that are equipped with digital components and are software-controlled, and of offering corresponding services via the internet. This technical basis alone would not suffice to trigger a fourth industrial revolution. There are a few technologies that have been available for a longer time but have received a completely new significance in connection with the Internet of Things and Services. And regarding the utilization of these technologies, Industrie 4.0 is a very real vision.

3.1 Artificial Intelligence

Among other sources, the beginnings of Industrie 4.0 traces back to research done by the German Research Center for Artificial Intelligence (DFKI). Prof. Wolfgang Wahlster, Director and Chairman of the Board of Directors at the DFKI, teaches and conducts research in the areas of artificial intelligence (AI) and computer linguistics in the Department of Information Technology at the University of Saarbrücken, Germany. In several publications concerning Industrie 4.0, including significant graphic images used for illustration, the DFKI and Prof. Wahlster or one of his many colleagues can be found as sources or authors. In Kaiserslautern, the DFKI, under the direction of Prof. Detlef Zühlke, established a smart factory to serve as a research laboratory a few years before the *Industrie 4.0* initiative was

U. Sendler (✉)
Mauerkircherstraße 30, 81679 Munich, Germany
E-Mail: ulrich.sendler@ulrichsendler.de

U. Sendler (ed.), *The Internet of Things*,
https://doi.org/10.1007/978-3-662-54904-9_3

founded. In October of 2015, Google took over a share of the DFKI. It is the only research enterprise in Europe to date in which Google participates with a capital contribution and a seat on the supervisory board.

The question as to whether Industrie 4.0 has anything to do with artificial intelligence is thus not far-fetched, but rather obvious. To understand the connection, let us have a brief look at the history of AI.

The term "artificial intelligence" has existed in that form since 1956, and thus predates the first courses of study in information technology. The computer had hardly entered the world stage and become economically applicable when it led to incredible expectations as to what problems it could solve: all problems on the planet, actually, thought a few people, and not the dumbest, to be sure. A few of the first AI experts presumed that, within a short period of time, it would be possible to store the entirety of human knowledge on computers. They took it even a step further by asserting that, once this happened, the biomass of the human brain would become superfluous, heralding a post-human age.

Just how presumptuous some of these specialists were can best be seen in a few of their prophecies. One of the pioneers of AI, Herbert Simon from Carnegie Mellon University, predicted in 1957 that, within the following ten years, a computer would become the world chess champion and would discover and prove a significant mathematical theorem. In fact, it took 40 years, until 1997, before Garry Kasparov could be defeated by the IBM system Deep Blue. And to date, no computer has discovered a mathematical theorem. Proving well-known theorems, on the other hand, has become a special area of AI (see e.g. [1]).

These initial expectations were much too high. Neither hardware performance, nor storage capacity, and especially not information science itself, still in its early years, was able to solve random problems. Several projects, which were partly initiated and funded by industry in the hopes of saving money on industrial processes, were abandoned without further ado. Yet, at the same time that the first freely-programmable computers were developed in the 1940s, ingenious ideas originated that only today have met the technology with which they can actually be put to practical use, such as artificial neural networks, which we will subsequently examine further.

A second phase of AI, beginning as early as the mid-1970s, was characterized by the development of so-called expert systems. Such applications, also known as knowledge-based systems, were fed with rule-based knowledge from a specific area of expertise. Sometimes incredibly efficient systems evolved, which, when given specific questions from precisely that related area of expertise, could lead to favorable results. Nevertheless, these attempts were also only useful in a limited way. One example was MYCIN, a system for supporting diagnostic and therapeutic decisions related to infectious diseases of the blood, developed in the 1970s at Stanford University [2]. It was capable of making decisions whose quality corresponded to those of medical specialists. Unfortunately, it also supplied therapeutic recommendations for blood infections when it was fed data pertaining to an intestinal infection, which required completely different therapeutic measures. It was only familiar with the area of expertise of blood infections.

Although a good deal of money was also put into the development of industrial expert systems in the 1980s and 1990s, this phase, too, exhibited no great breakthroughs. For instance, there were attempts in the automotive industry to develop systems to automate the construction of free-form surfaces, as this portion of the design process represented a monstrous cost pool at the time, while serving as the greatest obstacle to shortening vehicle development cycles. Even when enormous developmental efforts proved successful in individual cases, their economic costs were never reasonably proportionate to their results. In such cases as well, industry capped their investments, allowing expert systems—beyond information technology—to more or less be forgotten.

Interestingly, both of the first two phases of artificial intelligence were pursuing the storage of human knowledge and rules, as if human intelligence could be reduced to knowledge and following rules. These approaches failed on the one hand due to an insufficiency of computer capacity and software. On the other and, they were fairly limited in wanting to take on human intelligence.

A third phase did not begin until the turn of the millennium: based on findings of neurophysics and neurobiology, which, through chromophoric procedures of visualization, gradually enabled the architecture and neural construction of the brain to be examined and depicted. AI researchers harkened back to a model of artificial neurons presented as early as 1943 (!) by Warren S. McCulloch and Walter Pitts, which then became known as the McCulloch-Pitts neuron [3]. Those geniuses suspected how the brain was constructed and how it functioned without having been able to prove it at the time. Sixty years later, researchers have now begun with the development of neural networks. The system is intended to use the information architecture of the brain of humans and animals as a model, and develop learning processes similar to those of intelligent beings. This phase is not finished by far. However, especially in recent years, it appears to have reached results that have advanced its economic use, such as for controlling machines or robots, into the realm of possibility.

Computer performance, storage capacities and information technology research have progressed to such a degree that, around the world today, in addition to the research laboratories of institutes dedicated to research and development, numerous industrial enterprises are focusing on these topics in the hopes of achieving economic success. Quite a few developments are not even perceived as artificial intelligence anymore, even though it is AI that has provided the foundation for enormous economic successes: The most popular examples are certainly the search algorithms which have aided Google, Amazon and eBay in their success. Pattern analysis, pattern recognition, language recognition, robotics—all of these areas were originally subsections of artificial intelligence.

In February 2011, Ken Jennings and Brad Rutter, who up until then had been outstanding, record-holding champions on the quiz show Jeopardy, played against and lost to IBM's Watson system, which, for the first time, was able to independently and successfully weigh various solutions, winning by a mile. Jeopardy has been a popular television quiz show since the 1960s, where participants are presented with answers from various subject areas for which they must form the correct question.

One of the most recent examples of the performance capability of such systems is the five-match competition between humans and a computer in the Asian board game Go in early March of 2016. Almost 20 years after the victory of IBM Deep Blue over Kasparov, the system AlphaGo by Google DeepMind played against one of the world's best professional Go players, the 33-year-old South Korean, Lee Sedol.

DeepMind is a British start-up taken over by Google. With its software AlphaGo, it had already beaten a European Go master in the autumn of 2015. Then AlphaGo was pitted against a world champion and won in South Korea with a score of 4:1. Go is considered to be more than 10 times more complex than chess. Black and white playing pieces are alternately placed on a board of 19 × 19 squares. The object is to occupy as large a portion of the board as possible. What seems easy means, for instance: If Black and White each lay two pieces, there are 1.6 billion move possibilities. That is why Go is valued as a game which, in addition to strategic thinking and a high level of calculation skills, primarily requires human intuition, creativity, patience and a desire for playful battle. It is not enough to simply store rules and matches played in the unit's memory.

AlphaGo is based on layered artificial neural networks modeled after the human neural network system. If an action leads to success, the system remembers that success and adjusts the nodes involved, similar to how the human brain releases neurotransmitters to support the nerve synapses. After countless saved Go games are processed, the software was prepared for the game against Lee Sedol by playing against itself. And although the development team of DeepMind co-founder Demis Hassabis himself had not expected a victory for another few years, AlphaGo was already capable of winning. Artificial intelligence as a mixture of artificial neural networks and machine learning has beaten humans in a realm in which distinguished experts had predicted they would not reach until at least ten years.

According to Hassabis, what was developed in a playful way is nevertheless targeted at very real applications. For example, the same type of systems is to be employed in medical operations. And of course, machine learning and robots will be used in industry itself. In 2013 and 2014, Google invested a total of 17 billion US$ for corporate acquisitions. In eight separate cases, the enterprises taken over were robotics companies, including the military robot manufacturer Boston Dynamics.

When Demis Hassabis had Google promise him before taking over his company that the software and algorithms of DeepMind would not be used for arms production or intelligence assignments, it demonstrated where he himself saw the dangers. Whether the promise made by Google was ever made official in the form of a contract is not known.

The software learns to learn using the methods of artificial intelligence. AI can be used to allow a robot that moves on two or four legs like a human or dog to pick up an object, bring it somewhere and put it down in a specific place, for instance. There are videos made by Boston Dynamics showing a human kicking the robot or pushing it over violently. The robot gets back up, picks up the piece it is to transport and continues carrying out its task. Thus, it has already been made capable of overcoming a series of unanticipated obstacles that may hinder it in carrying out its task.

According to Google DeepMind, it also works together with the Future of Humanity Institute at Oxford University in developing possibilities to allow autonomous machines to be switched off again while they are in operation. This possibility is called interruptibility. This is significant, because why shouldn't it be possible for a learning machine to recognize that, in order to perform a task, it must at least be switched on? Thus, why shouldn't it also be possible to teach the machine how it can prevent itself from being shut off?

That is a considerably alarming view of the future, and humans will have to make sure that such developments move in the right direction. For the time being, however, it is important to note: It will most likely take several years or even decades before robots will be capable of replacing human workers through autonomous learning and action. Training robots through machine learning is currently much too expensive and complex to be used in a profitable way in comparison to standard programming of robots to perform the precise movements required—not to mention that it will take even longer until machines can communicate with other robots or people as humans can.

Nevertheless: In late 2014, British physicist and astrophysicist Dr. Stephen Hawking—unable to speak since 1985 due to an incurable muscle disease and, with the aid of artificial intelligence, able to formulate words using eye movements—expressed the fear, taken very seriously by experts, that the development of artificial intelligence could lead to robots becoming equal to humans and even surpassing them. "Humans, who are limited by slow biological evolution, couldn't compete, and would be superseded," said Hawking in an interview with the Financial Times. Thus, the advice to take seriously the possibilities of AI from all sides is not overstated.

By the way, it is not only Google currently showing so much interest in artificial intelligence. On March 25, 2016, the New York Times published an article headlined "The Race Is On to Control Artificial Intelligence, and Tech's Future" [4]. The authors saw the AlphaGo game as more of a statement from Google to its competitors than to the world Go champion. And this competition was specified, with reference to the technology analysts at International Data Corporation (IDC): The market for applications involving machine learning, according to the IDC, will grow to a value of 40 billion dollars by the year 2020, and 60% of those applications will run on the platforms of Amazon, Google, IBM and Microsoft.

Regarding this prediction, a fight has now broken out about who will win this recent platform competition. Not only are the big guys considered potential winners. There are several small start-ups which are not afraid to take on the large corporations. In the article, a professor at Stanford University reports of one doctoral candidate who was offered employment before he even took his final exams. He was offered one million dollars per year. Yet it was not one single company, but four, that were competing for him. The prospective employee ranked the larger companies vying for him lower than the others, both with regard to how exciting he thought his tasks would be as well as the salary.

At any rate, the large corporations invest large sums of money to maintain their position. With its System Watson, IBM has begun to develop an international business around the Watson system in which the former computer producer and current system integrator sees great promise. Along with 500 large and small partners, David Kenny of the Watson Division is quoted in the New York Times as defining the long-term goal to be "to have hundreds of millions of people use Watson as self-service AI." The German newspaper *Süddeutsche Zeitung* noted shortly afterward that one of those large partners is SAP [5]. The ERP supplier, whose business is also being threatened by the cloud services of Salesforce, hopes to expand its real time database SAP HANA using the analytical capabilities of IBM Watson.

In 2015, Microsoft supplemented its own cloud platform Azure with machine learning capabilities and is now offering 18 related services. Amazon has also been taking similar measures to expand its web services since 2015.

With a basis in artificial intelligence, the deck seems to have once again been reshuffled. So, after the PC platform and the internet platform, do we now have an AI platform? The development of AI in recent years certainly shows that it is also ready for broad usage in industry. In connection with other technologies that have also reached a certain degree of maturity, it will surely play a growing role within the context of Industrie 4.0.

3.2 Big Data

It is difficult to speak of Industrie 4.0 without coming across the term "big data." When several billion devices are networked, a plethora of data naturally accumulates in addition to the data already generated without this development. If you go looking for reliable figures on how much data is verifiably generated, stored or analyzed per year or per day, you will find all sorts of information, except for evidence that would stand up to being investigated. Quite simply, there is already far too much data, and the development of information technology and computer hardware is much too fast to be able to obtain an overview of it all.

According to information from IBM making its rounds on the internet, we currently produce 2.5 quintillion bytes of data per day worldwide. One quintillion is 1 with 18 zeros. This may be true; the progression of digitalization is causing an unimaginable flood of data, which is multiplying by the hour.

But the term "big data" not only refers to the pure volume of data. Rather, there are three criteria which must be fulfilled in order for the employment of special software solutions to seem appropriate for big data. These criteria are the "three Vs" of volume, velocity and variety.

The sheer volume is thus one of the three criteria, and, of course, for Industrie 4.0 and the Internet of Things, the following applies: The more digital components that are installed in devices which can theoretically supply data via the internet, the larger the volume of available information is, the faster the volume of that information will grow, and the more varied the data types are that can only be used when a concrete piece of information is derived from a piece of digital data.

The second criterion, the speed at which data is generated or collected, is also on the mark. Whether it is movement data from mobile products or measurement data from production plants during operation in real time—the data volume that goes out into the world via networked devices pro nanosecond cannot be monitored or evaluated by any human with conventional means.

The multiplicity and diversity of data is also a criterion which pertains to all sorts of devices connected to the internet. For instance, there is so much diverse data collected from motor vehicles, be it in relation to the operation of the vehicle, from the GPS system, from connected mobile phones or other subsystems, that we can justifiably speak of a special variance.

Thus, there is no question that the criteria for employing big data solutions have principally been fulfilled for data from products connected to the Internet of Things. However, a closer examination of individual cases is still worthwhile.

All data from industrial devices originates either from the installed software or is generated and collected by installed components. The manufacturers of these devices usually know very well which data is or could be involved. After all, the software was programmed either by that manufacturer or a supplier, and in general, every sensor and actuator comes from the company that puts the device on the market. So, the engineers, designers and software specialists of the producer will know what type of data they should expect and in what quantities from which source.

That is why there is a considerable difference between data from industrial devices and, let's say, personal or individual-specific data as it relates to business in electronics stores and internet advertisements. Industrial data usually has a clear, known relationship to itself as well as to the device and its use. In the consumer realm, a rational relationship must first be established. The fact that people looking for a particular product have also searched for other particular ones is just such a relationship that lends search engine providers the possibility of offering advertising space to product suppliers. To bring together such non-correlating data in a context that is useful cannot be accomplished without big data solutions.

On the other hand, for the evaluation of the data of their machines and robots, industry has learned from the past decades to write ever better programs that deliver important analyses faster. As it is known which values can be obtained at which times from which devices or components built into those devices—because, after all, that data is nothing more than target data from engineering—the corresponding, in the meantime very sophisticated industrial analysis programs can focus on those values that are unknown: the runaway values, the malfunctions, the special, unexpected data. That is why, despite the large volume, variance and speed of data flow, it is still possible for the previously used software to be sufficient when the device is connected to the internet and is also has integrated services.

A further aspect must be tested to decide if and for what data a big data solution would be the right means: Before the data generated in or collected by the device is analyzed, it must first be sorted and thoroughly and locally filtered. Just as a person only absorbs and processes a small fraction of the information that flows into his or her brain, so, too, can data coming from various devices be superfluous and useless due to the large volume. It depends on the purpose for which such data is collected, and on the relationship and relevance to the business model behind it. In addition, the internet would not even be able to process all theoretically possible data transfers from all networked devices. Thus, the data must first be thoroughly filtered in the device to determine what exactly should be transferred. Then, the filtered data, reduced to a valuable and relevant information flow, must ultimately be checked to determine the best method and correct tool for the analysis.

To put it bluntly: You shouldn't take a big data sledgehammer to crack a data nut if any of your own existing software will do the job. On the other hand, it is obvious that, with the Internet of Things, new and possibly economically prudent applications of big data solutions can now also be considered for industry. In addition to the information scientists who are tending to the development of embedded software, in the future, specialists may also be required who are familiar with big data. Since the end of the 1990s, completely new courses of study have crystallized out of information technology that teach data science. In the 1960s, data science was originally a term used as a synonym for information technology. Today, it signifies the science of statistical analysis of large volumes of data.

By the way, Germany is by no means a blank area on the map of this field. For example, in 2001, student assistants in the Department of Artificial Intelligence at the TU Dortmund began developing an open-source development environment for machine learning and data mining, which is basically the deep drilling and recovery of valuable treasures in unending data mountains. In 2007, it turned into a start-up called RapidMiner, which offered software of the same name as a free download. Today, the company employs more than 100 people in its locations in Dortmund (Germany), Boston (USA), London (UK) and Budapest (Hungary). Cleverly, the downloadable software is only the tool, but using it correctly requires the help of specialists. In the meantime, the system is used by industrial giants such as Lufthansa, Cisco, eBay and the marketing research institute GfK. In total, at about 600 customers worldwide, 35,000 active implementations with more than 250,000 users and 40,000 downloads per month—the numbers show why for years RapidMiner has been rated as a global leader by international analysts. More and more customers come from industry and are looking for opportunities to use this solution to obtain meaningful information from their partially unresearched mountains of data. The statistics department at the TU Dortmund offers a master's program in data science.

3.3 The Cloud

Digitalization is a very clear example of how technical progress often—if not always—solves humankind's problems while, at the same time, more or less exchanging them for new ones. From the start, the computer has helped to make large problems small and to master tasks which previously seemed insurmountable, from mathematics to automation, with the wave of a hand. From the very first model, it has been a significant component of progress, with which humans have begun to take control of natural dangers and catastrophes at a much earlier stage. Today, we not only know more specifically what the weather will be like and can, for instance, optimize the timing of sowing and harvesting crops or even more precisely plan an outing; we are also beginning to recognize much earlier when and where an earthquake or tsunami may occur. At the same time, the computer is intensifying competition, increasing the speed of development and of daily life and forcing people to increasingly adapt to its possibilities.

The first computers were not only gigantic, they were also expensive, such that only the largest corporations could afford them. The smaller enterprises had to resort to external computing centers or do without using them at all. Then along came midsize computers with various versions of the operating system Unix, which, for example, could be used for several work stations in various realms of engineering. CAD, CAM, all of those systems which in the past 40 years have taken industry by storm, first ran on Unix operating systems of various producers. In the mid-1980s, Microsoft introduced the operating systems for the PC, first DOS and subsequently Windows. The Unix system producers, from Apollo to Digital Equipment to Silicon Graphics, Sun Microsystems and Siemens Nixdorf, that employed tens of thousands of people in their heyday, soon disappeared from the market, with hardly a trace.

The whole world, from private persons to large corporations, began to use the PC. All important software systems were now available for the PC. That solved an important problem in industry: The enormously high costs for computers and software had shrunk to the extent that there would soon be PCs on every desk—not only of the smallest companies, but also every private person, and almost every task in a company could be performed or processed digitally.

However, a large problem emerged that has not yet been solved, but whose solution is now technically possible: The multiplicity of hardware and software in a company and the large to colossal IT infrastructures, the staff needed to maintain and it and the management involved has caused new costs of unforeseen dimensions. Today, it is hardly possible for many companies to keep up with the several new versions of their countless systems, not to mention interfaces between the systems. And neither hardware nor software tends to meet the requirements for individual workplaces, much less the entire enterprise. Sometimes it is too little, but it is mostly far too much. Users generally only employ a fraction of software functionality and the performance capability it provides. However, if it ever becomes too little, because a certain task requires a large amount of processing power or special software, a short-term solution is hardly possible.

The next step in the computer evolution then took place, and it is no wonder: This step brought the digitalization and virtualization of the computer itself—because that is essentially what the cloud is.

The first cloud service came from Amazon. Its core business, internet trade, is the largest e-commerce platform in the world, with millions of customers and transactions per day. In order to have a highly-scalable and highly-available IT infrastructure and to offer its customers a reliable service at all times, Amazon developed the cloud technology for its own needs. However, Amazon Web Services (AWS) presented a service right from the start that particularly caters to enterprises.

Highly scalable and highly available means that instead of installing the maximum required computing capacity in a company, those features of external computers are used which are required at any given time. And theoretically, an unlimited capacity is available. Right from their own screens, users have access to computers about which they know nothing, not even where they are situated, and, most importantly, these computers are not their problem. This concept works for hardware as well as storage space and software, because, from a technical standpoint, cloud technology comes in three service varieties.

The first variety is the one described above. Using official terminology, it is known as infrastructure as a service (IaaS). Customers rent a virtual server and use it as needed. They can add or subtract capacities as it corresponds to their respective requirements.

The second model is the platform as a service (PaaS). Customers include, for example, suppliers of software applications that use the finished platform for development, testing and also as a runtime environment. The platform is somewhat more virtual than the infrastructure model, in which a customer is at least allocated to what resembles a virtual server of varying capacities. In the platform model, the customer has absolutely no idea which server structures run which parts of his or her application, or, for example, which parts are re-used for testing and compilation, and which ones for the finished application itself.

The third model is called software as a service (SaaS). Here, a customer uses a software program via his or her end device. For instance, the ERP software by Salesforce works according to this principle, as well as every kind of web app started from a random device connected to the internet. Almost every app on every smartphone is based on this principle.

These three models are built on each other. The internet-based software needs a platform that will allow it to work on the internet, and the platform needs an infrastructure of servers that will meet its demands.

From an organizational standpoint, a further differentiation is made between a public and private cloud. While the public cloud is open to every end user on the internet, the group of users in a private cloud is clearly defined. Examples include the employees of a company, additional business partners or additional customers. Operators of a private cloud partition it off from the rest of the internet. The rules of access by a defined group are completely independent from the place in which the cloud services are operated.

Now, it is easy to understand that the cloud has quite a bit to do with Industrie 4.0 and the Internet of Things. Those who wish to analyze and use data from machines, systems or other products via the internet cannot know when implementing an internet-based service how many of their customers will take advantage of such services. They are in a similar situation as suppliers of consumer goods or services for end users. They require a highly-scalable and highly-available platform.

Only a few large corporations will independently establish such a platform for their customers and partners. It makes sense that a series of suppliers—such as described in the chapter on artificial intelligence—will take shape for whom cloud services will become the core business.

Just which of these platforms will be among the most popular in industry remains to be seen in the coming years. It is possible that industrial companies that actively put their products on the Internet of Things and wish to offer the corresponding apps will either decide on one or two of these platforms or will have to use the ones their customers prefer. It will probably be similar to today's smartphone apps: A producer develops an app either more or less exclusively for the platform of one or another smartphone provider which then is not available to users of other devices. Or, such a producer will have to go to the trouble of making and keeping his app runnable on all important mobile operating systems.

The only thing that is clear at the moment is: Without cloud technology, the Internet of Things would not work. Industry must grapple with it. The responsible persons in German companies are sometimes accused of being against the cloud on principle. It is true that a fear of surrendering control over company expertise and operational knowledge, as is the case for evaluation apps, may very well be greater in Germany than elsewhere. The answer, however, can only be to use suitable measures and select reliable platforms for that degree of security which will lead the cloud to become popular, even in industry. In that case, the IoT can turn Germany into an export success. If this does not succeed, German Industry will not take on a leading role in the Internet of Things.

References

1. Plaisted, D. A., & Zhu, Y. (1999). *The efficiency of theorem proving strategies—A comparative and asymptotic analysis*. Wiesbaden: Springer Vieweg (e-book).
2. Educational Technology. (1991). *Expert systems and intelligent computer aided instruction*. New Jersey: Educational Technology (ISBN 0-87778-224-5).
3. Nauck, D., Klawonn, F., & Kruse, R. (1996). *Neuronale Netze und Fuzzy Systeme—Grundlagen des Konnektionismus, Neuronaler Fuzzy Systeme und der Kopplung mit wissensbasierten Methoden*. Wiesbaden: Springer (978-3-528-15265-9, 978-3-663-10898-6 (e-book)).
4. Markoff, J., & Lohr, S. (2016, March 25). The race is on to control artificial intelligence, and tech's future. *New York Times*.
5. Martin-Jung, H. (2016, April 7). Schneller in die Wolke. *Süddeutsche Zeitung, Wirtschaft*.

The Initiative in Germany

4

Ulrich Sendler

Abstract

A period just short of five years is not a lot of time for an initiative such as *Industrie 4.0*, on which several industrial enterprises, research institutes, associations and the federal government of Germany are cooperating. The time constraint becomes even more pronounced if you consider that all of these participants are representatives of companies, organizations and institutes which must often deal with heavy competition on a day-to-day basis. Just the collaboration alone between the three industrial associations BITKOM, VDMA and ZVEI represents the first cooperative activity ever of its kind. That makes the results achieved in this short span of time even more astounding. At the same time, however, things are moving much too slowly for an initiative of such significance and in an environment of such internet speed. This chapter will describe the development of the initiative and look at the collaboration involved, the structure of the platform and its central fields of work, its turnover to the federal government and initial concrete results, including international activity.

4.1 From an Association Platform to a Government Platform

It was industrial representatives in the working group *Industrie 4.0* from acatech and a research union which wanted to have their associations in the same boat. For a plan that was to be cross-industrial and cross-disciplinary in character, it seemed reasonable to involve at least the most important associations right from the start.

U. Sendler (✉)
Mauerkircherstraße 30, 81679 Munich, Germany
E-Mail: ulrich.sendler@ulrichsendler.de

U. Sendler (ed.), *The Internet of Things*,
https://doi.org/10.1007/978-3-662-54904-9_4

BITKOM represents 1500 members, primarily from the IT and telecommunications industries. BITKOM refers to the project as the digital economy. The VDMA (German Mechanical Engineering Industry Association), with more than 3100 members from primarily midsize companies of the investment goods industry, is the largest industrial association in Europe. ZVEI (German Electrical and Electronic Manufacturers' Association) has 1600 members divided into 22 specialist associations, including those for automation and consumer electronics.

The *Die Plattform Industrie 4.0* was presented by those three associations at the 2013 Hanover Trade Fair. At that time, they had already activated their own, joint website. The structure of the platform basically included a steering committee, comprised of representatives of member enterprises, sponsor associations, a speaker from the scientific advisory board and the managers of the working groups. The steering committee was entrusted with the task of setting up working groups and, in cooperation with the managers of those groups, steer the platform. The executive board consisted of CEOs of medium-sized companies, and was responsible for providing ideas for the strategic direction of the platform. The scientific advisory board was made up of professors from departments relevant to Industrie 4.0.

An office was established to serve as the implementation and communication institution comprising a few permanent employees from the three associations. Rainer Glatz, managing director of the Software and the Electrical Automation groups of the VDMA and director of the Information Technology department of the VDMA, was appointed as the director of this office.

Based on the definition of Industrie 4.0 by the platform (see Sect. 2.1) and according to the implementation recommendations by acatech and the research union, in the second half of 2013, working groups were established. The idea was to cover the topics of standardization, job design and organization, security, research and the regulatory framework. Soon after the platform was established, these topics were able to be specified and the working groups formed.

Working Group 1 (AG 1), Strategy and Framework, was made up solely of steering committee members and was dedicated to the overall concept, the work plan, and the goals and principles of the platform: They asked themselves what goals they should target within what periods of time, and how and using which steps they wanted to achieve them.

Overview

The following were identified as significant goals:

- Additional annual monetary benefit (such as an increase in efficiency or turnover) for the economy
- Evolutionary implementation through an incremental retro-fitting of the existing infrastructure
- Confluence of knowledge and the setting of standards and the development of common quality standards for the quality seal I40
- Only pre-competitive cooperation and a strict observance of cartel laws

The implementation strategy for the platform, which now stands, explains the individual goals under the moniker "Comprehensive Overview of *Industrie 4.0*."

The topics of reference architecture and standardization became the most comprehensive set of tasks of the second working group, AG 2. It involved various reference architectures, details of interfaces, object and service descriptions, data models and communications standards, as well as the initiation and coordination of official standardization activities. This working group and its various sub-committees, as well as the committees of other consulted organizations, have already produced extensive results.

The AG 3, Research and Innovation, has also already attained significant results. It produced a research and innovation roadmap in cooperation with the scientific advisory board and in consultation with the German Federal Ministry of Education and Research (BMBF) and the Ministry for Economic Affairs and Energy (BMWi). This roadmap contains the innovative and research-related activities that the platform sees as vital in implementing Industrie 4.0.

Finally, the AG 4 has taken on the topic of the protection of networked systems. Its primary goal was the generic depiction of IT security aspects for processes and value creation chains as well as the value creation networks in Industrie 4.0. Its results were to be integrated in the reference architectures, as well as deliver test procedures for security testing.

At first, no further working groups were created for the other topics. The regulatory framework question was to be pursued within the BDI/BDA (Federation of German Industries/Confederation of German Employers) task force called *Zukunft der Arbeit* (Future of Work), in the working group Legal Foresighting. The topic of humans and work was also placed in the Future of Work group of the BDI/BDA.

There was also no separate working group for the topic of new business models, on the one hand, because this topic is relevant to competition and thus does not qualify as one of the strategic topics of *Industrie 4.0*. On the other hand, discussions arose concluding that it would be better suited to the future project "Smart Service World—Internet-based Services for Business," initiated by the federal government and acatech.

Two years of intense work followed, and in April of 2015, the official takeover of the platform *Industrie 4.0* was announced at the Hanover Trade Fair. Simultaneously, the results of the working groups and other participants became available. The implementation strategy of *Industrie 4.0* was distributed as a result report of the platform at a press conference [1].

On the website of the BMWi, the new *Plattform Industrie 4.0* is announced as follows:

> The more business is digitized and networked, the more interfaces emerge—in development, production and distribution, both nationally and globally. This requires the cooperation and input of several participants. A coordinated design of the digital structural change is the guiding principle of the new *Plattform Industrie 4.0*.

The existing platform of associations was expanded under the direction of Federal Economic Minister Sigmar Gabriel (BMWi) and Federal Research Minister Johanna Wanka (BMBF)—in addition to political representatives, agents from professional associations (VDMA, ZVEI, BITKOM, BDI, VDA, BDEW), trade unions (IG Metall) and science (Fraunhofer Society) also took part [2].

Figure 4.1 shows the new structure of the expanded platform. With the German organizations BDI (Federation of German Industries), the VDA (Automotive Industry Association) and the BDEW (Federal Association of the Energy and Water Industry), three large industrial associations came together; added to them are IG Metall as the largest independent trade union of the Confederation of German Trade Unions (DGB) and, by the way, the largest trade union of a single industry in the world, and the Fraunhofer Society, one of the largest research societies. In the new *Plattform Industrie 4.0*, the German production and processing industry, including its employees and research and development, are quite comprehensively represented.

Along with the expansion, the topics of the regulatory framework, as well as employment and training and advanced training were added to the existing topics of the working groups, now five in number. The last topic is especially significant, such that the Federal Ministry of Education and Research (BMBF) belongs to its

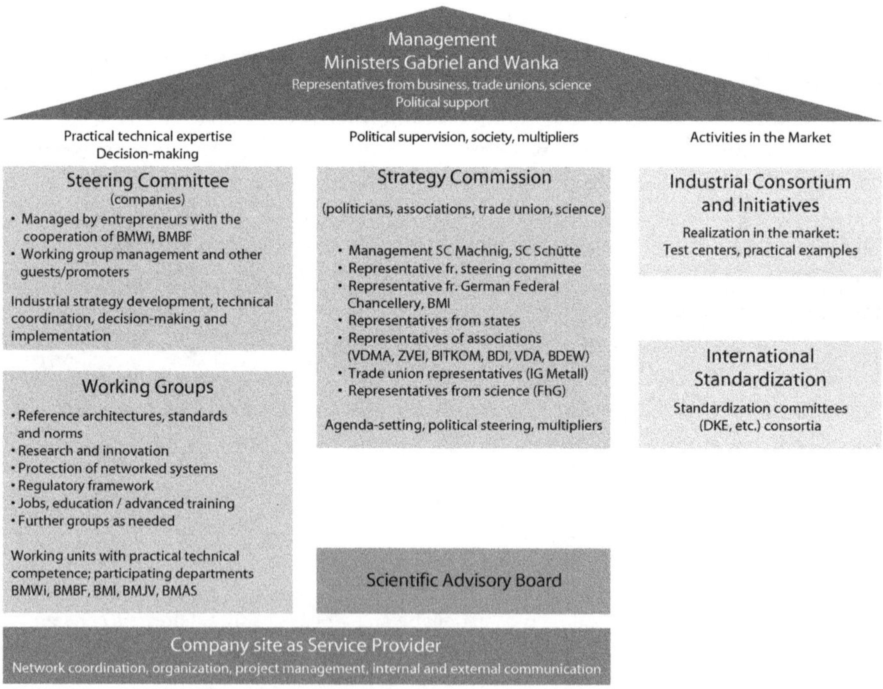

Fig. 4.1 New structure of the platform following its transfer to the German federal government. *Source* BMWi

management committee—because without a change in the general educational and higher educational curricula, the next step of digitalization, which envelops all of industry and business, would not be possible. And even if, according to German law, it is the responsibility of the individual states, an issue of such central importance must come from an initiative from the federal ministry. The paradigms taught to young people have become obsolete. E-learning is all but absent from classrooms. University departments are too still too rigidly oriented toward individual disciplines. School children and university students must still decide on their area of specialization too early. Yet, for changes which must be decided and implemented at the state level, Germany as an industrial location cannot wait for every state administration to recognize the exigency of the challenge.

What was good twenty years ago is too little for the future, because the established paths are too narrow. Industrie 4.0 needs a large and quickly growing number of experts capable of understanding and steering the interrelation of the various disciplines and able to manage multidisciplinary projects. In all, the working population of our society will have to transform extremely rapidly with the increasing digitalization of business if it does not want to risk this development being coupled with an increasing number of unemployed.

When the platform was introduced in Hanover, in addition to the federal economic minister and federal research minister, representatives from the directing boards at Festo, SAP and Siemens, as well as the IG Metall, were also on the podium (Fig. 4.2). But aside from the innovations in the composition of the platform and the expanded goals mentioned above, the speakers did not have much else to report. Especially absent were concrete steps for the coming period.

Georg Giersberg, a technology expert for the newspaper *Frankfurter Allgemeine Zeitung*, followed on the next day with a bitter commentary having the headline "The Wasted 4.0 Opportunity." The article states:

> A speaker of the platform's executive board who sold the establishment of an internet address and the creation of several working papers as proof of the success of the previous work, and an economic minister who reported on the roots of the German education system in a corporate state. With 300 participants, 600 valuable hours were wasted on the way to Industrie 4.0 [3].

Fig. 4.2 Presentation of the new *plattform industrie 4.0* in Hanover in April 2015. (Sendler)

The fear that the new management would not provide the necessary boost to the project and the platform is not completely unfounded. The federal government—in addition to a wealth of other, no less pressing matters—has taken on an extremely important task for Germany as an industrial location. It will have to continually give high priority to the project if it wishes to carry it out successfully. It is certainly one of the projects against which politics will have to be measured in the coming elections. Of course, it is in no way clear how a change of administration will affect work on the platform.

However, one year later, on April 26, 2016, once again at the Hanover Trade Fair, the results of the first year of the new platform were presented, showing that a series of topics had been worked on, evidently to the satisfaction of all involved.

It is also a project for which international cooperation must prevail. As early as in October of 2014, a campaign between the German and the Chinese government was established, having the title "Shape Innovation Together." Among other points, the agreement for this campaign states:

> The digitalization of industry (Industrie 4.0) is of great significance for the further development of the German and Chinese economies. Both sides agree that this process must primarily be stimulated by the companies themselves. The governments of both countries will politically support the participation of companies in this process [4].

Such political support measures certainly also include further government consultations and agreements such as those previously concluded with China. In July of 2015, the *Frankfurter Allgemeine Zeitung* reported under the headline "Germany also implements Industrie 4.0 with China":

> Germany and China wish to cooperate more closely with one another in the realm of modern digital industrial technologies. German Economic Minister Sigmar Gabriel (SPD) and Chinese Minister for Industry and Information Technology Miao Wei signed a corresponding statement of intent for cooperation in "intelligent manufacturing" this Tuesday in Beijing. [...] Miao Wei spoke of "winning a stage of the race" and a new phase in industrial collaboration between the two countries [5].

Representatives of industry and science are also involved in talks and consultations on the administrative level. In both countries, visits to companies are coupled with the project to ensure a connection to real industrial situations. Nevertheless, from the standpoint of outsiders, few concrete measures have been established which could serve as examples of practical cooperation.

4.2 Research

At the Hanover Trade Fair of 2014, the scientific advisory board published 17 theses in the categories humans, technology and organization. The four theses on the topic of humans comprised possible and desirable effects of Industrie 4.0 on humans as employees in industry. For instance, Thesis 1 states: "Diverse opportunities for a human-oriented design of work organization will emerge, also with regard to self-organization and autonomy. In particular, opportunities will open up for work planning oriented toward the aging and the aged." The largest block of nine theses was dedicated to technology. They focused on the technical aspects of Industrie 4.0, such as Thesis 9, where intelligent products were described as "active information carriers and addressable and identifiable over all lifecycle phases." The last four theses address organizational structures in industry. They mainly concern the new forms of value creation and cooperation.

At the same time, in a whitepaper on research and development topics, the issues necessary for the implementation of the theses were named and a rough schedule given. This whitepaper was integrated into the implementation strategy in an updated version of April 2015 in the form of Chap. 5, Research and Innovation. It contains a research roadmap for implementation in the time period from 2015 to 2035 (see Fig. 4.3).

Five topic areas were defined for this roadmap, which partially influence each other:

- Horizontal integration via value creation networks
- Consistency of engineering over the entire lifecycle
- Vertical integration and networked production systems

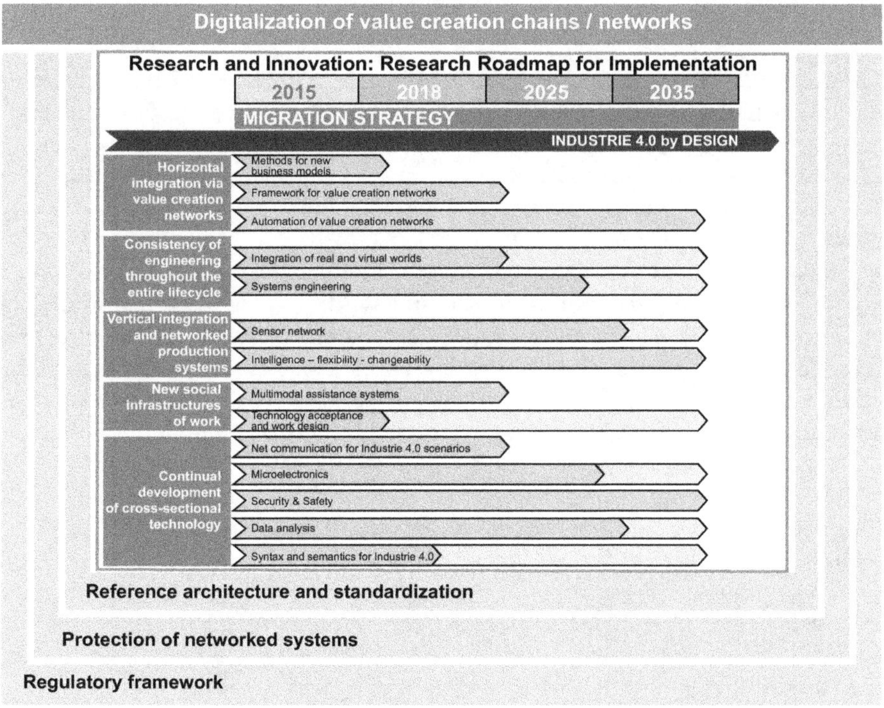

Fig. 4.3 Core components of the research roadmap for Industrie 4.0. (BMWi)

- New social infrastructures for work
- Continual development of cross-sectional technologies

These five topic areas of the implementation strategy are described in detail in Chap. 5, with a brief profile of the contents of research and innovation, and including an explanation of the expected results and major milestones.

When the point of consistency of engineering over the entire lifecycle is observed, it can be divided into the "integration of the real and virtual worlds" and "systems engineering." It is one of the components of the implementation strategy in which the role of engineering and product and systems development, and not production, specifically take center stage.

Several institutions at various universities and research centers have begun work in the meanwhile. Forty-six projects listed in the platform are up and running under the heading of research and development alone. The most important task of all of these projects is the cross-company development of methods and tools with which even midsize companies can master the initial hurdle in transforming into a digital industry. Technology transfer is taking place, and the way is being paved for Germany as an industrial location. A few outstanding representatives of such research present their work in their own chapters of this book.

4.3 Reference Architecture, Standardization

The goal of Working Group 2 was the definition of a fundamental reference architecture for Industrie 4.0 and the resulting necessity for standardization. The reference architecture in this context refers to a model which supplements the previous tasks and procedures of production companies to include Industrie 4.0 aspects. The intent was for it to be as generic as possible, in order to be applicable to any possible product and branch of industry.

The issue required expertise from other institutions. The experts from the Society of Measurement and Automatic Control (GMA) of the Association of German Engineers (VDI) and the German Association for Electrical, Electronic & Information Technologies (VDE) working on the committees "Industrie 4.0" and "Cyber-Physical Systems" offered to serve as partners for the development of the approaches. At the same time, the so-called SG2 mirror committee was founded in the Association for Electrical, Electronic & Information Technologies (ZVEI), which also contributed content to the association. The German Commission for Electrical, Electronic and Information Technologies (DKE) was also involved, such that standardization became a part of the association as well.

The result is the implementation strategy detailed in Chap. 6 on the one hand, and, on the other, also published as a status report of the VDI, VDE and ZVEI with the title "Reference Architecture Model Industrie 4.0 (RAMI40), sometimes shortened to RAMI [1].

The three-dimensional RAMI40 (Fig. 4.4) is based on the smart grid architecture model (SGAM), which is internationally recognized. Various perspectives, such as the functional description or communication behavior, are depicted on the levels of the vertical axis. The horizontal axis represents the product lifecycle and its value creation chains. The third axis of the hierarchy levels arranges the functions and responsibilities between devices and device classes within a factory.

The term "Industrie 4.0 components" was coined for the individual elements within the architecture. To differentiate them from other objects and components, an initial version of a reference model has been defined for Industrie 4.0 components (Fig. 4.5), which is to be more closely defined in the coming years.

A reference model in accordance with the requirement discussed in the working group is to be used to describe how the superordinate IT system of a component can provide a so-called administration shell. This refers to a communication interface between modules that contains all data of the real module, serving as its "digital twin."

In addition to the reference models, there are recommendations for the use and development of norms and standards for Industrie 4.0. The DKE has issued a standardization roadmap for this purpose, and in Chap. 6 of the implementation strategy, there is an open list of standards potentially relevant for Industrie 4.0. Experience has shown that this step will be the lengthiest one. However, the working group assumes that "the definition of technical requirements in globally valid standardization systems [is] especially important for the globally-active and exporting German industry."

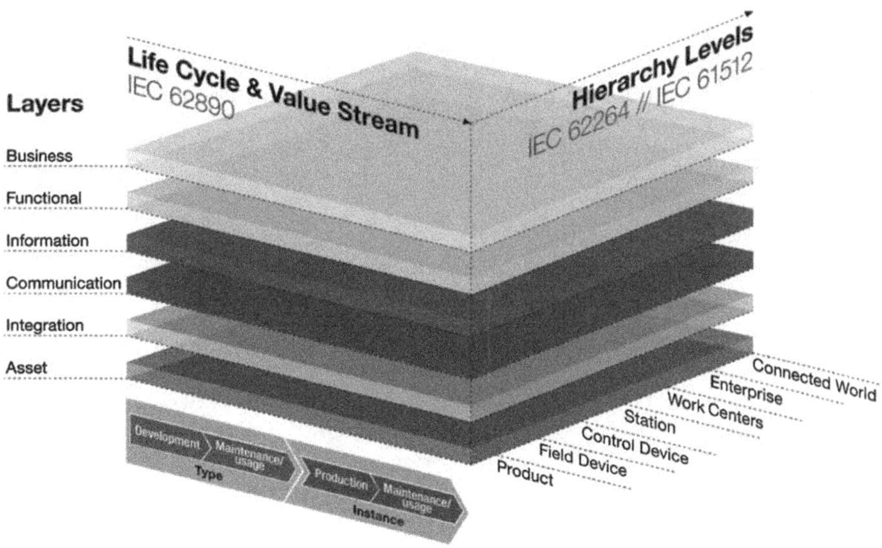

Fig. 4.4 Reference architecture model RAMI40. (Implementation strategy Industrie 4.0 [1])

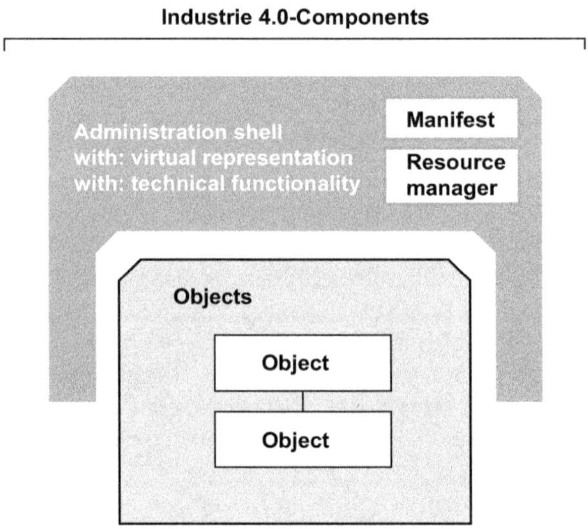

Fig. 4.5 Reference model Industrie 4.0 components. (Implementation strategy Industrie 4.0 [1])

4.4 Safety and Security of Networked Systems

The increasing and comprehensive digitalization poses growing problems to industry with regard to security. In April of 2015, a brochure of the Open IT competence center of the Fraunhofer Institute for Open Communication Systems (FOKUS) was published, whose foreword states:

> The term "security" within the context of infrastructures stands for protection against attacks from the outside, but also for safety in the functioning of ever more complex and interdependent structures upon which, in the meantime, we are dependent in our daily lives. Due to the persistent permeation of our society by information technology (IT), not only is the border between safety and security becoming increasingly blurred, but they are also influencing each other [6].

The use of standard software in production or in the control and monitoring of machines and systems has dramatically increased the degree of danger, because it means that industrial processes are now exposed to the same risk from hacking attacks as office PCs. Through the use of cyber-physical systems and mobile end devices in factories, this risk has multiplied even further. Today, billions of devices are already networked over the internet, and thus capable of being networked with each other. Embedded software in devices, machines and products of all types makes remote control via mobile devices possible.

Security as opposed to safety is not only a question of the authentication of a user or operator through a password or the installation of a firewall for a PC. When devices can be controlled by the software of other devices, then devices must also be able to authenticate each other. Otherwise, the door will be open to undesired intervention in industrial processes, as well as in the use of products by end users.

Just how far security and safety overlap in the meantime is clear in this question: If insecure communication is possible between devices, then protection of the technical systems and products of a plant, including protection of people from accidents or other hazards, cannot be guaranteed. Thus, secure communication must take place.

The magnitude of this challenge is apparent in the fact that the seventh and last chapter of the Implementation Strategy Industrie 4.0 concerning the protection of networked systems, despite its good 20 pages, does not really contain any concrete measures. It does include all the more hypotheses, exemplary measures and recommendations on how to react to described threat scenarios—even though the introduction of the chapter states:

> Security is the "enabler" for Industrie 4.0 value chain networks. [...] Trust is generated when the information and data can be safely and correctly verifiably exchanged between the actual authorized parties. Ensuring this is the task of security in Industrie 4.0. Without guaranteed security in office and production systems, Industrie 4.0 cannot be implemented, as no trust can be generated for the sensitive communication processes [7].

The fact is, the topic of (data) security has not become smaller with increasing digitalization, but rather larger. However, many of the questions posed as a result remain unanswered, and there is much doubt as to whether or not these questions can be answered at all. With the increasing role of software and the networking of everything and everyone via the internet, the risk potential is growing, even when the greatest possible degree of discretion and caution is observed. Accepting this is one of the challenges of Industrie 4.0. It is not only impossible to completely protect society from terrorist attacks, it is also becoming increasingly impossible to protect factories, employees and product users from unintentional or willful causation of the failure of technical systems.

However, this cannot lead to people closing their eyes to possible hazards and security vulnerabilities and hoping that one's own factory, product or system will not be affected. On the contrary, it is high time that industry dedicated itself to exploring this question intensively and thoroughly; more meticulously than it has done in the last 30 years of digitalization.

Solutions that are being developed by leading industrial enterprises and research institutes range from physical unclonable functions (PUF), with which things on the internet can be definitively identified, to security solutions for networks and application security, to the safeguarding of industrial communication points.

Methods for weak-point analysis as well as permanent safety monitoring are intended to aid in more quickly identifying attacks and undesired activities, in order to be able to react more swiftly. The implementation strategy states:

> Currently, the average time needed to identify an attack amounts to several hundred days, whereby an increasing number of attacks are not being recognized by the affected enterprises [8].

Every enterprise must develop its own security strategy. The use of technical and systematic solutions is just part of the necessary measures. The second important aspect comprises organizational measures with which security holes can be patched or reduced. In this regard, training of all employees is critical. Only if they know what they can do and when to uphold security can they be capable of contributing to the solution.

The third aspect pertains to the complexity of products, devices and thus also machines and systems themselves: Their development can no longer only serve to implement functional requirements. They must also exclude (or at least try to exclude) the possibility that other functions than those planned can be executed. Where software allows the control of a device via mobile end devices, it must also protect these devices from inadvertent actuation. Where software can be updated through automatic flashing (updating and reprogramming during operation), it must be ensured that it cannot be changed to an undesired status from an unauthorized location. And, of course, not only does the mechanical model and the circuitry of the electronics need to be protected from intellectual property theft, which is part of these elements, the software, too, the source code of the control, must be kept just as safe from undesired access and alterations.

This means that security is not only a question of IT security. It is a permanent task of all participants in development and production. The infrastructure needed has a type of data management at its core which safely stores data in encoded form over its entire lifecycle and makes it available to authorized persons at any time in its current form. Product lifecycle management (PLM) is not becoming less important with Industrie 4.0, but more important, including for the protection of networked systems.

4.5 Projects in Practical Application

After so many explanations of the theoretical foundation upon which the platform *Industrie 4.0* is driving the initiative, let us have a look behind its first websites to get an idea of the extent to which its practical application has flourished, which can in fact already be stated using example products and projects. To foreshadow: A factory or company network that has fully implemented Industrie 4.0 still does not exist five years after the start of the initiative, but this was not to be expected anyway. The transition which has begun is too comprehensive, there are too many areas involved, and the process of this transformation is too complex. However, there are several projects which started under the flag of Industrie 4.0 and of which significant parts have already been completed.

In addition to the *Plattform Industrie 4.0*, which will be discussed in further detail in this regard, there are two further opportunities to become familiar with projects that have already been successfully completed.

1. Corporate consulting firm Pierre Audoin Consultants (PAC) has placed a PAC Innovation Register online which lists tested and evaluated company profiles, supplier data and case studies on Industrie 4.0 and the Internet of Things. According to PAC information, the database, which numbered almost 200 projects at the end of 2015, is growing by about 30 examples per month. The projects are then verified, categorized and, if they fulfill basic maturity criteria, published. Anyone can register and enter their own projects, and the project list is freely available for download [9].
2. The top cluster it's OWL (which stands for "Intelligent Technical Systems Ost-WestfalenLippe"), supported by the German federal government, has assisted in the implementation of a total of 47 projects in which industrial companies from the mechanical engineering, electrical engineering and electronics and automotive supply industries, together with regional research institutes, render new products, technologies and applications market-ready. In addition, 73 so-called transfer projects have already been started or completed, and a hundred more are scheduled to be completed by the end of 2017. These projects are intended to also enable small and midsize companies, which themselves have no or insufficient resources of their own, to use modern technologies. On the homepage of the cluster, you can read profiles and detailed descriptions of several of these projects [10]. Chapter 12 of this book provides a detailed look at the work of it's OWL.

The website of *Plattform Industrie 4.0* provides a good overview of the progress of practical projects as well as research and development activities. Under a section dedicated to practical applications, there is a map of Industrie 4.0 [11], which currently shows 207 running projects, subdivided according to application examples and test and competence centers, including their geographical base on a map of Germany. Via this map, visitors can access a list of the projects, which not only offers a brief profile but also a detailed explanation of every individual project. In these detailed explanations, readers will also find significant answers to the following questions:

- What challenges needed to be mastered and what concrete uses resulted?
- How can the Industrie 4.0 approach be described?
- What was able to be achieved?
- What measures were used to achieve the solution?
- What can others learn from it?

On the other hand, filters can be set which allow certain types of projects to be displayed. This is very useful, because these filters enable a differentiation according to application areas, such as producing industries or logistics, according to value creation sector such as production and supply chain or design and engineering, or according to state, development stage and corporate size.

If you look at application instances, the manufacturing industry, as expected, is clearly the most heavily represented, with 104 projects. Infrastructure and logistics each have 15 projects, and only a handful are representatives of education and advanced training (6), agriculture (6) and other projects (4).

It is shocking that, up to now, only a dwindling number of projects have been dedicated to education and advanced training. There are three in the state of Bavaria and one each in Baden-Württemberg, Hesse and Rhineland-Palatinate. Only the Academy Cube in Rhineland-Palatinate, created in 2013 on the initiative of SAP as an advanced training and network platform in the realm of MINT (mathematics, information technology, natural science and technology), addresses the lack of experts and the qualification gaps identified by specially funded business communities. An intelligent matching system connects advanced training offers with open positions, which increases the chances for finding employment. More than 50 partners from industry, politics and academics support the platform.

The projects are primarily concentrated in the three German states of Baden-Württemberg (38), North Rhine-Westphalia (30) and Bavaria (24). The high number in North Rhine-Westphalia is surely largely due to the activities of the top cluster it's OWL. If we only look at the application examples from the manufacturing industry, the ranking is almost identical; the top three spots go to the same states in the same order.

The largest ratio by far of the promoted work is in the value creation realm of production and the supply chain. A total of 99 projects are listed under this sector, followed by design and engineering with 30, logistics with 21, service with 20 and other areas with 16. The active companies are largely and evidently successfully focused on a quick implementation, because 79 projects have already reported market-readiness or productive use, and a further 31 are in the market introduction or pilot phase. In contrast, there are 20 each of research and development projects and demonstrator projects.

A look at the magnitude of the participating enterprises very clearly shows what great challenges Germany as an industrial location faces in Industrie 4.0. The largest number of projects (63) comes from companies with more than 15,000 employees. Only 37 projects are taking place in firms of 250 to 5000 employees, and 59 in the smallest category of one to 250 employees. More than half of the projects is thus allocated to large corporations, while by far the most companies come from the SME sector in Germany. This disproportion becomes even clearer if the projects of the manufacturing industry are filtered out. Here, 66 projects come from firms with more than 5000 employees, and 44 come from smaller enterprises.

A few companies are especially active, and are leading in a large number of projects: Siemens (16), Bosch (14), ABB (10) and Telekom (8). The restraint of the automotive industry is conspicuous. As the only large manufacturer, Volkswagen is on the list with four projects. Their distinct focus is on the optimization of production planning and control, and not on the innovation of products and services. One of the projects deals with a virtual planning table, another with intralogistics and virtual commissioning, another with countermeasures in planning. Only one single project, M.A.R.S. (markerless augmented reality system), concerns the use of modern digital technology for validating design data.

In addition to the application examples, there are 25 test and five competence centers on the map. The five competence centers, in Berlin-Brandenburg, Hesse, Lower Saxony, North Rhine-Westphalia and Rhineland-Palatinate, were brought to life last year by the BMWi within the context of the core focus area "SME Digital—ICT Applications in Business," which is designed to support companies in their efficient use of modern information and communications technologies. They already comprise 15 funded projects on the topic of e-standards and 15 under the motto of "Usability for SMEs." The five competence centers on the Industrie 4.0 map represent a third thematic area, "SME 4.0—Digital Production and Work Processes." They were augmented in 2016 by another competence center for small trade. Other centers are in planning, and four so-called SME 4.0 agencies are intended to provide additional expertise. Thus, these centers are designed to primarily help small and medium-sized companies to gear up for Industrie 4.0.

The 20 test centers are ranked differently than the application examples. With six test laboratories, North Rhine-Westphalia is in first place, followed by Baden-Württemberg with five. Yet with one test lab, Bavaria is tied for last place with Bremen and Brandenburg. The testing environments are largely laboratory-like facilities at universities and research institutes. Why none of the Bavarian universities has of yet participated in the activities of the platform with their own centers remains a mystery.

A look at the map of the projects of the *Plattform Industrie 4.0* teaches us a great deal. There are already a lot of practical results; industry has produced a number of products, components, software systems and other things in several efforts. The market has been augmented by a few Industrie 4.0 products in the first five years of the initiative. With Siemens, Bosch, ABB and Telekom, a few of the most important players are leading the pack, and that is good for Germany as an industrial location.

The focus of the activity is clearly on the optimization and flexibilization of production planning and thus fits in with the unfortunately very limited focus of the entire initiative. Companies are paying much too little attention to their innovative capability for their products and especially to associated services. And that is bad for Germany as an industrial location. If industry becomes even better and more flexible in the manufacturing of their products and the related necessary factories and plants, it is good for everyone who wishes to do business with these products in the future. This does not necessarily apply to the manufacturers themselves. For instance, creative service providers could be more successful who better understand software apps, the cloud and the internet. this does not necessarily apply to Germany as an industrial location.

The fact that SMEs, in contrast to their significance for the country, are wholly underrepresented, is confirmed by the many statements coming from politicians, analysts, researchers and IT providers, who are more likely to be confronted with skepticism, caution and a lack of knowledge in the smaller companies than enthusiasm for Industrie 4.0. Whether, on the other hand, the five competence centers of the German Federal Ministry of Economics and the SME 4.0 agencies can provide enough leverage is questionable.

4.6 Industrie 4.0—not Manufacturing 4.0

It has taken a few years for Industrie 4.0 to be noticed internationally. In the meantime, however, it has become a driving force of the discussion on technological progress in industry. The fact that, in Germany, the focus has been placed so distinctly on production and not the entire value creation chain has led to Industrie 4.0 also becoming known internationally as an initiative focused on manufacturing, fabrication and automation, while other countries and their industries are more broadly positioned and have claimed the Internet of Things and Services for themselves.

In 2014, five enterprises in the USA established the Industrial Internet Consortium (IIC), which, by the end of 2015, gained as many members in fewer than two years as the *Plattform Industrie 4.0*. And scores of important companies are members of both initiatives. In mid-2015, there was a heated debate, especially in various trade media, about which of those two associations was more important, and which was a step ahead regarding standardization and reference architecture. Awkward statements by representatives of both organizations fired the debate, even though they wanted to remain subjective.

Then, a constructive discussion began which ultimately led to a meeting of representatives of I40 and IIC—that is, from Bosch, Cisco, IIC, Pepperl + Fuchs, SAP, Siemens, Steinbeis Institute and ThingsWise—in Zurich. On March 3, 2016, the representatives of the BMWi and both groups then announced their future collaboration at a joint press conference in Berlin. Cooperation between the two architecture models RAMI40 (reference architecture model for Industrie 4.0) and IIRA (industrial internet reference architecture) is intended to facilitate future interoperability. Both basically want to cooperate in standardization and utilize joint testing environments. A common roadmap has been designed for this purpose.

The press release for this on the homepage of the *Plattform Industrie 4.0* goes into somewhat more detail. For instance, it includes a statement by Stan Schneider, CEO of Real-Time Innovations (RTI) and a member of the IIC steering committee:

> The Plattform Industrie 4.0 approach, with its strong anchor in industrial manufacturing, is a perfect complement to the approach of the IIC, which puts a stronger focus on IoT applications for the realms of healthcare management, transportation, energy and smart cities [12].

Using the example of the automobile, it describes where the borders run: For motor vehicles and their production, RAMI40 is good; for everything happening on the Internet of Things pertaining to motor vehicles, IIRA is better suited. Technicians have agreed in their mutual discussions that they consider their activities as mutually complementary. In the future, the informal group wishes to make efforts to become closer.

It is possible that—from the viewpoint of Germany as an industrial location—with these efforts, a step is being taken in the wrong direction. The manufacturing industry is not the same as manufacturing. For companies in Germany and their role in the Internet of Things, the decisive factor is whether they are looking at digitalization in a comprehensive manner and consider the IoT, develop their products for it as well as their own business models. Otherwise the *Plattform Industrie 4.0* and German enterprises will become a mere accessory to the protagonists of the Internet of Things from the USA—an accessory that deals with the special area of manufacturing.

At the 2016 Hanover Trade Fair, there was another meeting with a further initiative, the *Alliance Industrie Du Futur*, which had previously been introduced as the "French Industrie 4.0." A common action plan of both initiatives was submitted to German economic minister Sigmar Gabriel and French economic minister Emmanuel Macron. Among other things, it announces an initial version of an action plan for international standardization to be finished by the end of 2016, which is based on RAMI40. It further cites the particular importance of providing information about concrete application examples to companies in both countries—"primarily current examples of manufacturing processes and pilot and research projects." In this document, too, the "primary" focus is on "manufacturing processes."

There are several consultations with China on a number of levels in which various federal ministers and representatives of *Plattform Industrie 4.0* are involved. To date, however, it seems that the main focus is a mutual signaling of a basic willingness to cooperate. From the German side, as participants in such consultations report, there is great fear in some areas that, in practice, this cooperation may lead to an unintended drain of know-how.

References

1. Umsetzungsstrategie Industrie 4.0—Ergebnisbericht der Plattform Industrie 4.0, (Implementation strategy Industrie 4.0—result report of the plattform industrie 4.0), BITKOM, VDMA, ZVEI, editors.
2. http://www.bmwi.de/DE/Themen/Industrie/industrie-4-0.html. Accessed 12 May 2016.
3. Die Vertane 4.0-Chance, Frankfurter Allgemeine Zeitung, Georg Giersberg, 15 April 2015.
4. http://www.bundesregierung.de/Content/DE/Pressemitteilungen/BPA/2014/10/2014-10-10-aktionsrahmen-dt-chin-konsultationen.html. Accessed 12 May 2016.
5. Deutschland setzt Industrie 4.0 auch mit China um, Frankfurter Allgemeine Zeitung, 14 July 2015.

6. S²: Safety und Security aus dem Blickwinkel der öffentlichen IT, Kompetenzzentrum Öffentliche IT, Fraunhofer-Institut für Offene Kommunikationssysteme FOKUS, April 2015.
7. Umsetzungsstrategie Industrie 4.0—Ergebnisbericht der Plattform Industrie 4.0, (Implementation strategy Industrie 4.0—result report of the plattform industrie 4.0), BITKOM, VDMA, ZVEI, editors, pp. 71 ff.
8. Umsetzungsstrategie Industrie 4.0—Ergebnisbericht der Plattform Industrie 4.0, (Implementation strategy Industrie 4.0—result report of the plattform industrie 4.0), BITKOM, VDMA, ZVEI, editors, p. 74.
9. https://www.pac-online.com/innovation-register-profiles-and-use-cases. Accessed 12 May 2016.
10. http://www.its-owl.de/projekte/. Accessed 12 May 2016.
11. http://www.plattform-i40.de/I40/Navigation/DE/In-der-Praxis/Karte/karte.html. Accessed 12 May 2016.
12. https://www.plattform-i40.de/I40/Redaktion/DE/Pressemitteilungen/2016/2016-03-02-kooperation-iic.html. Accessed 12 May 2016.

The USA

5

Ulrich Sendler

Abstract

The history of industrialization is not one that progressed in a harmonic way internationally. The USA's pursuit of European trailblazers quickly led to them assuming the top spot as an economic power. Yet just a few decades later, the next technological driver, the computer, brought with it the beginnings of a separation of global industry into hardware and software. US industry was capable of setting the tone for subsequent digitalization. Now, it looks as though, through digitalization, a new decision is on the horizon for the manufacturing and systems industry: Who will dominate the industrial data business? Will the Industrial Internet Consortium help? Now, the USA's temporary vanquishing of positions in the hardware industry could prove to be a weakness. For that reason, too, a re-industrialization has been set into motion. But the long concentration on hardware in Germany could also backfire in contrast to a US industry that is gaining strength and leaning on its leading position in the digital realm.

5.1 The Latecomer Takes the Lead

US industry entered the international arena with a considerable delay in comparison to England, France and Germany. In 1769, the USA was busy with its own formation and in no way finished with conquering all parts of the land of the Indians when James Watt, in the United Kingdom, made the steam engine the core of the Industrial Revolution. In 1765, for the first time, nine of the British colonies refused to continue paying taxes to England. In 1773, American patriots raided

U. Sendler (✉)
Mauerkircherstraße 30, 81679 Munich, Germany
E-Mail: ulrich.sendler@ulrichsendler.de

U. Sendler (ed.), *The Internet of Things*,
https://doi.org/10.1007/978-3-662-54904-9_5

British tea ships and destroyed their payload in the Boston Tea Party. The Declaration of Independence was signed in 1776, and in the same year, a war began between the colonial power and the colonies, which did not end until the recognition of the USA by England in 1783. At that time, France and Germany had also built the steam engine and were already in the middle of developing an industrial society.

And while the core countries of Europe expanded their industries while simultaneously implementing their new strengths stemming from those industries in the conquering of further colonies on all continents, the USA was in the process of completing its constitution as a nation. The continual growth of national territories from the northeast to the southwest led to several wars with Mexico. The fight over the American constitution in the 19th century was colored by the fight over slavery, which the southern states, who subsisted on the agricultural and cotton industries, lost the four-year Civil War in 1865. The military and political reconstruction of the new nation took another ten years.

Only then was the USA able to concentrate fully on industrialization. In 1869, the first transcontinental railroad was opened between the Atlantic and Pacific oceans, and other lines were established in the early 1880s. The race to catch up, which had then begun, was boosted by the wealth and easy accessibility of iron ore, coal and a number of other natural resources. At the end of the 19th century and in the early 20th century, European emigration to the USA reached a pinnacle, which was subsequently limited in the Immigration Act of 1924. During the period between 1870 and 1920, the overall population of the USA increased from 38.5 to 106 million. US inventors were quick at registering patents for innovative products. From the beginning of industrialization, the American outlook, in which one forges his own destiny, played a great role in its development. In only four decades, US industry surpassed its European competition. By the end of World War I, the USA was the strongest economic power in the world.

That was also the point in time defined as the beginning of the second industrial revolution. In this case, it was Ford and the American automotive industry that set the tone. Electricity, oil as an energy source, assembly line production and mass production formed the core of a development which enabled the manufacture of mass products at a price which masses of people could afford. At the same time, Taylorism had established itself. Frederick Winslow Taylor formulated methods to organize work processes that were based on work studies and, for the first time, enabled the scientifically-founded management of industrial work [1]. The division of labor, and with it, the specialization of experts on particular tasks and areas of work were born, transforming industry around the world from the USA.

Automobiles, airplanes, trains, machinery—up to the middle of the last century and considerably beyond the victorious end of World War II for the USA, products from the USA and the methods to develop and produce them set the pace for global industry. At the same time, the American way of life, synonymous with prosperity, was underpinned by Hollywood films, accompanied by jazz and rock & roll music.

The next technological surge came in the Fifties and Sixties with the invention of the computer. Subsequently, programmable microelectronics, the miniaturization of integrated, electronic circuits and the triumph of software became technologies that would fundamentally change the world. German industry had regained strength after the war thanks to the Marshall Plan and multifarious help from the USA, and enjoyed their famous *Wirtschaftswunder*, or economic miracle. It used the computer and storage-programmable logic control for the swift automation of production and the operation of factories of all kinds. Today, this is what is primarily considered the start of the third industrial revolution in Germany. In fact, in the following decades, German industry would succeed in achieving international market leadership in a series of industrial branches, while more or less giving up other branches to the industries of other countries.

But the computer itself also continued to be developed. Software, originally an integral component of computers, became autonomous. Hardware became smaller and smaller, while its performance, with regard to processing speed as well as storage capacity, experienced what seemed like unstoppable growth. The computer industry, however, was not one of those branches of industry in which Germany was able to attain a leading position; on the contrary: Even individual areas within this industry which had had their origins in Germany—just as the computer itself—disappeared in the course of the second half of the last century. And it was this industry—the high-tech industry—in which the USA placed its emphasis.

After the mid-20th century, the development of industrialization took at least two different tracks; at least because the further separation of hardware and software led to an additional fork in the road for the high-tech industry. With regard to computer and peripheral device production, this can be traced to the fact that, here too, US manufacturers switched to outsourcing, ultimately leading to the contemporary dominance of Asian producers in this realm. But the first splitting of the industry took place when computers and microelectronics became available. Some—most recently with Germany leading the international market—used computer technology especially to develop and produce high-quality mechatronic products of the most varied of kinds. Others—to date dominated by the USA—concentrated on the further development of high technology itself. This split between two fundamentally different industrial developments is illustrated in Fig. 5.1. By 1970 at the latest, when computer technology had advanced so far that it could be used for programmable logic control in automation, the two paths diverged.

5.2 The Land in Which Software Grows

The development from hardware via software and the internet to data, mentioned elsewhere in this book, can be illustrated quite well using two examples. At the same time, it becomes easy to see why the USA led the world in digitalization, if not every realm, unchallenged for so long.

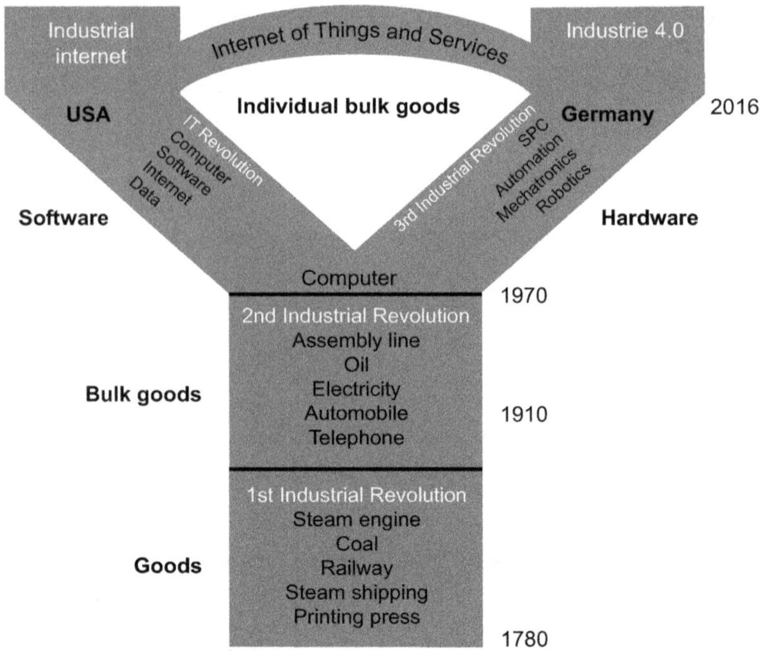

Fig. 5.1 With the onset of computer technology, the development of industry split into hardware and software. (© Ulrich Sendler, 2016)

The first example is IBM. Herman Hollerith founded the Tabulating Machine Company in 1896, whose business was using machines to enter and evaluate data using punchcards. In 1910, he established a German subsidiary called DEHOMAG, for *Deutsche Hollerith-Maschinen Gesellschaft* (German Hollerith Machine Association). In 1924, the enterprise was renamed "International Business Machines", or IBM for short, because the product line consisted of machines such as keypunch machines, testers, sorters and mixers for punchcards and other office machines. By the way, these machines were generally leased by customers.

The second example is Hewlett Packard. William Hewlett and David Packard, both graduates of Stanford University, founded the company in 1939. Their first product was an audio-frequency oscillator. One of their first customers was the Walt Disney Studios. Devices of the most varied of kinds for measurement technology and later medical technology, were the initial backbone products before HP became an international computer corporation.

In as early as the Fifties, IBM began producing computers. The first transistor-driven and storage-programmable IBM computer was put on the market in 1960. HP began producing tabletop computers in the Seventies, and in the Eighties, PCs.

The garage in which Hewlett and Packard put together their first inventions is considered to be the first building of what became known as Silicon Valley. The actual start of Silicon Valley was in 1951, with the establishment of Stanford

Industrial Park, a research and industrial zone next to Stanford University, not far from San Francisco. Former employees of electronics firms and university graduates founded small companies there and developed innovative ideas and products. With the proliferation of computer technology from the 1960s, these were increasingly high-tech companies.

Thus, at the same time in which German industry was focusing on computer-supported automation, the USA was developing its own high-tech sectors which would soon overtake traditional industry. In the 1950s, every fourth American still worked in processing trades. Today, this number is not even one out of ten. Between 1989 and 2009 alone, almost six million industrial jobs were lost. The percentage of processing trades contributing to the gross domestic product was almost 12%, only half of what it was in Germany. On the other hand, the USA has assumed a position in the realm of digitalization which is even more astonishing than the slump in traditional industry: 80% of software turnover worldwide was earned by companies with their headquarters in the USA [2]. The German newspaper *Süddeutsche Zeitung* states:

> For this new "best of the world," perhaps no land is better suited than the USA. The entrepreneurial spirit of its citizens, its willingness to break with traditions, its enthusiasm for computers have provided it with a head start [2].

In fact: Following mainframe computers, tabletop computers and pocket calculators came on the scene, then PCs and Unix computers, and then, the USA invented the internet. While the small, handy mobile telephones of the first generation, with their temporarily big names such as Nokia and Sony-Ericsson, were more likely to be based in Europe or Asia, the Nineties, bolstered by the internet, saw a new surge from inventors from Silicon Valley: With its iPod, iPhone and iPad, Apple defined an innovative take on consumer electronics and communication. Once that was established, Google, Amazon, Facebook and several other companies represented suppliers who no longer focused on hardware for this new development, but rather only on the internet and its available data.

Business in data in the first twenty years was a business dealing exclusively in customer data. Providers supplied never before seen apps for free or a very low price designed to make daily life easier and more pleasant. In return, users of mobile end devices connecting to the internet didn't ask what would happen with their user data. The knowledge filtered and sorted from millions of user data sets became the basis for various types of business developed by the new, quickly growing corporations together with consumer goods manufacturers. The chief business consisted of offering advertising space on the internet, for which ever more companies were and are prepared to pay more and more money.

In 2013, Coca Cola was bumped from the top spot by Apple on the list of companies worth the most, and now Google, or more specifically, the new corporate holding Alphabet, is challenging Apple for that spot. Thus, a consumer product (a drink) was followed by computers (smartphones and tablets), and hardware and software are now followed by purely data-based business (search engines as advertising space). For a few decades, doing business with software and data was big enough to more than balance out the USA's loss in leadership in the traditional industry of machine and plant engineering.

With the new standard for internet addresses, IPv6, it has now become possible to expand the business of selling data by several dimensions. If every product can be supplied with its own internet address, device data can also be the object of business models, because innovative services can be conceived and offered for all types of devices. It is another kind of business, because it primarily concerns the data of products and investment goods, which only contain consumer data in special cases. But who would be more predestined to define this new type of business than the inventors of the software and data business in the USA?

Microsoft conceptualized business with software and easily outran the pioneers of the computer age, such as HP and IBM. Apple surpassed Microsoft with mobile devices and internet business. Google overtook Apple with pure data business. There have always been new founders of companies, resourceful startups, and courageous new thinkers who have redefined the leading position of US business for more than a hundred years. HP and IBM are fighting to find a new place in the new age and succeed as consulting and IT providers. But for the upcoming round, the big name and new brand may not yet be known.

5.3 The Industrial Internet Consortium

On March 27, 2014, AT&T, Cisco, GE, IBM and Intel announced in Boston that they had formed the Industrial Internet Consortium, in order to "improve integration of the physical and digital worlds," as the headline of their first press release stated. The sub-headline cites a further goal as "more reliable access to big data," to promote business.

Thus, a telecommunications corporation, a leading networking company, an electronics and transportation company and two IT giants were the initiators. US Secretary of Commerce Penny Pritzker was quoted in the press release as follows:

> The Administration is looking forward to working with public-private collaborations like the new IIC to turn innovative Industrial Internet products and systems into new jobs in smart manufacturing, health care, transportation and other areas [3].

The provision of 100 million dollars per year for research and development in the environment of cyber-physical systems by the US government was also named as part of the support from politics. However, unlike in Germany, politics did not take over leadership of the initiative. It still remains on the outside.

The five founding members have each secured a permanent seat on the steering committee, which was augmented by six further members: two so-called supporting member companies, each elected for a period of four years, currently being SAP and Schneider Elektrik until 2019; two members from big industry and one member from small and medium-sized industry, each elected for one year; and finally, one member each from a non-profit organization and from the realm of science and research, also elected for one year.

Management of active business of the consortium was transferred to the Object Management Group (OMG), whose chairman and CEO Richard Soley is now also the managing director of the IIC. He additionally manages the work of the steering committee, of which he is a non-elected, twelfth member.

The OMG is a consortium founded in 1989 which focuses on the development of standards for producer-independent, multi-system, object-oriented programming. At the time of its founding, the OMG included IBM, Apple, Sun and eleven other companies. In the meantime, the OMG has more than 800 members, and develops internationally recognized standards, such as the Requirements Interchange Format (ReqIF), developed a few years ago, especially requested by the German automotive industry. The OMG has its headquarters in Needham, Massachusetts [4].

Familiar at least to IT specialists is the Common Object Request Broker Architecture (CORBA), which facilitates the generation of distributed applications in heterogeneous environments, and the Unified Modeling Language (UML), which enables the modeling and documentation of object-oriented systems using normal syntax.

The IIC has thus sought out an extremely competent and internationally recognized organization to steer activities. It is no wonder that the international expansion of the consortium did not take very long.

For the election of the steering committee in September 2014, the IIC had 68 members, and for the following elections in early September of 2015, membership had grown to 200 from 26 countries. Several companies that are active in *Industrie 4.0* have also joined the IIC, such as the companies ABB, Bosch, SAP and Siemens.

Just as in the *Plattform Industrie 4.0*, work in the consortium is organized into working groups. The IIC also has a reference architecture in the meantime, the Industrial Internet Reference Architecture (IIRA). Although it is somewhat reminiscent of the reference architecture of *Industrie 4.0*, it is much more general (see Fig. 5.2). It was published in June of 2015 and can be downloaded through the website of the Consortium [5].

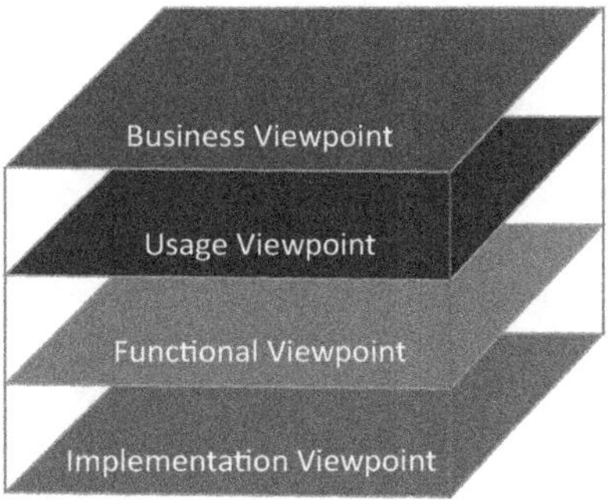

Fig. 5.2 Industrial internet reference architecture (IIRA). (IIC)

The IIRA makes a less technically detailed impression than the German architecture. The illustrations published for the reference architecture are more strongly reminiscent of software architectures and flow charts. At the same time, the IIC published the first version of an industrial internet vocabulary. In it, terms and definitions are explained and cited with their respective sources, as they are used in all documents of the IIC.

The main work of the consortium concerns the so-called testbeds, for which a separate working group was established. These testbeds are intended to be environments where the innovation and opportunities of the industrial internet, new technologies and applications, new products and services are initiated, reviewed and tested for their usability for the market.

Six such testbeds (of eight planned) have been publicly released so far. We can use a specific example to explain what they are and how they work: system efficiency. The testbed has a management member, in this case Infosys, and supporting members, here Bosch, GE, IBM, Intel and PTC. This testbed targets the market segments high tech, industrial manufacturing, discrete and manufacturing industry, automotive, aircraft and other segments with high-quality, stationary and non-stationary systems. The challenges are described for which solutions are being sought. In this case, for example, only 15% of all operators are implementing systematic measures for securing optimal efficiency. A targeted goal is cited as the efficient and precise collection of device data in real time and its analysis for reaching correct decisions. Finally, the concrete example of the "testbed in action" will be presented and explained, in this case, using the example of aircraft landing gear [6].

Two years after its founding, the Industrial Internet Consortium has already come relatively far in implementing very pragmatic approaches that facilitate and support the development of new products and services. The procedure seems to be more based on the development methods of IT and internet corporations in the USA. It is, however, especially the marketing of the ideas—which is to be expected from an American initiative—that has been very effective and professional. On the IIC website, you can immediately find what you are looking for and, naturally, the respective contact person as well.

5.4 Who Will Win the Battle Over Industrial Data?

At the 2016 Hanover Trade Fair, the USA served as the partner country. The German newspaper *Frankfurter Allgemeine Zeitung* published a special issue shortly before the start of the trade show with the headline "Production of the Future" and the sub-heading "America is calling the shots."

US President Barack Obama, together with German Chancellor Angela Merkel, opened the trade show. Packaged in flattery for the hostess with a great deal of praise, Obama emphasized the strengths of the US economy and its industry. The chancellor answered with a smile: "We are prepared. We love competition. But we also like to win."

With 465 exhibitors, the USA had about five times more representation than on average in recent years, in all halls and of course in the automation and IT halls of the Digital Factory.

It is difficult to see what the subject of the competition actually is. Of course, the manufacturing industry, including machine and plant engineering, has been depleted in the USA over the course of half a century. Even a shot in the arm in the amount of a hundred million dollars a year cannot undo the damage. The lead of German industry in development, production planning and manufacturing is enormous and hard to catch up to. Yet the lead of the US high-tech industry, internet and data companies is just as large and just as difficult to overtake.

A new game has begun, and a new hand will be dealt. Elections in the USA are based on a simple majority vote. The principle of "the winner takes it all," a clear distinction between winners and losers, is very widespread there and in no way limited to politics. It seems to be perfectly natural that, in a country that has for decades led the digitalization of the world with its internet and data business, is now dominating business with industrial internet data. Yet that would be overlooking the fact that industry in the USA, due to the complete concentration on the internet, does not exhibit the degree of digitalization considered to be normal in Germany. The USA is the world market leader in digitalization. However, most products of daily life are far from the modern product world for the Internet of Things: bad mechanics, bad mechatronics. Even the infrastructure for the use of the internet is miserable in large parts of the USA, and hardly better than in Germany. In both countries, there are giant areas where easy access to broadband networks with a rapid data flow is not a matter of course. In both countries, it hardly seems possible to improve conditions in a short period of time. And as long as there is no internet connection on large chunks of a train ride, we cannot speak of an Internet of Things as a mass market.

But several responsible persons in German industry also think that nobody could challenge the success of their products on the world market anytime soon. Yet that is just as incorrect; because the digitalization of their companies is based on isolated applications, and is not universal, not to mention not networked and internet-based. However, the new networking opportunities provide an Achilles heel to the process of networking their products, via which creative software specialists can hack into the system—and these weak spots are invisible.

Elevators in operation, whether for passengers or freight, have a long service life. During that time, they need to be regularly maintained. Nevertheless, parts of the systems can malfunction from time to time, which are more or less serious, depending on their importance. Many malfunctions show signs well in advance. The noise made when the elevator is in motion can change. The doors may not open or close normally, which can also cause perceptible noises. Display elements and electrical components may also exhibit noticeable changes. All of these things are symptoms that can be detected through external observation or through measurements and sensors. For this, neither the product data of the manufacturer needs to be known nor must the corresponding measuring devices be integrated in the elevator. A small, smart device on the outer wall is all that is needed.

Almost all data pertaining to the use of a device can represent such gateways through which third-party service providers under certain conditions can mediate between manufacturer and customer with special offers and take care of the business of maintenance and service, which would otherwise greatly inhibit and undermine the relationship of the manufacturer to the customer.

It is more difficult for third-party service providers to develop a business with original product data from the manufacturer, because it is not necessarily easily accessible, but rather belongs to the producer, who can additionally secure such data. In contrast, linking original data from engineering, simulation and testing is a great advantage for the manufacturer, because he or she can then use the data to offer completely different services than everyone else. Because the elevator manufacturer knows which data represents target values and which indicate malfunctions, he or she can predict a malfunction early with only that data; he does not have to wait until strange noises or other peculiarities can be determined. However, the manufacturer must have a continuous data chain allowing him or her access at all times to the engineering data and its connection with data from the factory.

Thus, it is a downright minefield that has to be traversed. Neither is all of the data which could theoretically serve as the basis for services known and accessible, nor are all services known that could result through the use of product data. Finding your way in this field requires a knowledge of products, engineering and production, as well as many ideas and the willingness to push forward into unknown territory.

The USA has proven to be a favorable location for business with software, the internet and data. It is ahead of German industry at this stage of advanced industrial development. A few important differences in approaches to new business have become evident:

- The first of ten principles that Google lists for its own company philosophy on its homepage states "Focus on the user and all else will follow" [7]. The most famous print advertisement of a German automobile manufacturer is from Audi, which was also printed in US magazines in the German language: "Vorsprung durch Technik" ("Advancement through technology"). Can we be more specific in describing the difference between the approaches of the software and hardware world champions?
- While creativity and the willingness to try new things and drop them again if they are not good enough are part of the core characteristics of a Silicon Valley startup, engineers, the most important employees in industry, in Germany are still characterized by being very thorough and sometimes working meticulously on a single detail until the competition has successfully placed a somewhat lower-quality model on the market.
- The startup in California mentioned above is itself the counterpart to the German family-run company, part of the thousands of midsize industrial enterprises. A comparable financing network such as the one which churns out new startups in the USA, and out of which firms like Google and Facebook are repeatedly produced, does not exist in Germany.

In the coming years, it will be exciting to observe the competition between these so very different industrial nations in this new battlefield. Right now, nobody can predict who will win.

References

1. Taylor, F. W. (2006). *The principles of scientific management.* New York: Cosimo. Reprint of the edition: London: Harper & Brothers, 1911.
2. Die Maschinen sind zurück, Süddeutsche Zeitung, Thema der Woche, April 23/24, 2016.
3. http://www.iiconsortium.org/press-room/03-27-14.htm. Accessed 12 May 2016.
4. http://www.omg.org/gettingstarted/gettingstartedindex.htm. Accessed 12 May 2016.
5. http://www.iiconsortium.org/IIRA.htm. Accessed 12 May 2016.
6. http://www.iiconsortium.org/asset-efficiency.htm. Accessed 12 May 2016.
7. https://www.google.com/intl/de_de/about/company/philosophy/. Accessed 12 May 2016.

China's Comeback

6

Ulrich Sendler

Abstract

Since the end of the 1970s, China has increasingly become an industrial country. With "Made in China 2025," the goal has been expressed to become the Number 1 industrial nation. Although doubts about it are justified, a look at individual sectors will show that this goal is not out of reach. A German/Chinese collaboration offers the greatest chances for both sides.

6.1 Made in China 2025

When, in 1911, the more than two thousand years of history of the Chinese empire came to an end with the announcement of the Republic of China through the national revolution of Sun Yat-Sen, the second industrial revolution had already begun in the western world. China, however, had hardly any industry; rather, it was almost a purely agrarian state. Following wars and civil wars, the nation once again gained its full sovereignty with the establishment of the People's Republic of China in 1949.

The past several decades in China were characterized by a swift catching-up with industrialization. Villages became cities with millions of inhabitants, the agrarian state became an industrial nation. Among the 13 cities listed on the internet as having the largest populations of the world, the People's Republic of China alone is home to four, including Beijing (20 million), Shanghai (19.2 million), Guangzhou (11.1 million) and Shenzhen (10.6 million). Hundreds of millions of people found jobs, and a middle class began to develop. Yet, for years, it has been clear that this development is now in a rut. Labor expenses are climbing, growth is

U. Sendler (✉)
Mauerkircherstraße 30, 81679 Munich, Germany
E-Mail: ulrich.sendler@ulrichsendler.de

U. Sendler (ed.), *The Internet of Things*,
https://doi.org/10.1007/978-3-662-54904-9_6

slowing, and China is ceasing to be the seemingly unstoppable engine of international economic growth.

On May 19, 2015, an initial national ten-year plan to transform China was presented, called “Made in China 2025.” Two more plans were to follow, “in order to transform China into a leading manufacturing power by the year 2049,” as it stands in the official announcement [1]. By the 100th anniversary of the founding of the People’s Republic, China hopes to become the top industrial nation in the world. They worked on this plan for two and a half years with the support of 150 science and business experts. The new five-year plan for the national economy, started in 2016, is also focused on the radical modernization of industry. The initiative *Industrie 4.0* is seen by the Chinese as a positive example and inspiration (see Sect. 7.3). The following account will be supplemented with much more detail and more specifically in Chap. 7, which Xinhuanet has contributed to this book.

Overview
Made in China 2025 has identified nine tasks to be approached as priorities:

- Improvement of innovation
- Integration of information technology and business
- Strengthening of the industrial base
- Promotion of Chinese brands in the world
- Environmentally-friendly manufacturing
- Promotion of breakthroughs in ten important industrial sectors
- Restructuring of the processing trade (from mass to class)
- Promotion of service-oriented producers and service providers
- Internationalization of production

The ten important industrial sectors listed below represent central branches of the manufacturing industry and the high-tech and electrical industries.

Overview
The ten sectors include:

- New information technologies
- (C)NC machines and robotics
- Aerospace technology
- Seafaring technology and high-tech ships
- Railway technology
- Environmentally-friendly vehicles
- Drive assemblies
- New materials
- Biomedicine and medical devices
- Agricultural machines

The adopted plan calls for massive financial support about whose extent no figures have been disclosed. Initially, Made in China 2025 will concentrate on five large-scale projects. These include the expansion of an innovation center for the manufacturing industry, the bolstering of the industrial base and the promotion of environmentally-friendly production. By 2020, a further 14 innovation centers are to be added, with a total of 40 by 2025.

In the publication, it was announced that the plan will primarily rely on the market, but that the government will also support it. The goal is to have 40% of all components and materials of new products come from China by 2020, and 70% by 2025. Intellectual property rights are to be more strictly protected, especially for small and medium-sized companies. Intellectual property is to be able to be employed more heavily for business strategies, and companies are to receive the permission to define technological standards themselves, and their position on international standards committees is to be strengthened.

This initiative is seen as the key to allowing economic growth to "maintain a medium to high level and to allow China's industry to push the global value creation chain higher," as the publication of the Chinese State Council asserts. Premier Li is quoted as saying that "the country must double its efforts in order to transform China from a manufacturer of great volumes to a manufacturer of great quality" [2].

In the USA, an article on "Made in China 2025" appeared on June 1, 2015 at the Center for Strategic and International Studies (CSIS). CSIS is an independent think tank in Washington with a focus on the foreign policy of the Unites States. Scott Kennedy, the author, provides an evaluation of the Chinese and German initiatives. According to Kennedy, Made in China 2025 has gotten its inspiration directly from the German initiative *Industrie 4.0.* He then compares it to the Chinese initiative, writing:

> The Chinese effort is far broader, as the efficiency and quality of Chinese producers are highly uneven, and multiple challenges need to be overcome in a short amount of time … [3].

Yet neither the government nor the industry of China are attempting to simply copy *Industrie 4.0.* As will become clear in Chap. 7, China is searching for its own way, which picks up on interesting components of all approaches observed in currently leading industrial nations. But it is also clear that, in the German initiative, a more than fitting approach is seen, or, as stated in Sect. 7.3.2:

> However, Germany's manufacturing industry possesses a strong technological foundation and can thus directly implement Industrie 4.0. China, on the other hand, has to juggle Industry 2.0, 3.0 and 4.0 at the same time, as well as achieve a restructuring of its traditional industries. In addition, China's economy must keep pace, even in its skyrocketing development in the high-end sector. These tasks are even more complicated and more difficult than Germany's implementation of *Industrie 4.0.* Ultimately, however, China and Germany will meet in Industrie 4.0.

6.2 China's Starting Position

It is difficult to ascertain where industry in China stands on the whole. Some observers say it is on the way from Industry 2.0 (that is, mass production on the assembly line) to Industry 3.0 (computer-controlled automation). In truth, however, its development is much too varied for such a simplified assessment.

Very large portions of industry, insofar as it has promoted mass production of cheap products in the recent past, are not even at the level of Industry 2.0, if they have even emerged from a pre-industrial manufacturing stage. Thousands of unskilled workers hammer and screw products together at individual workstations at high speed. That is not the type of electrical mass production on an assembly line that ensued in the western world with the advent of Industry 2.0.

Other sectors have quickly assumed a great deal of expertise from western partners as well as western competitors. In robotics, in the construction of high-speed trains and the aerospace industry, China does indeed shine. The country is home to companies that are already far ahead of enterprises in the USA and Germany. However, this part of industry is the exception, not the rule, for most companies. Yet these are exceptions that show how quickly development can advance. And between these two extremes, anything goes: from companies comparable to our state of the art, to startups in e-commerce and internet services which compete with the big guys from Silicon Valley.

Let's have a look at the electrical industry, for example. According to the definition given by ZVEI, it includes the suppliers of assembly parts, information and communications technology, automation, household appliances, energy management, consumer electronics, lighting, electromedicine and others. This industry was the second strongest in the world in 2013, at € 3703 trillion, following the chemical industry (€ 3841 trillion), far ahead of the automotive industry (€ 2831 trillion) and mechanical engineering (€ 2225 trillion). Globally, the industry employed more than 24 million people in 2013—14.5 million in China alone. Within ten years, the number of Chinese electrical industrial workers had tripled. Even more impressive is the picture you get when you compare the development of the world's largest electrical markets. In 1995, the Chinese electrical market was only half as large as the German market. Around the turn of the century, China held third place behind the USA and Japan. Yet in 2013, China's market, at € 1293 trillion, was 2.4 times larger than the USA (€ 540 billion), and all together larger than the next four markets of the USA, Japan, South Korea and Germany put together.

Also with regard to global electrical production, China leads by far, as shown in Fig. 6.1. A look at global market shares provides a similar picture. China's global market share for the electrical industry in 2013 had climbed to 34.9%, with the USA a distant second at 14.6%. Ten years before, the relationship had been reversed: the USA at 23.9%, and China at 13%. Germany only played a small role at 2.9%, and in the meantime, has slipped behind South Korea. The year 2011 is seen as that point in time in which the so-called newly-industrialized and developing countries,

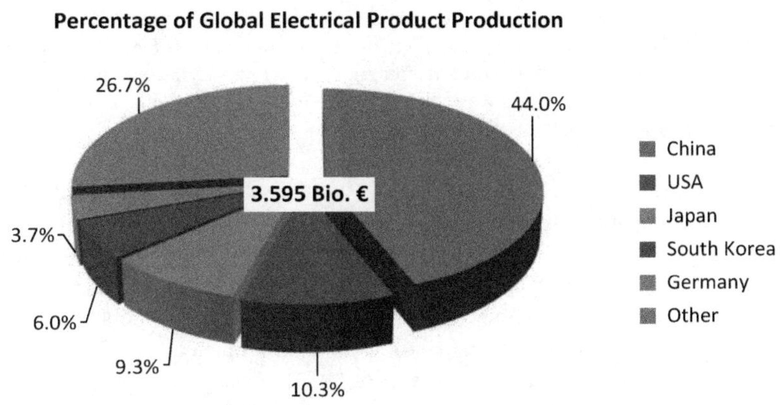

Fig. 6.1 China is by far the leading producer of electrical products in the world. *source* Elektroindustrie weltweit—Branchenstruktur und Entwicklung Electrical Industry Worldwide—Industry Structure and Development, ZVEI, 2014

of which China is one, caught up in the world electrical market. In 2013, they had already reached 53% [4].

It would be false to believe that giant companies such as Foxconn, contract manufacturers for Apple, Dell, Hewlett-Packard, Microsoft, Nintendo and Sony, among others, having 1.3 million employees in 2015, most on mainland China, although their headquarters is in Taiwan, make up the main portion of this development. Especially companies like Haier (70,000 employees) and Huawei (170,000 employees) are also outrunning their international competition—with value creation processes that their competitors would love to have; and with products that are closer to the visions of Industrie 4.0 than most in Germany. Since 1984, Haier has partnered with technological companies such as Liebherr in Germany, offering household appliances. As the world market leader for major household appliances, the company achieved a turnover of $24.2 billion in 2011. With its use of IT for a continuous, digital value creation chain, Haier is a significant reference customer for Siemens PLM. Huawei is a telecommunications supplier with its home office in Shenzhen, China, which, in 2015, made a profit of € 5 billion and a turnover of more than € 56 billion. In selling more than 100 million smartphones per year, their focus is on the development and manufacture of communication technology devices, such as mobile phones, but also optical networks and end devices.

A further example is the automotive industry. The strength of the electrical industry described above plays a significant role, because it is precisely the combination of the electrical and high-tech industries with the automotive industry comes into play. In a study conducted by MERICS Mercator Institute for China Studies, in the China Monitor No. 31 of March 2016, the focus is directed at a fundamental change of development in China:

> Digitisation of the automotive sector is progressing very differently in China than it is in Europe or the US—the tone is not being set by Google or Apple, but by innovative *Chinese* companies with influence. These upcoming firms are rapidly pushing their way into the Chinese automotive sector with radically new business models and are changing the market environment as they go [5].

The study continues to state that especially young companies in the internet sector are transferring their dynamic work processes to the automotive sector. Their strengths are short product cycles and the rapid development of new business sectors. This process is aided by the great interest of Chinese car buyers in digital applications: In answer to the question as to whether they would choose a car from a different producer for better access to apps, data and media, only 20% of German customers said 'yes.' In China, it was 60% [6].

Motor vehicles can be networked in China faster than in Europe, and China could soon set the pace internationally and pass the USA, warns the China Monitor. Only a serious economic crisis could slow this trend.

The buzzword is the "Internet of Cars." In addition to autonomous driving, it focuses on embedding a digital infrastructure in the vehicle, including communication between

- car and driver (or the driver's smartphone)
- car and car
- car and intelligent traffic infrastructure
- car and internet
- car and mobile communications network
- car and satellites (satellite navigation)
- car and online services for car-related services.

Within the context of the 13th five-year plan, the Chinese Ministry of Industry and Information Technology (MIIT) is currently working on a strategy for the promotion of the Internet of Cars. Together with the industry, a separate digital ecosystem for cars is to be created with the Chinese infrastructure. The government wants to spread Chinese standards throughout the world. This pertains to both hardware and software systems for intelligent traffic systems as well as satellite navigation and the telecommunications infrastructure. And the more interfaces a car obtains through networking with this Chinese infrastructure, the more the technical framework on the Chinese market will differ from those in the USA and Europe [5].

In this regard, a special challenge is developing for automobile manufacturers in Germany, Japan and the USA. Not only is the urgency of equipping vehicles with internet services rising, as is the need to promote their networking, but the ecosystems currently being established will be very different from those in the western world. Those companies wishing to successfully offer motor vehicles on the Chinese market in the years to come must know how to work within that ecosystem of the Internet of Cars.

Against this background, it is amazing how little the relationships between various aspects of China's economic development are taken into consideration in individual cases. The newspaper *Süddeutsche Zeitung* published a leader comment in the economic section on May 13, 2016, with the headline that translates as "Beijing keeps blowing (up the balloon)," which states:

> 4.7 trillion yuan. That converts to 632 billion euros. China's leadership wants to invest this sum in the country's transportation network in the coming three years for even more high-speed train routes, airports, highways. [...] The problem of Beijing's leaders are their own guarantees. The economy is supposed to grow by at least 6.5% - no matter how. The trillions invested may provide temporary assistance in reaching that goal. In truth, however, they represent a confession of failure [7].

A good portion of this enormous investment is going directly to the realm of infrastructure, which will be a prerequisite for the Internet of Cars. This is anything but a balloon about to pop.

However, it is correct to say that, considering its full spectrum, the Chinese manufacturing industry is only limitedly automated and far from a digital value creation chain. According to the China Monitor of March 2015 with the title "*Industrie 4.0*: Will German Technology Help China Catch Up with the West," approximately 60% of companies utilize industry software such as Enterprise Resource Planning (ERP), Manufacturing Execution Systems (MES) or Product Lifecycle Management (PLM). In China, there are currently about 14 industrial robots for every 10,000 industrial workers. In comparison, there are 282 in Germany. Nevertheless, the study comes to the following conclusion:

> According to an unpublished study by the Chinese Academy of Engineering, the PRC could be on an equal footing with the USA, Germany and Japan as a progressive industrial producer by 2045. [...] Digitisation is the fitting stepping stone for China. By Chinese estimates, *Industrie 4.0* could increase China's productivity by 25 to 30 per cent and lower unforeseen production losses by 60 per cent [8].

According to the above, since 2005, investments of producing industries in the IT sector have doubled. In the meantime, China is the world's largest key market for industrial robots. By 2017, it is predicted that China will operate the most industrial robots. The key markets for radio frequency identification chips (RFIDs), sensors and embedded software systems are booming.

The initiated German/Chinese cooperation on an administrative level and on many levels of research and industry, could be very profitable for both sides. To a large degree, there are countless firms which can plan their digital transformation almost as if in a greenfield approach, without the inherited burden of a growing IT island landscape that has developed in recent decades in Germany, among other places, which is hard to integrate. Technologies and tools from Germany would certainly be advantageous for this. China would have examples that could be broadly spread. And technology transfer would have showcase projects which would show the partly-digitized companies in one's own country what can be expected at the end of the vision of Industrie 4.0.

References

1. http://www.chinadaily.com.cn/bizchina/2015-05/19/content_20760528.htm. Accessed 12 May 2016
2. http://german.china.org.cn/business/txt/2015-03/31/content_35203958.htm. Accessed 12 May 2016.
3. http://csis.org/publication/made-china-2025. Accessed 12 May 2016.
4. http://www.zvei.org/Verband/Publikationen/Seiten/Elektroindustrie-weltweit.aspx. Accessed 12 May 2016.
5. http://www.merics.org/fileadmin/user_upload/downloads/China-Monitor/MERICS_China_Monitor_31_End_of_the_road_for_international_car_makers_in_China.pdf. Accessed 12 May 2016.
6. Competing for the connected customer—perspectives on the opportunities created by car connectivity and automation, McKinsey&Company, Advanced Industries, September 2015, p. 17.
7. "Peking bläst und bläst", Süddeutsche Zeitung, May 13, 2016, p. 17.
8. https://www.merics.org/fileadmin/templates/download/china-monitor/China_Monitor_No_23_en.pdf. Accessed 12 May 2016.

"Made in China 2025" and "Industrie 4.0"—In Motion Together

7

Tian Shubin and Pan Zhi

Abstract

On October 29, 2015, China's national news agency Xinhua received official permission to publish the communique of the fifth committee conference of the 13th Central Committee of the Communist Party of China. Via Xinhua's online platform Xinhuanet (www.new.cn), a media portal with the most influential power and range in China and beyond, this communique increasingly caught the attention of the international public. Simultaneously, the paper was consulted as a programmatic document in the analysis, explanation and evaluation of Chinese development.

One of the most important demands in the communique states: To achieve the development goals in the period of the 13th five-year plan, China must approach all difficult development challenges with enthusiasm and to base its superiority in its own development on a more stable and deeply-rooted foundation. The document also asserts that the concepts of an innovative, coordinated and green development, characterized by an opening to the outside and mutual profiting, are to be achieved. The Chinese government further announced it would begin working on forming a new industrial system. Its targets are to more rapidly develop a strong domestic manufacturing industry, to realize the initiative "Made in China 2025" and to bolster the industrial foundations of the country. In future, a series of strategic industries must be developed, driving the cultivation of the modern service sector.

T. Shubin · P. Zhi (✉)
Xinhuanet, 8th Floor, Jinyu Building, No. 129, Xuanwumen Weststr, 100031 Beijing, China
E-Mail: panzhi@xinhuaeurope.com

U. Sendler (ed.), *The Internet of Things*,
https://doi.org/10.1007/978-3-662-54904-9_7

7.1 Overview

On October 29, 2015, China's national news agency Xinhua received the official permission to publish the communique of the fifth committee conference of the 13th central committee of the Communist Party of China. Via Xinhua's online platform Xinhuanet (www.new.cn), a media portal with the most influential power and range in China and beyond, the communique increasingly attracted the attention of the international public. Simultaneously, the paper was consulted as a programmatic document in the analysis, explanation and evaluation of Chinese development.

One of the most important demands in the communique states: To achieve the development goals in the period of the 13th five-year plan, China must approach all difficult development challenges with enthusiasm and to base its superiority in its own development on a more stable and deeply-rooted foundation. The document also asserts that the concepts of an innovative, coordinated and green development, characterized by an opening to the outside and mutual profiting, are to be achieved. The Chinese government further announced it would begin working on forming a new industrial system. Its targets are to more rapidly develop a strong domestic manufacturing industry, to realize the initiative "Made in China 2025" and to bolster the industrial foundations of the country. In future, a series of strategic industries must be developed, driving the cultivation of the modern service sector.

The initiative "Made in China 2025", officially introduced for the first time in 2015, is part of the Chinese government's "Five Developments" concept. "Made in China 2025" is an action plan scheduled over a period of ten years, designed to ultimately implement the strategy of "developing a country with a strong manufacturing industry." This comprehensive campaign comprises a variety of topics and concrete goals.

China's government has clearly recognized the key role of modern industry in further development, which also becomes clear in the introductory chapter of the action plan for "Made in China 2025." In it, we read: "The manufacturing industry represents a pillar of the economy. It not only serves as a foundation for the development of the nation, but is also a central instrument for the cultivation of a flourishing economy, as well as a basic requirement for the strengthening of the nation. […] The only way for China to build up an internationally competitive manufacturing industry is to increase its extensive potential to ensure the general security of the country and thus establish an influential nation within the world community." Therefore, it is clear that "Made in China 2025" will receive a central role in achieving the goal of the Chinese government to revitalize the country as a nation in a great way.

On the other side of the globe, the German government officially presented its strategy *Industrie 4.0* in April of 2013 at the Hanover Trade Fair. This future-oriented project is directed at preparing German industry well for the future of production. In addition, the German administration hopes to use the project to find answers to a large series of global development issues. These include a shortage of natural resources, an increase in the average age of employees and land consumption in metropolitan areas, in which a spatial separation between residential and industrial areas is increasingly reaching its practical limits.

Although the two strategies recently put forth by China and Germany bear different names and do not correspond one hundred percent regarding content, they still reflect the ambition of both nations to play a leading role in global development by further developing their manufacturing industry to a large extent, thus increasing their general economic strength. "Made in China 2025" and "Industrie 4.0" thus have several common points.

The fact that "Made in China 2025" and the German initiative "Industrie 4.0" exhibit so many potential interfaces is no coincidence, but rather the logical consequence of current development. Based on a series of positive results which could be achieved during Chinese President Xi Jinping's visit to Germany in March of 2014, China's Prime Minister Li Keqiang and German Chancellor Angela Merkel initiated the government consultations of both countries, which had entered their third round, where the new campaign "Shaping Innovation Together" for the German/Chinese cooperative effort, was presented. In this campaign, China and Germany express four common perspectives. Viewed from a global perspective, all countries of the world not only see several opportunities in the new industrial revolution, but also a number of challenges. A new hand will be dealt for the division of international industries. Against this background, it seems perfectly reasonable both for China, as a representative of the developing nations, as well as Germany, as a traditional, strong industrial nation, to jointly search for development possibilities.

It cannot be denied that, in the course of German and Chinese development, a certain competition has also taken root. Germany, with its leading role in global industry, has long since served as a role model for China. However, there is also no question that the People's Republic, which has shown rapid growth since the implementation of the reform and opening, today not only offers a giant market, with a potential the likes of which traditional economic powerhouses such as Germany have long dreamed, but has also matured into a competitor to be taken seriously in harsh international competition, as can be seen in the example of Chinese high-speed trains (Fig. 7.1). China surely hopes to get into a position to indirectly overtake its global competitors during the implementation of its strategy.

At the same time, Germany is becoming more and more aware of the existence of global competition. The implementation recommendations for the future-oriented project *Industrie 4.0*, published in September of 2013, state: "At the same time, global competition pressure for production technology is continually growing. Not only are competitors from Asia putting domestic industry under pressure, but the USA is also countering its own de-industrialization with promotional programs for advanced manufacturing."

However, this competition situation is in no way comparable to a soccer game, in which the focus is on either victory or loss. Instead, it can be seen as a kind of relay race, in which China and Germany encourage each other and are running toward the same finish line. Both countries are starting from their own pole position and thus seem destined to future cooperation.

Fig. 7.1 High-speed trains in China, 2015. (Xinhua)

Or, in the words of Xi Jinping in a guest editorial written for the *Frankfurter Allgemeine Zeitung* during his visit to Germany with the title "Good for China, Europe and the World": "Since China and Germany are the most important economies in Asia and Europe, their increased cooperation will mean the alliance of two strong forces, and the connection of the growth poles of Asia and Europe. This will greatly promote the formation of a large Asio-European market, it will influence the growth of the entire Eurasian continent and have extensive effects on the constellations of economy and trade all over the world."

7.2 From "Big" to "Strong": China on the Path to a Strong Manufacturing Industry

7.2.1 In "Three Steps" to a Country with a Strong Manufacturing Industry

On May 8, 2010, the Chinese State Council published the program "Made in China 2025," signed by Prime Minister Li Keqiang. It is an action plan with the goal of developing China into a country with a strong manufacturing industry.

In the 2010 "Global Manufacturing Competitiveness Index" of the American consulting firm Deloitte, China reached the top spot in the world. According to statistics from the Chinese Ministry of Industry and Information Technology (MIIT), China's manufacturing industry made up just 2.7% of the global manufacturing industry in the year 1990 (see Fig. 7.2). The People's Republic was thus

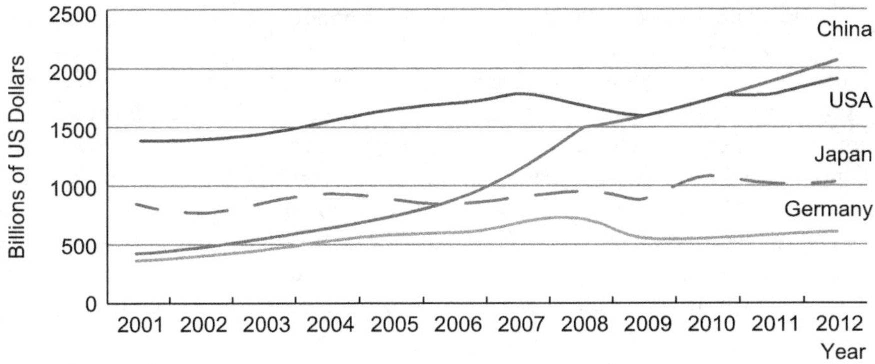

Fig. 7.2 Development of MVA (value added in manufacturing) of China, Japan, Germany and the USA from 2001 to 2012. (MIIT)

in ninth place. By the year 2000, this percentage had already grown to 6%, which moved China up to fourth place. And the trend did not stop there: In 2007, China reached 13.4% and thus second place in the ranking. In 2010, the People's Republic became the world's leading manufacturing nation, with a share of 19.8%. Since the mid-19th century, China, after 150 years, has thus regained the title of world's leading great power in the realm of the manufacturing industry.

In its roughly 150-year development, China's manufacturing industry has grown by impressive amounts, and yet it is not considered to have a strong industrial sector in a global comparison. The large gap that still exists becomes especially evident when we compare China's manufacturing industry with those of modern industrial nations like Germany. This can be seen, among other places, in China's independent innovative power, which, as of yet, is still weak. With regard to energy efficiency in the use of natural resources, too, China is still lagging behind. What is more, its industrial structure is not efficient, and the degree of utilization of information technology remains low. In addition, the People's Republic needs to catch up in the realm of economic efficiency.

China's task of transforming its domestic industrial structure, raising the level of industry and thus achieving an escalated development is proving to be an urgent and difficult task. In the meantime, however, China's manufacturing industry has entered a phase in which it certainly has the potential to achieve a historical transformation from an industry with a large product volume to one of strong performance.

According to many expert opinions, China's manufacturing industry has passed through three developmental phases since the implementation of the reform and opening: The first phase, primarily characterized by the use of active labor, began in the 1980s. The second phase came in the 1990s. Its focus was the modernization of plant production. The third phase, which started at the turn of the millennium and is ongoing today, is characterized by innovative products and the use of information technology.

In the course of societal progress, the advantages of the Chinese economy, which had long profited from low material and labor costs, have continually melted away in recent years. On the contrary, pressure, especially from the growing demands of environmental protection, is now growing uninterruptedly. At the same time, enormous changes can be seen on the demand side of the market. All of this is leading to the fact that the development model China previously implemented, which had been work-, resource- and energy intensive, can no longer be maintained. Simultaneously, the developed nations are currently working on a re-industrialization strategy, in order to revive their own manufacturing industries, and to move the construction of large-scale plants with comparably high technological standards into their own countries. Meanwhile, other countries with medium and low incomes, with their advantages regarding natural resources and work force, are taking over the tasks of labor-intensive manufacturing. Thus, China is feeling pressure from two sides and is faced with serious challenges.

On March 5, 2015, during the convention of the National People's Congress (NPC) and the National Committee of the Chinese People's Political Consultative Conference (CPPCC), China's Premier Li Keqiang officially presented the plan for the initiative "Made in China 2025" in his progress report. He said: "We should actively implement the plan 'Made in China 2025,' dedicate ourselves to an intelligent transformation, the strengthening of the industrial foundations and green development and thus transform China at an accelerated pace from a country with a big manufacturing industry to a country with a strong manufacturing industry."

Subsequently, Miao Wei, the Minister for Industry and Information Technology, said in an interview that the execution of the "Made in China 2025" initiative is the first step in transforming the manufacturing industry from an industry with big production volumes to one with high performance, because, indeed, although China is an industrial nation with a large production volume, it is not one characterized by high efficiency. "China lacks key corporations with competitive potential in the international market. In the realm of the autonomous production of a few technical systems, it is crucial to achieve a decisive breakthrough. A few significant products have not yet occupied optimal places on the market. We are not yet a country whose manufacturing industry demonstrates high efficiency."

In fact, China has planned to transform itself from "big" to "strong" within three decades. The initiative "Made in China 2025" serves only as the first action plan and a guidepost for the future. According to the mutual routine plan, China is striving to be put on the list of industrial nations with a high degree of efficiency. In the years to follow, the goal is for China's manufacturing industry to catch up with the level of those industrial nations which are situated among the average of countries with the most efficient industries. In a third step, to be completed by the 100th anniversary of the founding of the People's Republic of China (October 1, 2049), China's position as an industrial nation with high efficiency is to be even stronger. The country will then be in the front row of industrial nations with high efficiency.

7.2.2 Core Content of the Initiative "Made in China 2025"

The initiative "Made in China 2025" aims to transition from "big" to "strong" in three steps. The integration of information technology and industrialization is to contribute to the jump from an industry with large production volumes to one of high efficiency. For this process, the following four points have been defined as principles:

- In the initiative "Made in China 2025," the market is to take on the leading role, while the government only serves as a guide.
- Look to the future with a firm stance in the present.
- Target comprehensive advancement and breakthroughs in selective areas.
- Create autonomous development and cooperation, as well as win-win situations.

Considering the elimination of five serious insufficiencies, five significant guidelines were presented:

- The strategy of development driven by innovation
- The precedence of quality over quantity
- Green development
- Structural optimization
- Promotion of talent as a central issue

That is why five important projects have been determined in the following ten key areas: new-generation information and telecommunications technology, high-quality and digitally-controlled machines tools and robots, aerospace facilities, facilities for maritime projects and highly-engineered ships, modern facilities for railway transportation and energy conservation and vehicles, electrical plants, agricultural machines powered by new energy sources, new materials, biopharmacology and efficient medical devices and instruments.

In March of 2015, a special meeting took place to present the initiative "Made in China 2025." At this meeting, Su Bo, Deputy Minister for Industry and Information Technology, introduced the five important projects:

Firstly, the projects for the development of the innovation center of the manufacturing industry are to be conducted across the country. After the market-oriented reform, several state research institutes were converted to companies, and the corresponding research projects were cut back and innovation activity lowered. For basic research and projects related to industrialization, a series of national centers are to be established for the coordinated innovation of production, training, research and application. The innovation centers are to be created in the style of the 45 governmental innovation centers in the USA. That means that the centers are to be established with the support of companies, universities, research academies and research institutes. In the form of an alliance of industrial enterprises, they will be responsible for the core task of developing an industrial nation with high efficiency, orient themselves toward market demand and achieve results on a step-by-step basis.

Secondly, projects in the realm of an intelligent manufacturing industry are to be realized. The intelligent manufacturing industry is at the core of the next round of technical revolution. It is also considered the focus for technologies such as IT-supported networking, digitalization and artificial intelligence. The intelligent manufacturing industry can contribute to an improvement in the standard of digitalization and of artificial intelligence.

Thirdly, the project is intended to strengthen the industrial base. One of the main causes for the shortfall in the manufacturing industry is that the development and production of significant components and replacement parts, technological processes and material quality have not continued to evolve. At a meeting of the Chinese State Council, leading figures spoke in particular about fundamental technical processes. It was considered urgent to conduct the project to strengthen the industrial base.

Fourthly, green development projects were cited as significant. Environmental damage and a shortage of resources limit China's economic development. Since China's manufacturing industry has become the largest in the world, quality and efficiency of economic growth have become primary tasks. Natural resources are to be used economically and the environment is to be protected. In the realm of green development and emissions reduction, China still possesses great, yet largely untapped potential. That is why it is crucial to conduct projects promoting green development.

Fifthly, a high level of innovation in production plants is an important undertaking. This includes some projects which have already begun, such as in the area of nuclear technology, the internet, the production of high-quality and digitally-controlled machine tools and the production of wide-bodied aircraft. China still needs quite a range of new, special projects, in order to raise the level of the entire manufacturing industry in the realm of systems engineering.

7.2.3 Innovation as the Driving Force for "Made in China 2025"

Compared to the name of the industrial development plans and strategic documents in earlier periods, the name "Made in China 2025" is a small innovation in itself: This state strategy was given its name as a reference to the term *Industrie 4.0*, circulated by the German government. And innovation is precisely the driving force behind "Made in China 2025!"

It is common knowledge that the manufacturing industry is the main battlefield for innovation, that is, the area where innovation is fought out most intensively and enthusiastically. Technical innovation in the realm of Chinese industry has experienced various phases which can perhaps be described as follows: innovation through imitation, innovation through integration and innovation following takeovers and acquisitions. As fruit of the long-term collection of experiences, China's innovation factors in the meantime are now leading the world; the difference in levels of innovation which had long existed between

China and the developed nations has gradually declined; overall innovative power has been steadily increasing; the path which innovation is on has passed imitation and has reached a leading position. In 2014, expenses for science and research in China amounted to 1.3312 trillion Yuan. That equals 2.09% of GDP for 2014 and 2.88 times more than expenses in 2008, whose total was 461.6 billion Yuan. Internationally, China's expenses in this realm are ranked third. That makes China a leader among emerging markets.

In recent years, innovation as a driving force for development for China's enterprises has taken on an ever more important role: Corporate spending for research and development have rapidly risen, which has significantly strengthened innovative capability (see Fig. 7.3). Breakthroughs have been achieved in the areas of manned space flight, exploration of the moon, manned deep-sea diving, the development and construction of regional aircraft, the recovery and utilization of liquefied natural gas (LNG) and in high-speed travel. In the realms of transformer technology for ultra-high voltage, in the construction of plants for the highly-efficient ethane production, an important raw material for the chemical and plastics industries, in wind power plants and supercomputers, China is already keeping up with the global leaders.

Considering the fact that China is the largest production site in the world, with more than 220 of 500 major industrial products, the gap in the overall quality of the manufacturing industry and competitive capability between China and developed industrial nations is still very large. The most obvious problems are:

Fig. 7.3 China successfully launched a satellite in 2014. (Xinhua)

a lack of capability for autonomous innovation; core technologies are dominated and limited by other countries, and the results of scientific research cannot sufficiently support industrial production. All of these problems are limiting the development of Chinese industry. The ability to innovate in the realm of technology continues to develop weakly, and the number of patented products is low; the level of dependency on core technology is too high; high-performance plants, important replacement parts, components and materials must usually be procured from abroad. The level of dependency of the Chinese manufacturing industry lies considerably higher than 50%. CNC systems of the highest level of quality are imported at a rate of 95%, while 80% of integrated circuits and almost all first-class hydraulic components, seals and motors are imported. Still, China's industry, due to the international division of labor, is largely concentrated on "manufacturing—processing—installing." It only relies on modern technology to a small extent, and value creation is low. The competitive capability of Chinese industry in the realms of research and development, design, the contract-based takeover of projects, marketing and customer service is insufficient. The production of the Apple iPhone 6 mobile phone in China is a typical example: China earns fewer than five euros (or about six dollars) from the revenue of every unit sold, which amounts to less than 5% of the net profit.

Innovation as a driving force is one of the guidelines for the construction of a strong industrial manufacturing nation through "Made in China 2025," and the increase of innovative capability in the manufacturing industry is the main task. The project "Made in China 2025" cites definite demands: It is urgent that the innovation system of the manufacturing industry be improved, with the enterprises serving as the main supporters in market orientation. A competitive environment must be created in which production, learning, research and application are unified; the innovation chain should be oriented around the manufacturing chain, and the resource allocation chain around the innovation chain; research and development of complex core technology is to be emphasized; the implementation of results stemming from research and development in marketable products is to be promoted, and the innovative potential in core industrial areas is to be increased.

China's manufacturing industry has developed rapidly within the last thirty years. Its foundations lie in favorable production factors and an advantageous investment climate. However, in the future, the Chinese manufacturing industry should be sustained by innovation.

7.3 Different Initiatives, the Same Goal: A Comparison of "Made in China 2025" and *Industrie 4.0*

7.3.1 "Made in China 2025" and *Industrie 4.0*—Made for Each Other!

"Made in Germany" is not only a synonym for good quality in China, but all over the world. When Germany presented the concept of *Industrie 4.0*, the term, which is reminiscent of the most modern technology and German industrial products of the highest quality, became an instant hit in China.

Before the program *Industrie 4.0* was launched, it was discussed for almost ten years in scientific, economic and administrative circles. The preparations for the initiative "Made in China 2025" also took several years. Although it is hard to determine today which of the two initiatives saw the light of the world first, *Industrie 4.0* immediately won over the Chinese. Not only among executives in politics and business, but also management and company employees viewed the new idea from Germany with great admiration.

Leading politicians from China and Germany have long held the desire to further deepen the strategic partnership and number of collaborative efforts between the two countries. In the business sector, both countries already share close ties, with companies from the two nations having been cooperating for decades. All of this has contributed to the manufacturing industries of both countries starting to move in sequence. For many Chinese, the preference for "quality German workmanship" began in 1984, when the first German car, the VW Santana, appeared on Chinese roads. Today, the newest models from BMW, Mercedes and Audi can be spotted in Chinese cities on a daily basis. In the households of the Chinese middle class, there are increasingly more electronic devices from Siemens and Bosch, and in their kitchens products from WMF and ZWILLING. In addition, products from the German pharmaceutical industry, such as Merck Serono and Bayer, are protecting or restoring the health of many Chinese.

On March 28, 2014, China's President Xi Jinping said in a lecture to the Körber Foundation: "I think, with 'Made in Germany' and 'Made in China' wholeheartedly walking hand in hand, we can not only produce high-quality products, but even contribute to an increase in happiness and the formation of the ideals of the citizens of both of our countries."

In October of 2014, the action framework of the Sino-German joint action plan "Shaping Innovation Together" was presented during the state visit of China's Premier Li Keqiang. Regarding collaboration within the framework of the initiative *Industrie 4.0*, the plan states:

- The digitalization of industry (Industrie 4.0) is of great importance to the further development of the German and Chinese economies.
- Both countries shall establish a dialogue with the goal of exchanging information on Industrie 4.0.
- Both countries shall work together closely on standardization issues.
- In the realms of mobile internet, the Internet of Things, cloud computing and big data, both countries shall intensify their cooperation.

Just one year later, China's Premier Li Keqiang and German Chancellor Angela Merkel announced their agreement on the following at a press conference:

- China will promote the connection between "Made in China 2025" and *Industrie 4.0*. By "Made in China" and "Made in Germany" walking hand in hand, cooperation between the new industries of strategic importance will be further expanded.
- Germany will promote the collaboration between "Made in China 2025" and *Industrie 4.0*.

If you consider similar approaches in other countries, the German model is obviously more suited to China, because in China, the manufacturing industry is large, and in Germany, on the other hand, it is very strong. From a global perspective, Germany's strengths lie in the manufacturing industry, while America's clear advantage is its high-tech industry. In other words: The manufacturing industry plays the leading role in the project *Industrie 4.0*. With the increasing expansion of the Internet of Things, the standards of the manufacturing industry will be raised. Especially in the USA, the internet will play an ever more important role, enduringly influencing the manufacturing industry. The "National Strategic Plan for Advanced Manufacturing," initiated in 2012 by the U.S. government, cites one core issue: innovation. Through information technology, the structure of industry will be completely newly defined, providing important impetus to traditional industry.

The American bottom-up model, in which a complete renovation of the manufacturing industry is performed more or less from the bottom, starting with processors, computer systems, software, the internet and other information components, and reaching up to the assessment of big data, is fundamentally different from the *Industrie 4.0* model with regard to the approach. The latter represents a top-down model, which plans to turn around the existing manufacturing industry from the top down, using instruments such as new information technologies (Fig. 7.4).

That is why "Made in China 2025" and *Industrie 4.0* are made for each other!

7.3.2 "Made in China 2025" not Directly Comparable to Germany's *Industrie 4.0*

The goal of the initiative "Made in China 2025" is to ensure that, by 2025, China is among those nations with the strongest manufacturing industries. From that perspective, "Made in China 2025" is in no way just a Chinese-style copy of Germany's *Industrie 4.0*.

China's Minister for Industry and Information Technology, Miao Wei, provided a brief explanation in this regard: In reference to the promotion of a deeper integration of industrialization and information technology, "Made in China 2025" stands in harmony with Germany's *Industrie 4.0*. However, claims Miao, German industry is currently in a phase of development transitioning from Industry 3.0 to Industrie 4.0, while Chinese industrial companies need to catch up on the lessons learned from Industry 2.0 and Industry 3.0, before it can develop into Industrie 4.0. "We should pay attention to China's situation and the realities of Chinese

Fig. 7.4 A robot factory in China, 2015. (Xinhua)

industrial companies; then we can choose a good development path and develop better, faster and in a healthier manner."

In other words: For the execution of "Made in China 2025," value will have to be placed both on an abrupt as well as a gradual development of China's manufacturing industry. Against the background of rapid scientific and technological development, the initiatives of both countries represent significant strategic measures for the benefit of the manufacturing industry. However, Germany's manufacturing industry possesses a strong technological foundation and can thus directly implement *Industrie 4.0*. China, on the other hand, has to juggle Industry 2.0, 3.0 and 4.0 at the same time, as well as achieve a restructuring of its traditional industries. In addition, China's economy must keep pace, even in its skyrocketing development in the high-end sector. These tasks are even more complicated and more difficult than Germany's implementation of its *Industrie 4.0*. Ultimately, however, China and Germany will meet in Industrie 4.0.

There are several similarities between the strategies of both countries. One much emphasized core element of "Made in China 2025" is "intelligent manufacturing," which is also one of the key points in "Industrie 4.0." Starting there, China hopes to implement cyber-physical systems (CPS) as a basis for intelligent manufacturing, which is also a core element of "Industrie 4.0." Germany envisions about eight to ten years to achieve Industrie 4.0, and China plans to implement its strategy in the same amount of time.

In addition, both China's as well as Germany's strategy places great value in the role of the internet in modernizing and restructuring the manufacturing industry. With regard to the international upswing of industrial transformation and the challenges brought by new technologies, a deep-set integration of industrialization and informatization represents a new pinnacle for the manufacturing industry—a new industrial revolution which all countries of the world must face. That is another element of "Made in China 2025" which is repeatedly accentuated.

China's Premier Li Keqiang points out that "to put it briefly, the focus for a breakthrough for 'Made in China 2025' should be placed on integrating the 'Internet Plus' initiative, in order to accelerate the promotion of the rebirth of China's industry—directly following its trial by fire." This corresponds to the "Internet of Things," which the German strategy sees as having a significant role.

As mentioned, the primary goal of "Made in China 2025" is to transform China's manufacturing industry from one with a large production volume to one with a high degree of efficiency, while the primary goal of Germany's *Industrie 4.0* could be described by the motto "From a strong to an even stronger industry." The varying approaches of the manufacturing industries of both countries determine the various details of their respective strategies. However, since both strategies have the same goal, there are also several similarities.

7.3.3 Green Development Is One of the Main Directions of "Made in China 2025"

The high speed of the development of China's economy in the past 30 years has also generated several problems, the largest of which is probably environmental pollution. However, one of the five guidelines of "Made in China 2025" is "green development"—a clear sign of China's determination to coordinate the environment and development in the transformation of the country from a large to a strong manufacturing nation.

On March 5, 2015, during the conventions of the NPC and the CPPC, China's Premier Li Keqiang declared when presenting the government's work report: "The manufacturing industry is one of our strongest industries. We should implement the plan 'Made in China 2025,' adhere to innovation as a driving force for the knowledge-based transformation and green development and transform our country from one with a large manufacturing industry to a country with a strong manufacturing industry." This was the first time mention was made of "Made in China 2025." Emphasis on green development in the work report showed how important this topic is to the Chinese government.

Sustainability plays a significant role in the development of Chinese industry. Energy required by industry makes up more than 70% of energy consumption in the entire county, which means that there is great potential in energy conservation and a large margin for increasing resource efficiency. Green development in "Made in China 2025" is not just lip service for environmental protection, but rather a concept with clearly defined goals. In this strategic document, four standards have been set: energy consumption, carbon dioxide emissions and water consumption per producing unit should decrease by 34%, 40% and 41% respectively in comparison with 2015, while the recycling rate of solid industrial waste should reach 79%.

At the moment, dynamic changes are taking place in the development of the Chinese manufacturing industry in the realms of resources and energy, the environment and factor costs. China does not possess enough resources for its huge population—its fresh water, arable land and forest resources amount to only 28%, 40% and 25% per capita of the world average, respectively. The extent of exploitable reserves of important minerals lies at 7.7% for mineral oil, 17% for iron ore and 17% for copper, which is considerably below the international average. Environmental pollution is becoming increasingly evident following a lengthy period of overexploitation. Currently, approximately 70% of cities in China cannot meet the new standard for environmental and air quality. About 600 million residents in 17 provinces (including autonomous regions and immediate government cities) suffer from smog. Water and soil pollution are also becoming increasingly visible every day. Ever greater environmental events are taking place.

"Made in China 2025" is intended to transform the extremely resource-intensive development model of the Chinese manufacturing industry with regard to investments, energy demand and environmental pollution into a sustainable, "green" manufacturing model (see Fig. 7.5).

Gao Yunhu, the director of the Department for Energy Conservation and Efficiency of the Ministry of Industry and Information Technology, has issued detailed statements on the matter. In his opinion, the "green development" of the manufacturing industry would require an intelligent bridge between the current situation and a desirable future. The concrete measures include: first making the traditional

Fig. 7.5 New-energy vehicles in China, 2016. (Xinhua)

manufacturing industries, such as steel, nonferrous metals, construction materials, chemicals, paper, textiles and fabric dyes more sustainable. Equipping production with progressive energy conservation technologies to reduce emissions is an urgent task needed to reduce energy consumption and emissions in traditional manufacturing industries. Secondly, clean production, especially in core industries and in close proximity to important water divides, is to be guaranteed. By using technologies and processes for clean production, emissions can be prevented directly where they are produced. Thirdly, sustainable development in progressive manufacturing industries and strategic emerging industries are to be expedited. In doing so, value is to be placed on sustainable development right from the start, and the old way, that is, regulation after pollution, is to be avoided at all costs.

7.4 Winning the Future Together: The Many Highlights of the Sino-German Collaboration

7.4.1 Cooperation Model for Corporate Promotion: Companies as Driving Forces, the Government as a Coordinator

During his visit to Germany in March of 2014, Chinese President Xi Jinping wrote a guest article in the newspaper *Frankfurter Allgemeine Zeitung* (FAZ), in which he explained: "In recent years, Sino-German cooperation has always been at the head of Sino-European cooperation. Of the daily goods traffic between China and Europe at a value of 1.5 million dollars, almost one-third are traded between China and Germany. Every week, more than 70 airplanes travel between a good ten cities in each country. Of three direct freight train connections between China and Europe, two end in Germany, in Duisburg and Hamburg. And every year, more than one million tourists travel from Germany to China and vice versa. Both countries have not only become each other's largest trading partner in their respective regions, but they have also become the largest target regions for investments and the formation of enterprises. Currently, more than 8200 German companies have set up shop in China, and more than 2000 Chinese companies have established themselves in Germany."

The intensive contact between the German and Chinese governments has created favorable conditions for cooperation between companies of both nations on various levels, such that new space has also been generated for economic collaboration between China and Germany.

In the framework for action for Sino-German cooperation announced in October 2014 during Premiere Li Keqiang's visit to Germany, it states unmistakably: "The digitalization of industry ('Industrie 4.0') is of great importance to the further development of the German and Chinese economies. Both sides agree that this process must be expedited by the companies themselves. The governments of both countries will politically support the participation of the enterprises in this process."

While it is true that concrete collaboration between companies is to be conducted by the companies themselves, apparently, the support measures of both governments seem to be quicker, more active and more effective. On several levels, concrete results have already been achieved to promote cooperation between the companies of both nations.

In March of 2015, during the visit of Vice Premier Ma Kai in Germany, agreements between both governments regarding the strengthening of cooperation in the realm of Industrie 4.0 were made in six areas: First of all, a mechanism of cooperation is to be established. Between the German and Chinese government, a dialogue mechanism for Industrie 4.0 is to be created, in order to implement the action framework for Sino-German cooperation in practice. Secondly, basic and future-oriented research is to be conducted jointly. A further, significant point of *Industrie 4.0* is the setting of standards. A few new standards are to be formulated as the yield of their collaboration. Fourthly, cooperation in the realm of industrial design is to be bolstered. Fifthly, cooperation in the realms of intelligent manufacturing and pilot projects is to be strengthened. Sixthly, training and cooperation via a talent exchange is to be actively supported.

In August 2015, the Center for Talent Exchange of the Ministry for Industry and Information Technology in Beijing organized an event called "The Explanation of Germany's *Industrie 4.0* Strategy". A few experts from Germany, including Prof. Reiner Anderl, Chairman of the Board of the Scientific Committee of the *Industrie 4.0* initiative and a member of the German Academy of Technical Sciences, were invited to China to provide detailed explanations of *Industrie 4.0.* Also present were the heads of the responsible Chinese administrative departments, representatives of Chinese industry and the financial sector, corporate managers, media representatives and representatives from research and education. The goal of the event was to generally make people familiar with the development, implementation strategy and the action plan of Germany's *Industrie 4.0*, in order to offer a positive example and reasonable references for "Made in China 2025" and the promotion of the transformation and modernization of (Fig. 7.6).

In March of 2016, Shi Mingde, China's ambassador to Germany, shortly before German President Joachim Gauck's trip to China, said that "China and Germany have already established a working group and reached a preliminary consensus on developing a Sino-German platform for innovation cooperation in the province of Sichuan as well as an industrial park for high-end manufacturing in the city of Shenyang."

Within only two years (since 2014), cooperation between China and Germany on the topic of Industrie 4.0 has led to visible results.

7.4.2 Sichuan's Great Ambition: "Sustainable Thanks to Intelligent Manufacturing"

The following short story appeared under the heading "Sichuan" on Xinhuanet (www.xinhuanet.com.cn) in April of 2015: "The 20-year-old apprentice Yang Jinqiao blinked as he inspected a crack in a spark plug. He manually measured

Fig. 7.6 A modern factory in China, 2016. (Xinhua)

to see if the crack was longer than 0.5 mm and if the spark plug thus no longer conformed to the standard. A few yards behind him, 68-year-old Joschka Fischer, the former Vice Chancellor and Foreign Minister of Germany, was standing and waving to the crowd. Yang Jinqiao looked at Joschka Fischer and suddenly felt old—not because Fischer seemed so young, but because the sight of the German suddenly reminded him how old the technique he had learned and was using seemed to be. From the perspective of the most modern technology, it was becoming useless, no matter how he skilled he was at examining the crack with his eyes." Because in a discussion about the integration of "Made in China 2025" and the German *Industrie 4.0* at the Sichuan Institute of Industrial Technology, the apprentice Yang Jinqiao had just discovered that a robot with seven arms could supposedly accomplish zero-defect manufacturing. If, however, a robot makes no mistakes, then what was the point of the man's ability to precisely measure a crack having 0.5 mm? This thought filled Yang Jinqiao with concern.

The young apprentice's concern in reality is the panic of underdeveloped production capacities in the face of modern industrial production, but also panic of the workforce in the face of a modernization of industrial production. In the city of Deyang, they have found an antidote to this fear: They are working together with German organizations and assuming the achievements of *Industrie 4.0*. Simultaneously, apprentices and students are being encouraged to obtain technical certificates recognized both in China and Germany.

Sichuan is situated in the southwestern hinterlands of China, and is considered an important province from an economic and industrial standpoint. In 1993, the capital, Chengdu, was recognized by the State Ministry as a center for science and technology, trade and finance, as well as the hub for transportation and communication in China's southwest. Sichuan possesses 132 types of natural resources whose reserves have been verified as being present in the province. This means that 70% of all types of natural resources found in China can also be found in Sichuan. Based on this wealth of natural resources, Sichuan is also known as the "warehouse of nature," and the province is a significant industrial location.

Related to the "Sino-German cooperation platform for innovative industry" in the cities of Chengdu, Deyang and Mianyang, the province of Sichuan has initiated programs for Sino-German cooperation and founded the cooperation models "Platform + Industrial Park" and "Administration + Agency + Enterprise." This model is based on the jointly formulated cooperation mechanism and standard, and is driving the comprehensive integration of "Made in China 2025" and *Industrie 4.0*.

Let us look for example at the city of Deyang, which is not far from Chengdu. As an important location for the manufacture of high-tech tools and plants and one of the three locations for the construction of power plants, more than 45% of the large rolled steel plants in China are produced in Deyang. The city is also the largest production site for cast steel and boasts the largest production of power plants in the world, as well as the country's largest export of auger drills. A total of 60% of components produced in China for nuclear power plants, 40% of hydroelectric power plants, 30% of coal-fired power plants, 50% of the largest rolled steel plants and 20% of the largest cast iron and forging pieces for ships are produced in Deyang.

In April of 2016, more than 300 well-known persons, elite entrepreneurs and experts from politics, business and science gathered in Deyang and took part in the conference "Innovative Deyang—'Made in China 2025' meets 'German *Industrie 4.0*.'" They dealt with topics such as the contents and mechanisms of effective integration of "Made in China 2025" and *Industrie 4.0*, and jointly developed several effective formulas for the transformation of manufacturing in Deyang into an intelligent, green and service-oriented industry.

The city of Mianyang, situated near Deyang, also plays an important role in this collaboration. As an important location for scientific research in the arms industry and as a production site for the electrical industry, Mianyang is a state-recognized "science and technology city," and for quite some time has served as a model for innovation-driven development. Mianyang is home to more than 18 large research institutes, including the representative "China Academy of Engineering Physics," the backbone of 50 large and medium-sized companies such as the Changhong Group, Jezetek (Sichuan Jiuzhou Electric Group Co., Ltd.) and 14 colleges and universities, the most important of which being the Southwest University of Science and Technology. With all of these resources in science and technology, as well as a solid industrial basis, Mianyang is making efforts to accelerate the modernization and transformation of manufacturing. In recent years, Mianyang has already established a few progressively-led manufacturing industries in the areas of electronic communications, the automotive industry (including automobile components and accessories), biopharmaceuticals, new materials and new energies. As a consequence of the China (Mianyang) International Advanced Manufacturing Conference, Mianyang has attracted a few top-class international research organizations and companies—such as the Fraunhofer Society, Siemens and SAP—and has become a focal point of the Sino-German cooperation.

7.4.3 Sino-German Industrial Park for Machine and Plant Engineering Becomes a New Engine for the Revitalization of Northeastern China

As another significant cooperation project between China and Germany, the "Sino-German Industrial Park for Mechanical and Plant Engineering," is investing all its efforts and will do its best to become a new highlight and engine for the revitalization of northeastern China.

In early August 2014, the Chinese State Council first promised such an industrial park in a document. On December 23, 2015, the Council approved the plan. This represents the first strategic platform whose central theme is cooperation in the high-end manufacturing industry for mechanical and plant engineering, and at the same time serves as an important medium for the strategic integration of "Made in China 2025" and *Industrie 4.0.*

The city of Shenyang in northeastern China is an important site for state-owned enterprises with mechanical and plant engineering as the dominant industrial sector. Its industrial base has been stabilized, the industrial system completely developed, and the dominant industries such as mechanical and plant engineering, the automotive industry and its components, electrical information technology and aerospace, are competitive both domestically and abroad.

Shenyang has a solid foundation for cooperation with developed nations—especially with Germany. In 2014, the total volume of imports and exports between the city and Germany amounted to 4.5 billion euros, thus taking the top spot in export trade between Shenyang and 179 other nations and regions. At the end of 2014, 132 German companies had premises in Shenyang, and eight international top-500 enterprises from Germany invested in 14 consecutive projects there. The successful collaboration with BMW has already become a model for Sino-German cooperation.

The industrial park is situated in the Tiexi district of the city of Shenyang, an industrial region with mechanical and plant engineering as its dominant industry. Tiexi has a favorable basis for opening up toward and cooperating with Germany. In 2012, Tiexi was honored by the Chinese Ministry of Commerce and the German Federal Ministry for Economic Affairs and Technology as a "location for cooperation of Chinese and German enterprises." In 2014, the district became a member of the German-Chinese Consulting Economic Committee (DCBWA). Approximately 30 German automotive, mechanical, electrical and retail companies such as BMW, ZF Friedrichshafen AG, SEW, BASF, Heraeus and Metro have settled in the district.

Even shortly after commissioning of the industrial park, considerable achievements had already been made. To date, 35 German, European and American companies have settled in the park. German investments, such as the Center for Application, Research and Development of KULA Robots from Germany, Neugart Planetary Gearboxes (Shenyang), railway platform doors by Pintsch Bamag, components and accessories for railway cars by Schaltbau GmbH, the firefighting system by J. Wagner GmbH from Germany, electronically-controlled signal systems by Siemens and the production of cutting tools for CNC machines of EWS Weigele GmbH & Co. KG have either already begun or are in the development phase following the signing of contracts. The center for the Sino-German association of Industrie 4.0, as well as the innovation center for Chinese and German companies, have their headquarters in this industrial park.

Especially remarkable is the basic principle of the industrial park, in which "the market plays a leading role and the government a guiding role": The companies serving as an engine of economic development are to be highlighted. Plant manufacturers of both nations will be able to come together in the park in an exemplary cooperation model. At the same time, public services are also to receive more attention, to create a relaxed and beneficial political environment for the development of the companies. This corresponds to the strategic collaboration of both nations under the motto: "Companies drive the development, and the governments support the measures politically." The industrial park rejects the old models of government-dominated development and business management, taking a lesson from the experiences gained in the organization of the industrial park both domestically and abroad. The development and organization of the park are to be oriented toward the market. Through the admission of capital companies within the framework of the PPP model (public-private partnership), infrastructure development, the recruitment of enterprises and investments and a comprehensive administrative service are being promoted, so that a completely new development model can be tried out.

The industrial park is to assist in combining the respective advantages of Chinese manufacturing and German technology, in order to establish an international, intelligent and sustainable plant manufacturing park of high quality. "More than 3000 'hidden champions' from all over the world (1300 enterprises from Germany alone) and 200 suppliers of BMW are potential partners for our acquisition of investments," said Li Baojun, manager of the Sino-German Industrial Park for Mechanical and Plant Engineering. "We should employ the experiences gained in the industrial locations of Munich and Stuttgart and place high value in output efficiency per unit area, so that plant manufacturing can lead and guide the transformation and modernization of the manufacturing industry at a high technological level."

In the next ten years, the Sino-German Industrial Park for Mechanical and Plant Engineering will focus on developing five industrial sector groups, including intelligent manufacturing, high-end plants, automobile production, industrial services and strategically emerging industries, and generate a new engine for the revitalization of northeastern China.

"Made in China 2025" meets Germany's *Industrie 4.0*—which means a far-sighted strategic cooperation between both nations and a long process in which the industries of both countries can learn from each other, inspire each other and move forward together. This cooperation has already produced positive results and considerable achievements, and in future, can bring the people and the economies of both nations, and even the whole world, more happiness and welfare.

7.5 "Internet Plus:" Another Key Term in Understanding "Made in China 2025"

7.5.1 The Action Plan "Internet Plus" Is not Only Focused on the Manufacturing Industry

When Prime Minister Li Keqiang initially presented the plan for the "Made in China 2025" initiative on March 5, 2015 during a convocation of the National People's Congress (NPC) and the National Committee of the Chinese People's Political Consultative Conference (CPPCC) in an action report, he also mentioned for the first time the action plan "Internet Plus" (Fig. 7.7). Li Keqiang said: "We must elaborate the action plan 'Internet Plus,' in order to promote the fusion of the mobile internet, cloud computing, big data, the Internet of Things, etc. with the modern manufacturing industry. This will stimulate the healthy development of e-commerce, the industrial internet and internet finances and guide internet companies in expanding in the international market."

In early 2016, Li Keqiang drew special attention to the fact that breakthroughs in "Made in China 2025" should primarily lie in the integrated development of "Internet Plus," such that the Chinese manufacturing industry can "rise up" more quickly, "like a phoenix from the ashes." That is why "Internet Plus" is undoubtedly a further, extremely important key term in understanding "Made in China 2025."

Fig. 7.7 Internet Plus. (Xinhua)

In July of 2015, the Chinese State Council issued a directive for active promotion of the "Internet Plus" action plan.[1] This directive laid the groundwork in "Internet Plus" for the results of internet innovation and the economic and social sectors to be thoroughly combined with one another, in order to promote technical advances and an increase in efficiency and organizational changes. It also targets an increase in innovation in the real economy and an intensification of production power. In addition, the internet is to be organized even more comprehensively, such that it can serve as an infrastructure, and decisive innovative factors of new forms of economic and social development are to be pursued.

The implementation of "Internet Plus" is, of course, an extremely significant component of the manufacturing industry. However, the application sector of "Internet Plus" is evidently even more far-reaching. In the action plan "Internet Plus," a total of eleven primary measures are under development, including: "Internet Plus—Business Start-Up and Innovation," "Internet Plus—Cooperative Manufacturing," "Internet Plus—Modern Agriculture," Internet Plus—Intelligent Energy," "Internet Plus—Inclusive Financing," "Internet Plus—Beneficial Services for the Public," "Internet Plus—Highly-Efficient Logistics," "Internet Plus—e-Commerce," "Internet Plus—Comfortable Transportation," "Internet Plus—Green Ecology," and "Internet Plus—Artificial Intelligence."

In summary, one could say that the plan "Made in China 2025" is concentrated on the vertical axis of the manufacturing industry, to design a floorplan of the development and realization of the integration of informatization and industrialization. In that sense, "Internet Plus" takes the internet as the main characteristic of the development of informatization. Through the action plan "Internet Plus," a large-scale development is to be realized on the horizontal axis in several sectors, including the manufacturing industry, industry in a more comprehensive sense, agriculture, commerce, finance and the service sector.

At the same time, the realization of the goals of the action plan in all sectors can certainly be supported by the results of the manufacturing industry achieved within the context of "Made in China 2025." "Internet Plus" and "Made in China 2025" fuel each other, support each other and operate together.

7.5.2 "Small Internet Towns: An Example for Macro-Applications of "Internet Plus"

In order to achieve a deep connection between "Internet Plus" and other industries, in recent years, Xinhuanet has offered a service known as the "1000 Small Internet Towns Action Plan." This service is a macro example for the direct application of "Internet Plus." It is not only dependent on midsize and small cities that, according to the "Made in China 2025" plan, will exhibit development of their respective

[1] The directive to actively push the "Internet Plus" plan was published on July 4, 2015 on the website www.news.cn.

manufacturing industries, but also on the fusion of informatization, state affairs, public welfare and infrastructure. In this way, through the internet, efficiency can be promoted via integrated and coordinated development in all segments of a region.

At the "2015 China Internet Plus Innovation Conference Hebei Summit" in June of 2015, Xinhuanet officially defined the new concept of "small internet towns" and, with the aid of respected state institutions and leading corporations in this realm, also the "1000 Small Internet Towns Action Plan."

The "small internet towns" emphasize cooperation with local governments. On the levels of project positioning, top-level design, the introduction of resources and the increase in expertise, coordination and communication with local governments is being intensified. For the considerable development needs of the small towns, the forerunner of the development strategies of future small towns is being defined, and a completely market-oriented operating mode is being introduced. After that, relevant resources for the development of the community will be introduced, such as politics, financing, land, qualified personnel and other resources. This will achieve the informatization of public administration and services, as well as the qualitative changes and rapid developments following the uniting of the industries. In addition, the deep fusing of information industries and traditional industries and the restructuring and increase of the regional economy will be supported. To date, almost 300 units on the community or higher administrative level have applied for the establishment of "small internet towns." Furthermore, pilot tests are being conducted on a step-by-step basis.

In order to achieve a joint networking of and share in information, the four segments in establishing the "small internet towns" will be standardized; specifically: standardized infrastructure, standardized data platforms, standardized application platforms and standardized portals. All "small internet towns," however, will be constructed according to their own, special characteristics. For example, the town of Tangshan in the Hebei province, which has been considered a province of the iron and steel industry for quite some time now, has developed into a "small internet town for the iron and steel industry." The plans, which have already been implemented, correspond to the characteristics of the local, industrial organizations. Based on the current development of the iron and steel industry in Tangshan, progressive technologies and modern management are being introduced, to realize the innovative fusion of the iron and steel industry with the internet and to achieve the transformation and upgrade.

Based on the whole, the "small internet towns," as internet platforms for comprehensive applications of the solution "Internet Plus," represent the fundamental driver of innovative urbanization. They also serve as typical applications for "intelligent cities," and the "Internet of Things." The networking and complete integration of industry, agriculture, administrative services, security and education with the internet is being achieved through the comprehensive usage of "Internet Plus" solution plans in various sector models, such as cities, communities, villages, settlement communities, roads, development zones and schools. This will allow for the improvement of expertise in public administration and administrative services, as well as the advancement of the dynamics of economic development and the standard of living of the population. In addition, it will also allow energetic support of new business formations and innovations by the masses.

7.5.3 "Traceable China:" an Example for Micro-Applications of "Internet Plus"

In recent years, there have often been difficulties in China with food safety and the production and sale of counterfeit goods, which has caused enormous losses and damage to companies and consumers. Through the action plan "Internet Plus," in connection with the concrete requirements to the food production industry within the context of "Made in China 2025," Xinhuanet developed an open platform for the separation of foods and tracing of information about foods and goods, a service called "Traceable China." It has become an example for micro-applications of "Internet Plus."

The service "Traceable China" uses information technologies such as the internet, the Internet of Things, cloud computing and big data, etc., to spread and utilize information in all segments of manufacturing processes, sales and distribution. This strengthens the traceability of all processes from the beginning to the end of the system and the mutual exchange and access of information, and expands the uninterrupted range of the tracing system. The entire process chain of agricultural products, from "field to table," can thus be traced and the "safety of food eaten" guaranteed.

Currently, labels with QR codes are being used on the "Traceable China" platform. The information offered on the platform connects all sub-processes, such as goods production, inspection, quarantine, supervision and consumption. Customer-specific solutions are already being offered, including the cultivation of agricultural products and animal husbandry as a first step, food processing as a further step, and the tracing of the entire process of goods distribution by national industries as a final step. Other individualized solutions include the development of solution programs, such as: the tracing of the cultivation; the supervision and quality assurance of agricultural products; tracing all the way back to animal husbandry, slaughtering and processing; tracing of food processing and safety and marketing; tracing of goods information and transportation within the cold chain; the establishment of a platform for regional, electronic business traffic and the development of regional informatization and quality control, as well as other multi-dimensional, customer-specific solutions.

From the government level, the platform "Traceable China," based on offering traceable information, is developing a type of ecological interaction between government, producers and consumers. Due to all data stored on the "Traceable China" cloud platform, precise statistical analyses can be offered. Within the supply chain, the combination and exposure of large-scale production, the exchange of data and resources, the establishment of healthy production facilities, the distribution, marketing and direct sales are all bolstered.

With a strong hand, the project "Traceable China" took on state supervision of food safety and protection from product counterfeiting. That is why many state organizations prefer it for the informatization of supervision services. Through stringent monitoring of all goods processes on the platform, a favorable, closed circuit is generated in which the circulation system of especially local, trusted products can be logged from the development to the production stage, information can be retrieved, the path of the products can be followed and their quality traced, and products themselves can be recalled. This promotes the dissemination of "Internet Plus" even more effectively throughout the whole country.

After the platform "Traceable China" was put into operation (Fig. 7.8), it was met with wide acceptance. Xinhuanet has already worked together with several government offices to establish a national information and supervisory platform for corn seed, a platform for e-commerce in rural Hebai and an integrated information service system, which is primarily used for excellent agricultural products.

In addition, the project "Traceable China" offers companies even more comprehensive services in the realm of quality control, to provide consumers with true, transparent information on product tracing and tracking. Consumers can immediately receive information on their smartphones and other devices regarding tracing using the labels on products. This solves the problem of receiving asymmetrical information, and all types of security risks can be realistically and effectively limited.

Fig. 7.8 The official introduction of the platform "Traceable China" by Xinhuanet in 2015. (Xinhua)

Through the cooperation of administrative offices, the platform "Traceable China" is striving to monitor market functioning and supply and demand of products, to reorganize and standardize distribution and develop a modern distribution system. This will progressively lead to the establishment and perfection of an open, more competitive, modern market system, to guarantee consistent overall product quality and build up a new consumer environment for all of society.

Part II

Articles from the Research Sector

Industrie 4.0, the Internet of Things and Services, the industrial internet, and other similar terms have been and still are topics of interest for research. Although, in the meantime, there are initial practical pilot projects and even a series of productive applications in practical use, this does not change the fact that we are not talking about the state of the art, and not about what can be observed in the majority of companies today, but rather, about the future.

When we talk about "research," we mean everything: basic research, the applied research of scientific institutes in close connection with industrial enterprises, and, of course, research within industrial enterprises themselves, some collaborative, others company-specific. We also mean the networked research of various disciplines, which is becoming increasingly important in connection with the digitalization of industry and its products.

The following three chapters come from three research institutes which conduct research projects in close cooperation with industry. Some also involve other disciplines such as sociology or psychology, but the core of these efforts is the methodical and technological research surrounding engineering, production planning, production and operation. The three articles are included in alphabetical order of the names of the heads of the respective departments.

The chapter by Prof. Reiner Anderl (Dr.-Ing.), Oleg Anokhin and Alexander Arndt from the department of Data Processing in Construction at the Technical University of Darmstadt describes the Efficient Factory 4.0. With its demonstrators and practical solutions, this model factory is designed to aid small and midsize enterprises in particular to find their own way to implementing Industrie 4.0. The article presents application scenarios in which components and operating materials serve as information carriers, and scenarios pertaining to paperless quality assurance, digital value stream mapping or digital status and energy monitoring. As a practical example, worker assistance systems are also presented in their role in aiding industrial employees in the future to complete their increasingly complex tasks.

In his chapter, Prof. Martin Eigner (Dr.-Ing.) from the department of Virtual Product Development at the Technical University of Kaiserslautern, focuses on the industrial internet and the development of the engineering processes and IT solutions especially required for it. According to Martin Eigner, for the networked engineering of tomorrow, new construction methods and development processes are required. Similarly, in the realm of information technology and its employment in industrial value creation processes, new solutions are necessary.

Prof. Rainer Stark (Dr.-Ing.), Thomas Damerau and Kai Lindow of the Fraunhofer Institute for Production Systems and Design Technology in Berlin, present the concept of the information factory. This is an integrated production environment for information-driven development and manufacture which, through analysis of, control of and changes to technical systems and processes, leads to its increasing autonomy. Projects pertaining to virtual commissioning with smart hybrid prototyping, to cloud-based control and the metamorphosis toward an intelligent and networked factory are introduced and classified.

The three examples in no way represent the only activity on the German research landscape. Yet they provide a clear and telling view of research being conducted in Germany within the context of Industrie 4.0.

Efficient Factory 4.0 Darmstadt—Industrie 4.0 Implementation for Midsize Industry

8

Reiner Anderl, Oleg Anokhin and Alexander Arndt

Abstract

Industrie 4.0 has become a significant factor for success to companies in the manufacturing industry. Model factories as demonstrators are contributing greatly to its increasing prevalence. It is precisely here that the Efficient Factory 4.0 of the Technical University of Darmstadt begins its approach, demonstrating feasible solutions for the introduction of Industrie 4.0 into everyday industrial practice. It is thus a valuable aid in increasing the competitiveness of the manufacturing industry.

8.1 Introduction

Industrie 4.0 began in 2010 as a future-oriented project, stemming from the high-tech strategy of the German federal government. The result of this future-oriented project was published in the study "Recommendations for implementing the strategic initiative INDUSTRIE 4.0" [7, 8], leading to the founding of the *Industrie 4.0* platform, which was active from 2013 to 2015 under the umbrella of the German industrial associations BITKOM, VDMA and ZVEI. Through the so-called alliance platform, the fundamental definitions, goals and approaches for Industrie 4.0 were developed. In the year 2015, the alliance platform *Industrie 4.0* was converted to the present *Plattform Industrie 4.0*, which has since been preparing the way for Industrie 4.0 to be implemented in enterprises.

Industrie 4.0 stands for the fourth industrial revolution, a new level in organizing and controlling the continuous value creation chain over the entire lifespan of

R. Anderl (✉) · O. Anokhin · A. Arndt
Technical University of Darmstadt, Petersenstr. 30, 64287 Darmstadt, Germany
E-Mail: anderl@dik.tu-darmstadt.de

U. Sendler (ed.), *The Internet of Things*,
https://doi.org/10.1007/978-3-662-54904-9_8

products [7, 8]. It focuses on an increase in flexibility of production, based on individual customer wishes. Its foundation is the availability of all necessary information in real time, in order to optimally steer the value stream. Prerequisite to this are networked and communicable systems. This approach leads to the integration of production materials, components and employees into the networking and communication system. It is distinguished by the so-called vertical and horizontal integration of IT systems. Horizontal integration refers to the integration of IT systems for the various process steps of production and corporate planning, between which a material, energy and information flow runs, both internally as well as beyond corporate borders [10]. Vertical integration describes the integration of IT systems on the different hierarchical levels to reach a universal solution. The consequently generated dualism of information and material flow over various hierarchical levels and process steps in production and corporate planning requires new concepts which do justice to the horizontal and vertical integration of IT systems. These concepts have become known through so-called cyber-physical systems (CPS) [9], and imply that an individual, digital map exists for every real object and real process in production as well as for the subsequent operation phases.

Against this backdrop, Industrie 4.0 is characterized by the following technical basics [2, 3]:

Identification, localization and addressing of real objects. Objects in this regard can include operating resources, processes or construction elements (components).

- Identification refers to a distinct description and identifiability of objects via identification technologies such as barcodes, QR codes (quick response codes), RFIS (radio frequency identification), as well as an internet protocol address (IP address).
- Localization enables the location of an object to be determined. This can be accomplished via GPS technology (global positioning system) or via local position determination technology, such as are required on factory floors.
- Addressing serves to equip real objects with networking and communication capability using a distinct address. The most important technology used to achieve this is internet technology, enabling addressing to be done via an internet protocol address. With the aid of addressing via an IP address, real objects become communicable and can send data via web services as well as perform control functions via control services.

Internet technologies provide extremely efficient functions for networking and communication. The basis for this is provided by Internet Protocol Version 6 (IPv6), which offers addressing via an address range from 2**128 addresses. The addresses, converted to the decimal system, correspond to 3.4* 10**38 individual addresses.

The availability of IPv6 addressing represents a fundamental prerequisite to achieving the so-called Internet of Things (IoT). This means that all real objects equipped with an IPv6 address have network connectivity and communicability.

The Internet of Things is closely related to the Internet of Services and the Internet of Data. Internet-based services secure communication. Currently, two primary models are being pursued [12, 13]. These include the simple object access protocol (SOAP) on the one hand, and the representational state transfer (REST) approach on the other. The SOAP concept is based on the fact that XML (extensible markup language) is used as a format for queries and replies. The REST approach formulates queries with the aid of the URI (unified resource identifier), codes via the hypertext transfer protocol (http) and allows responses in any format, usually as HTML documents (hypertext markup language).

Furthermore, the Internet of Data (IoD) provides concepts with which to send large amounts of data within a short time from sensors of a real object to a server to be analyzed and to trigger control functions from the information gained.

Components and operating materials are information carriers [14–4]. This means that especially the components, modules and elements, right up to the finished product, must be individually, distinctly identifiable and carry information. Depending on requirements, components and operating materials can be equipped with identification, localization and/or an address. Addressing makes networking and communication with the component and operating materials possible. The information identifies the component itself, and, among other things, describes its manufacturing history. Similarly, operating materials, that is, manufacturing equipment (such as machine tools, tools, equipment), test equipment, assembly equipment and transportation equipment are also information carriers. They, too, are distinctly identifiable and carry information that indicates what tasks they have carried out at which times.

Through the understanding that components and operating materials are information carriers, an information network is created that comprehensively describes production. Thus, one can find out how production was undertaken in the past (semantic product memory [10, 14]), what the current state is and how future production steps are expected to be executed.

Concepts for a new security structure enable a high degree of resistance to factors interfering with production [6]. This security culture mainly includes four areas. These are IT security, reliability and robustness, privacy and knowledge protection.

The measures for ensuring IT security comprise comprehensive and well-developed methods such as firewalls, antivirus protection, restrictive configuration, data security, account-, password- and PIN code plans, data stream encryption, digital signatures, enterprise rights management, among others. Reliability and robustness serve to secure the constant operation readiness of networked systems and the availability of the overall system, even if individual sub-systems should fail. Privacy secures the authorized and accepted use of personalized data. Knowledge protection also secures the authorized use of data, and offers comprehensive protection mechanisms to block unauthorized access.

In addition, the new security structure also includes raising awareness in employees and management personnel for the high value placed in security for Industrie 4.0 production environments.

8.2 Efficient Factory 4.0 Darmstadt

In global competition, enterprises, especially small and midsize companies, are confronted with several changes in the German economic location due to the introduction of Industrie 4.0. New technologies and organization forms mean that companies have extensive opportunities and possibilities to increase production efficiency. In order to bring especially small and midsize companies closer to the new technologies and allow them to experience them, the project *Effiziente Fabrik 4.0* (Efficient Factory 4.0) was initiated at the Technical University of Darmstadt (see also www.effiziente-fabrik.tu-darmstadt.de). Investments for this project were facilitated by the European Union from the European Fund for Regional Development, from the state of Hesse and from the Wirschafts- und Infrastrukturbank Hessen (WIBank, "Economic and Infrastructure Bank of Hesse").

The goal of the Efficient Factory 4.0 is the analysis, development and implementation of information and communications technologies (ICT) and their combination with existing production technologies for the development of an efficient learning factory. In the Efficient Factory 4.0 plan, user and supplier companies as well as employee and corporate associations receive a descriptive depiction of the opportunities and potential resulting from Industrie 4.0. What is so special about this plan is that no new production environment is created, but rather, it uses the existing process learning factory *Center für industrielle Produktion* (Center for Industrial Production, CiP) at the TU Darmstadt (see also www.prozesslernfabrik.de). The process learning factory CiP represents the production of a small midsize company with the typical processes involved in metal processing as well as assembly and final inspection of the finished product. The product under observation is a pneumatic cylinder often used in industrial applications. The production of this cylinder consists of a component made in-house and purchased parts. It is a way for interested enterprises to receive a realistic look at the available opportunities. This provides users with an idea of which steps can be taken toward progressive and resource-efficient production using Industrie 4.0 solutions in an existing production environment.

In the Efficient Factory 4.0 project, a variety of implementation concepts were developed, based on a conducted study; see [5, 1]. These Industrie 4.0 application scenarios were integrated into the Efficient Factory 4.0 from both the hardware and the software sides. The scenarios in the project represent the starting points from which to enable an increase in efficiency in existing production systems through the integration of information and communications technologies. In total, the following five central application scenarios in the Efficient Factory 4.0 have been developed and implemented:

- Components and operating materials as information carriers
- Paperless quality assurance
- Digital value stream mapping
- Status and energy monitoring
- Flexible, intelligent worker assistance systems [1].

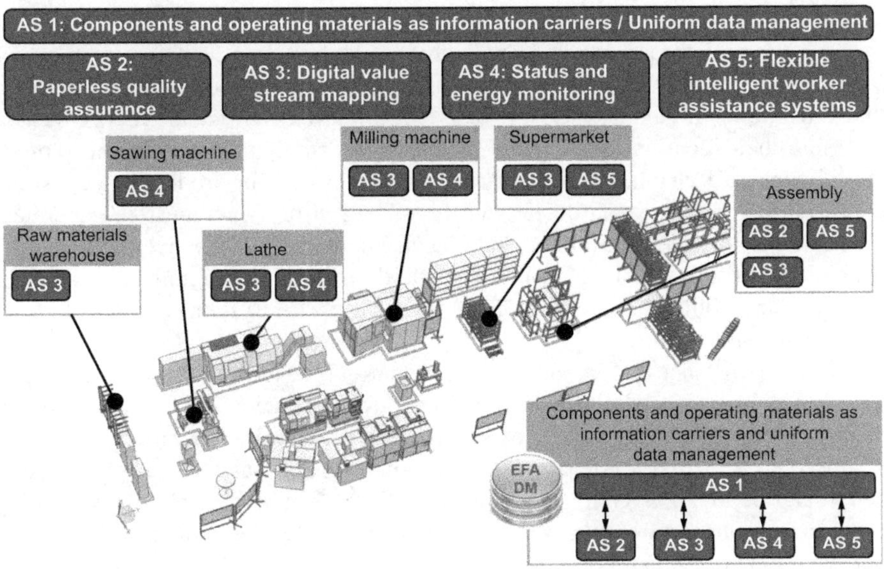

Fig. 8.1 Summary depiction of application scenarios (AS) of the Efficient Factory 4.0. (Source: Effiziente Fabrik 4.0)

Figure 8.1 shows an overview of these five application scenarios (AS), allocated to the individual stations in the Efficient Factory 4.0. These scenarios will be explained in more detail below.

Building on the implemented application scenarios, a project-based knowledge transfer takes place in the Efficient Factory 4.0. This transfer offers a platform upon which knowledge from a project can be presented and imparted to interested associations and enterprises. In addition, previously compiled implementation concepts and implemented solutions are didactically prepared and used to conduct workshops. The workshops are tailored to the requirements of employee interaction with the integrated Industrie 4.0 solutions in a newly-created socio-technical system, and also represent a content-based foundation for the SMEs 4.0 Competence Center in Darmstadt (see also www.mit40.de).

8.2.1 Application Scenario 1: Components and Operating Materials as Information Carriers

In order to achieve efficient and future-oriented production in the sense of Industrie 4.0, the collection and processing of data accumulating during value creation are decisive. In the factory of the future, such tasks are performed without media disruption, digitally and, in the best case, in a fully automated manner. Not only is it necessary to have technology in place for data collection and its integration into production, but also communication between all objects and involved persons.

As early as April of 2014, the Scientific Advisory Board of the *Plattform Industrie 4.0* adopted theses which were included in the implementation strategy of *Industrie 4.0* [8]. One of these theses is directed at future products, and states that they must be intelligent and serve as active information carriers, in order to be able to ensure their identifiability as well as their addressability over their entire product lifecycle. To enable the efficient use of such a CPS in production, a distinct allocation between the real object and the related virtual data must be generated, thus enabling the identification of the object. Therefore, the distinct and machine-readable identification of real components and products is a significant aspect for industry, since other requirements must be made to the system than those in the consumer realm.

Once all instances of production are identifiable, the collected data can be linked to them. Especially the linking of various information in real time with real objects makes it possible to employ components as information carriers, thus rendering today's textual accompanying documents superfluous [10]. It becomes evident that, due to the diversity of products and industrial sectors, simply examining components within this context is not sufficient to meet the demands of Industrie 4.0. Many factories, especially of medium size, are not familiar with the development of the product that they manufacture. The structural integration of identification in a component required for production thus cannot be their responsibility. That is why operating materials have been included in the concept itself. This means that individual data can be linked to a piece of operating material connected to the component, such as loading equipment. This procedure is also suitable for tracing products whose individual information is not significant, but is combined into lots, batches or packages.

These considerations were taken into account during the implementation of the system in the Efficient Factory 4.0. The technologies for identification of objects as well as the process steps in which they are used were defined in such a way that the highest possible cost efficiency can be achieved when the overall system is employed. While the raw material is marked with barcode stickers and can be identified with optical reading devices, RFID is used for loading equipment and components. The distribution of the various reading devices in the Efficient Factory 4.0 can be seen in Fig. 8.2.

The superordinate goal in implementing this application scenario in the Efficient Factory 4.0 is the direct linking of process information to the corresponding physical components, which are described in more detail through this information. This makes it possible to collect and process data accumulating in the value creation process in an efficient and future-oriented manner. Furthermore, this concept also enables the component- or operating materials-related forwarding and provision of data for various process steps in production, thus forming the basis for several further application scenarios which can profit from this data flow.

On the long term, the use of components and operating materials as information carriers could also lead to the linking of production processes that are temporally and spatially separated, without the need for a central control process. This aspect not only enables an improvement in efficiency in one's own product

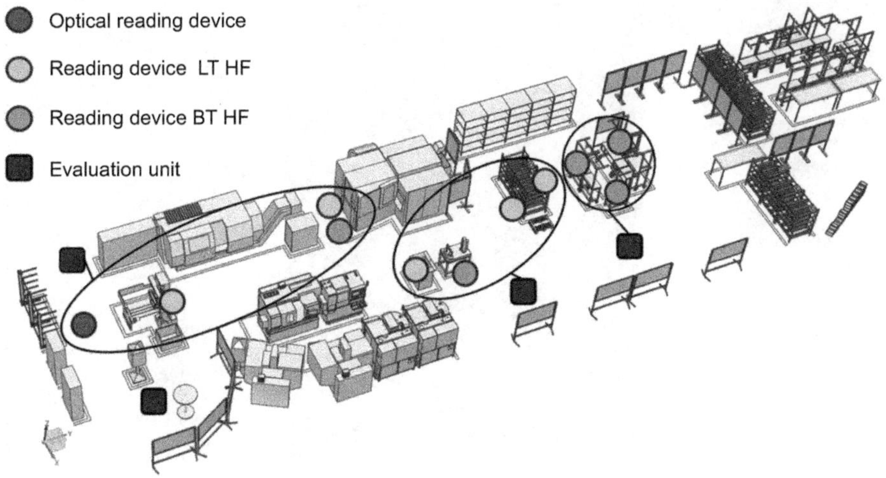

Fig. 8.2 Overview of identification devices in the Efficient Factory 4.0. (Source: Effiziente Fabrik 4.0)

environment, but also represents great potential for data processing over the entire product lifecycle and a new level of cooperation between enterprises along the value creation chain.

8.2.2 Application Scenario 2: Paperless Quality Assurance

Through the digitalization of data and information flow in production, we can already make several processes more efficient, as shown above. In this application scenario, we will demonstrate the application options of Industrie 4.0 concepts in the Efficient Factory 4.0 for automated quality assurance in manual assembly. The components to be assembled are used as information carriers to provide the tools employed with the necessary data. The concrete implementation is performed at an assembly workstation in which an electronic screwdriver station is used (see Fig. 8.3).

When a component is placed at the workstation, specific variant information can be immediately retrieved for the workstation and employees via RFID. On the one hand, information is displayed to the acting employee regarding further process steps, and on the other hand, the screwdriver station is told which programs to run.

Based on the distinct identification of a component, specific screwdriver programs can be retrieved and a visual image can be provided to the employee as to which assembly steps are to then be carried out. This procedure alone can contribute greatly to quality assurance, because the correct screwdriver program is always selected for a particular component. Thus, errors in the manual settings of the screwdriver parameters cannot occur.

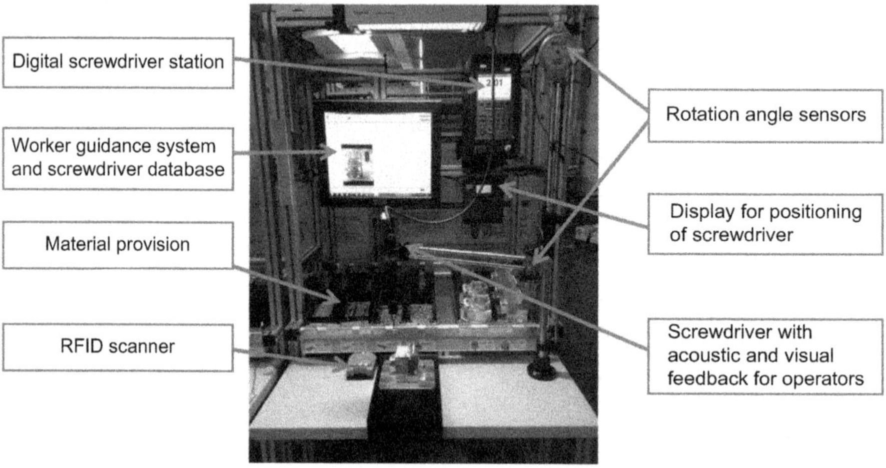

Fig. 8.3 Assembly workstation with screwdriver station and RFID scanner. (Source: Effiziente Fabrik 4.0)

The assistance system uses illustrations to assist the employee through step-by-step assembly. In order to further increase the quality, the integration of further sensors in the mounting parts of the assembly tool enable a precise recognition of its position. This makes faulty screwing impossible, as the screwdriver tool is only enabled by the system when the correct position is indicated.

Another significant advantage of this application scenario compared to conventional methods is made possible by the bidirectional data flow between the control system and the assembly station. In addition to the control of the assembly process through the provision of information, the collection of sensor data also enables automated, paperless documentation of the assembly process. The positions of the tool during individual screwing tasks as well as the torque and the course of the angle of revolution of every screwing procedure are digitally collected, stored and linked to the respective product via RFID identification. Thus, the fully automatic logging of all screwing tasks for the corresponding product can be achieved.

8.2.3 Application Scenario 3: Digital Value Stream Mapping

As a result of the networking of components and operating materials, a broad database for production is made available, with which a digital map of the participating process steps and described value stream can be generated. In the process, the areas of application of a digital value stream map do not greatly differ from that of an analog value stream map. It primarily serves to generate a transparency of the overall process, to assist in making efficient decisions and identify optimization potential. In contrast to analog value stream mapping, the central component of digital value stream mapping is the vertical integration of collected real time information in superordinate systems of the company. Only through the processing of the collected data into adequate information can the transparency of the process be increased and the basis for efficient decisions established. A high degree of transparency is not only achieved through the mapping of current process values, but in fact through the calculation and provision of superordinate key figures which illustrate relevant aspects of the process to the observer and thus represent significant input for the decision-making process. The automated collection and processing of data in real time can considerably increase data quality with regard to up-to-dateness, traceability, consistency, unambiguousness and comparability [11].

For the implementation of this application scenario in the Efficient Factory 4.0, especially the following key figures and areas were considered:

- Lead time
- Cycle time
- Setup time
- Wait time
- Inventory
- Overall equipment effectiveness (OEE)
- Quality
- Adherence to schedules
- Productivity
- Security

The current values of these key figures can be provided and calculated in real time with the aid of components and operating materials serving as information carriers as well as machine data collection by a process control system. A comparison of the previously set target values of these key figures can allow a current evaluation and visualization of production status. Figure 8.4 shows the visualization of production in the process control system employed in the Efficient Factory 4.0.

This offers a rough overview of the entire production process. For instance, current machine statuses can be determined at a glance. Depending on the role of the operator, the displayed information can be varied with regard to level of detail. In order to prevent a sensory overload, the visualization is structured in several levels. The image displayed represents the top level of the overall process. Using the button "Detailed information," the user can access further levels of visualization to receive more precise data on the process-specific key figures.

8.2.4 Application Scenario 4: Status and Energy Monitoring

One of the factors vital to success with regard to the efficiency of companies is the quality of information exchange. In order to provide information to the right place at the right time, new paths are necessary within the framework of Industrie 4.0. The classic automation pyramid represents a hierarchical communication system. This means that an exchange of information within one level or between levels

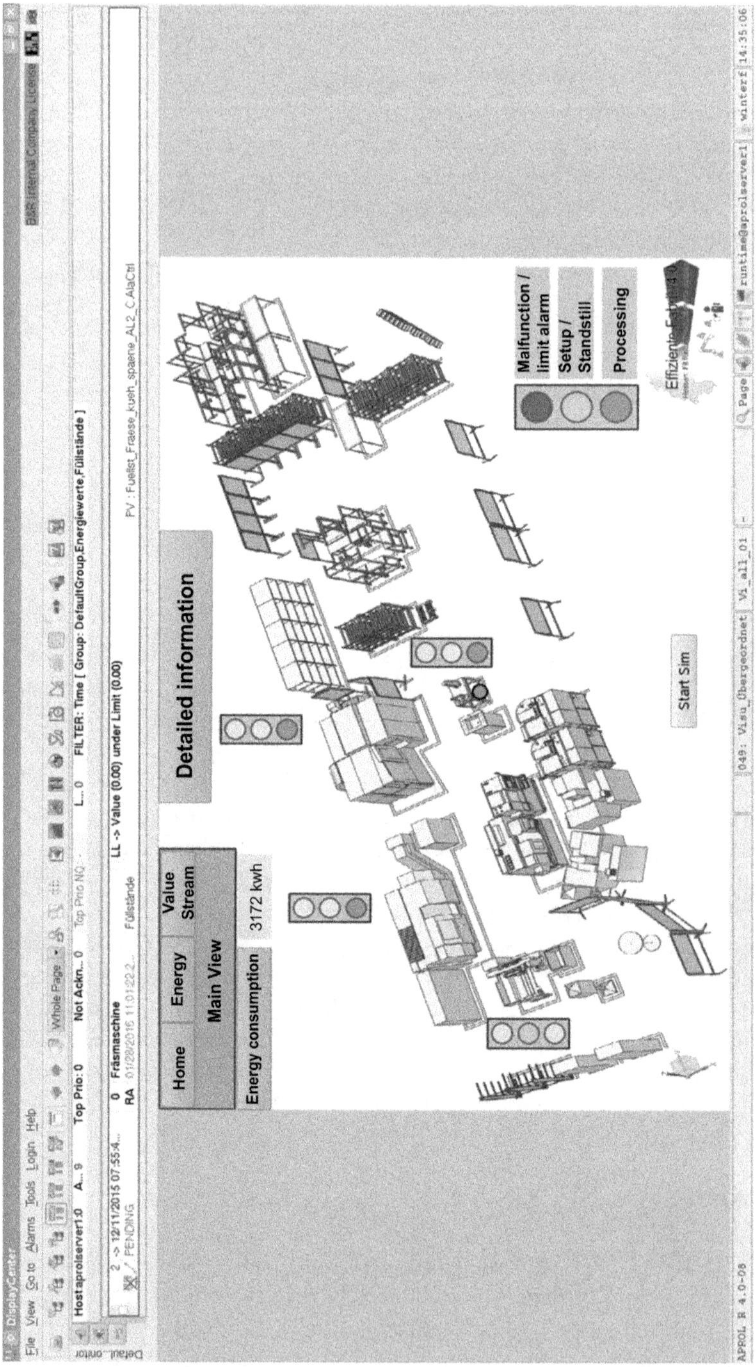

Fig. 8.4 Statuses of various production processes of the Efficient Factory 4.0. (Source: Effiziente Fabrik 4.0)

is possible. Industrie 4.0 solutions dissolve these traditional hierarchies, since the horizontal as well as vertical integration of IT systems in production systems takes place. This enables communication between any end points in the entire value creation chain. These essential transformations in production result in a variety of new possibilities and chances for status detection. Due to the onset of Industrie 4.0, sensor and actuator equipment even receives its own computing power and interfaces, such that active communication can occur in the entire network. In the Efficient Factory 4.0, these possibilities for status and energy monitoring of machines, products and even processes can be implemented and displayed. By examining these three levels, a comprehensive picture of the quality of the manufacturing process is generated; see also Fig. 8.5.

The product level serves the monitoring and mapping of a real-time product status, with which the product quality can be guaranteed over the entire production process. This feature is based on the components and operating materials serving as information carriers. Any occurring errors in the development process are quickly located and can be prevented. Among other things, the possibilities of digitalization enable integrated quality control, the forwarding of error messages in real time and their role-specific visualization for the respective operator. The primary goal of the machine level—in this case, machines and systems are the information carriers—is the prevention of machine damage, human injury and environmental damage in the course of facility operation. This enables the elimination of unplanned down times, and wear to tools can be identified in a timely manner. Furthermore, machine monitoring forms the basis for status-dependent maintenance, which ultimately leads to a reduction in costs and standstills. Identifying energy consumption during component processing means that energy consumption data during the production of a component can be allocated to each

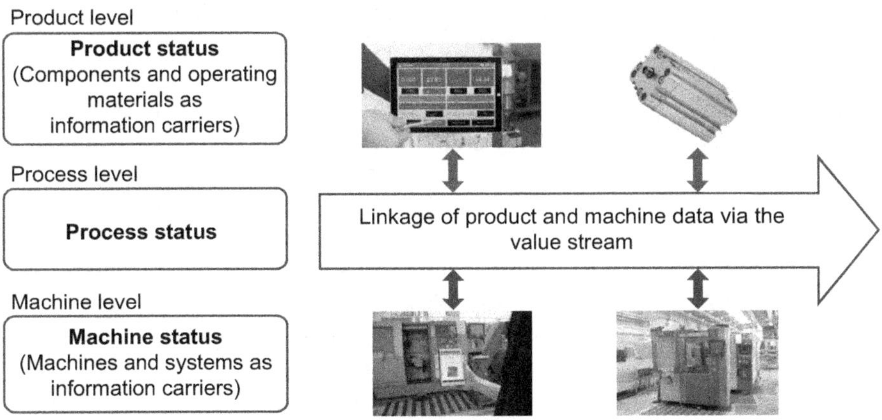

Fig. 8.5 The three levels of status and energy monitoring in the Efficient Factory 4.0. (Source: Effiziente Fabrik 4.0)

individual component. The collected data from the product and machine levels serve as input for enhancing process data on the process level. The goal of process control is to map the current status of a process, that is, the progress of a process, and the physical location of components. Unifying product status data and machine status data leads to a comprehensive, value stream-oriented process observation. For instance, the increased energy consumption of a milling machine (machine status) in a specific product variant (product status) can lead to the analytic conclusion that the milling machine or the tool is worn (process status).

In the Efficient Factory 4.0, various applications are implemented to generate data from the levels (product, machine and process). For example, external components in the form of sensors are attached to the machines or the information is directly retrieved from the control units of the machine. The various communication technologies are used on the one hand to illustrate to companies various means of data access and on the other hand, to provide the main functions of status and energy monitoring. To sum up, implementation in the Efficient Factory 4.0 enables the following functions with their associated uses:

- Integrated quality control including process security
- Real-time visualization of product quality indicators
- Active process intervention, even beyond corporate borders
- Real-time mapping of machine and process statuses (determination of machine failure, switching processing programs on/off, analysis of coolant fill levels, display of energy consumption, etc.)
- Knowledge of component location, status and history
- Energy consumption and quality verification per component
- Linking of product and process quality for the identification of correlations

8.2.5 Application Scenario 5: Flexible, Intelligent Worker Assistance Systems

In a number of production areas, there is already a high degree of digital information. They include processes, products and operating materials, among others. However, people are not yet scrutinized so comprehensively. Consequently, employees as part of the overall system have been previously disregarded in the development of intelligent assistance systems. The assistance systems successfully employed in practice react in a situation-based manner, but not in a user-related way, and do not collect data about employees. Solutions which pay more attention to employees and store specific information about employees are rarely used. One important reason for this is the yet relatively unspecified legal status regarding employee data collection. Within the context of the Efficient Factory 4.0, an assistance system has thus been developed whose primary goal is to make Industrie 4.0 solutions available to employees with the aid of a socio-technical design, thus making them more familiar with the attainable advantages. Such attainable advantages and opportunities include:

- The flexibilization of work
- The informatization of the working world
- The development of excellence among employees
- The assistance of employees

Based on the requirements for an assistance system in assembly, on the employee data model to be developed and the quality of the assembly information, a concept for a flexible intelligent assistance system has been developed. Figure 8.6 shows a schematic depiction of the developed assistance system.

Every employee possesses a distinct identification (ID); in our example, the combination of user name and password was chosen. Of course, other possibilities are conceivable, for instance logging in with a QR code or RFID chip. Employee information is made available to the assistance system based on the employee ID. The development of the employee data model represents a primary component of this application scenario, thanks to the active cooperation of the IG Metall union and various works councils. Once the worker assistance system has employee information available, an employee can then log in at the workstation where a component is to be assembled. The component as an information carrier has a distinct identification, read out via RFID, so that the specific assembly information can then be provided. Now the assistance system is able to assist the employee as needed, based on the component and assembly information as well as the qualification status of the employee.

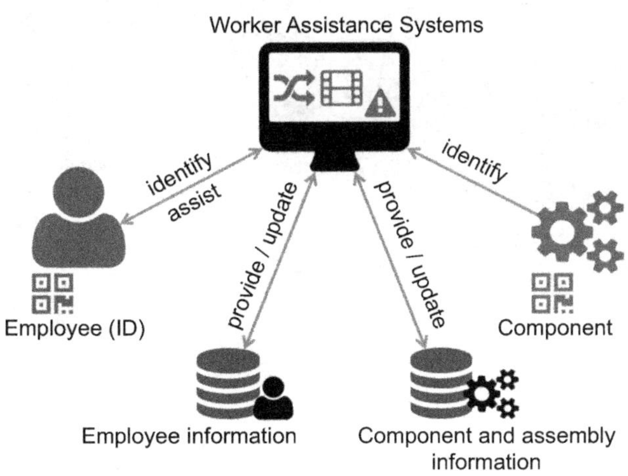

Fig. 8.6 Schematic construction of the assistance system. (Source: Effiziente Fabrik 4.0)

Figure 8.7 shows the implementation of the application scenario in the Efficient Factory 4.0. The photo on the left depicts the real structure of the assistance system, including the workstation itself and a tablet for employee communication. Once the employee has logged into the system, he is shown a user interface (see Fig. 8.7b). He now has a visualization of where he must scan the component to be assembled. Then, the assembly assistance begins. Depending on the application case, whether it is a large or small assembly lot size, the information can be generated and shown virtually, based on 3D CAD data or a real video recording (see the differences in assembly information, Fig. 8.7c).

The intelligent linking of employee information and assistance system enables a need-based provision of assembly information, no matter whether virtual or real. Need-based in this case means that every employee, based on his or her stored information, receives the assistance desired and prioritized by the system. For implementation, it is important to put the focus on the employee. For instance, he or she should independently decide on cycle times and types of information.

The introduction of the application scenario "Flexible, intelligent worker assistance systems" enables a person-based assembly assistance to take place, based on components and operating materials as information carriers. This supports and promotes assembly issues such as job rotation, that is, the flexible use of employees, and learning on the assembly job.

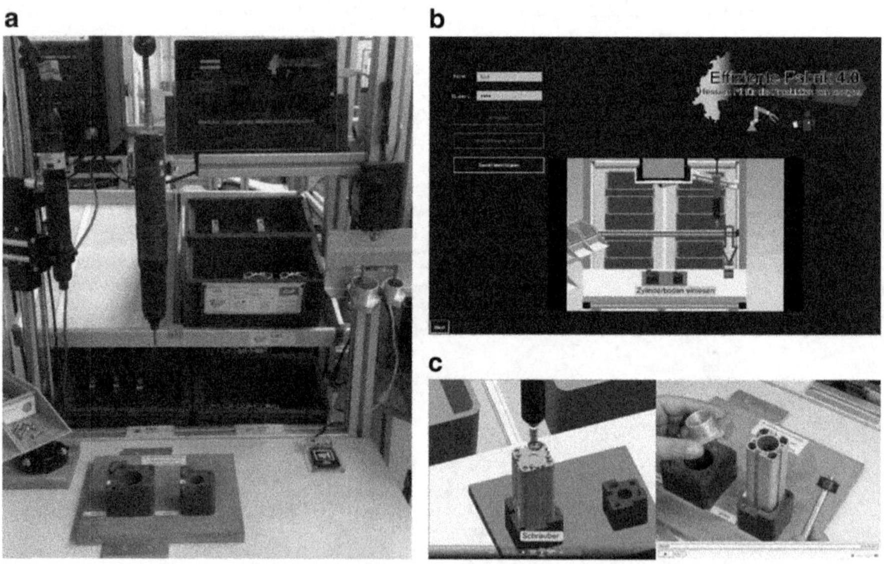

Fig. 8.7 The implementation of flexible, intelligent worker assistance systems in the Efficient Factory 4.0. **a** Physical construction, **b** User interface, **c** Assembly information (*left*: virtual—*right*: real videos). (Source: Effiziente Fabrik 4.0)

References

1. Abele, E., Anderl, R., Metternich, J., Wank, A., Anokhin, O., Arndt, A., et al. (2015). Effiziente Fabrik 4.0—Einzug von Industrie 4.0 in bestehende Produktionssysteme. *ZWF—Zeitschrift für wirtschaftlichen Fabrikbetrieb, 2015*(3), 150–153.
2. Anderl, R. (2014). Industrie 4.0—Advanced engineering of smart products and smart production. Technological innovations in the product development, 19th International Seminar on High Technology, Piracicaba, Brazil.
3. Anderl, R. (2015). Industrie 4.0—Technological approaches, use cases, and implementation. *Automatisierungstechnik, 63*(10), 753–765.
4. Anderl, R., Strang, D., Picard, A., & Christ, A. (2014). Integriertes Bauteildatenmodell für Industrie 4.0. Informationsträger für cyber-physische Produktionssysteme. *Zeitschrift für wirtschaftlichen Fabrikbetrieb (ZWF), 109*(1–2), 64–69.
5. Anderl, R., Abele, E., Metternich, J., Arndt, A., & Wank, A. (2015). *Industrie 4.0—Potentiale, Nutzen und Good-Practice-Beispiele für die hessische Industrie*. Bamberg: Meisenbach Verlag.
6. Grimm, M., Anderl, R., & Wang, Y. (2014). Conceptual approach for multi-disciplinary cyber physical systems design and engineering. Proceedings of the 10th International Symposium on Tools and Methods of Competitive Engineering, Budapest, Hungary, pp. 61–72.
7. Kagermann, H., Lukas, W.-D., & Wahlster, W. (2011). Industrie 4.0: Mit dem Internet der Dinge auf dem Weg zur 4. industriellen Revolution. *VDI, 13*(1), 2. https://www.wiso-net.de/document/VDIN__476866.
8. Kagermann, H., Wahlster, W., & Helbig, J. (2013). Recommendations for implementing the strategic initiative INDUSTRIE 4.0. Securing the future of German manufacturing industry.
9. Lee, E. A. (2010). CPS Foundations. Design Automation Conference (ACM), pp. 737–742.
10. Plattform Industrie 4.0: Umsetzungsstrategie Industrie 4.0 (2015).
11. Neubig, N. (2015). Besser managen mit Kennzahlen. *Mosbach QZ, 59*(9), 34–36.
12. Picard A., Anderl R., & Schützer K. (2013). Controlling smart production processes using RESTful web services and federative factory data management. 14th Asia Pacific Industrial Engineering and Management System, December 3–6, 2013.
13. Steinmetz, C., Christ, A., & Anderl, R. (2014). Data Management based on Internet Technology using RESTful Web Services Conference: 10th International Workshop on Integrated Design Engineering. IDE Workshop 2014, in Magdeburg.
14. Wahlster, W. (2013). The semantic product memory: An interactive black box for smart objects. In W. Wahlster (Ed.), *SemProM. Foundations of semantic product memories for the internet of things* (pp. 3–21). Berlin: Springer.

The Industrial Internet

Engineering Processes and IT Solutions

Martin Eigner

Abstract

Engineering is currently undergoing a massive transformation: smart systems and technologies, cybertronic products, big data and cloud computing within the context of the Internet of Things and Services, as well as Industrie 4.0. The media is falling over itself with reports on the new, fourth, industrial revolution. However, the American approach of an "Industrial Internet" describes this (r) evolution far better than the limited and very German-influenced term "Industrie 4.0." The industrial internet takes the entire product lifecycle into consideration and addresses consumer and investment goods, as well as services. This article illuminates this future-oriented topic, offering well-founded looks the networked engineering world of tomorrow, its construction methods and processes, as well as its IT solutions.

9.1 Introduction

The Internet of Things—Kevin Ashton used the term "Internet of Things" (IoT) for the first time in 1999—comes from internet-based, networked physical objects (things). By 2020, based on the internet protocol V6, approximately 37 billion things (generally products and systems with implicit communicability) will be connected to the internet. These things are also called cyber-physical or cybertronic products or systems. Based on them, new, often disruptive, service-oriented business models are being developed for the respective applications, e.g. smart products, smart factories, smart energy, smart mobility, smart farming and smart

M. Eigner (✉)
Technical University of Kaiserslautern, Gottlieb-Daimler-Straße, Building 44, 67663 Kaiserslautern, Germany
E-Mail: eigner@mv.uni-kl.de

U. Sendler (ed.), *The Internet of Things*,
https://doi.org/10.1007/978-3-662-54904-9_9

buildings. Services within new overall systems are becoming the central factor for success (→ Internet of Services, IoS). The value-based share of electronics and software for these types of products will continually increase. According to conservative estimates, $ 500 billion are predicted to be invested internationally in this market segment by the year 2020.[1] Optimistic forecasts for value creation of this sector by 2030 lie at up to $ 15 trillion worldwide, provided that the corresponding investment efforts are made in the realms of politics and industry. In Germany, the potential for a rise in cumulative GDP by 2030 is predicted to be at least $ 700 billion.[2]

The targeted directions mentioned were assumed through prework done by industrial associations, the research union and acatech in the future-oriented projects *Industrie 4.0* and *Internet-Based Services for the Economy* of the German Federal Ministry of Education and Research (BMBF) and the Federal Ministry of Economics and Technology (BMWI). These activities are generally welcome, yet, due to a strong focus on production automation, they do not exploit the actual potential to the fullest. The American approach of the Industrial Internet (www.industrialinternetconsortium.org/) covers the spectrum of possibilities far better than the limited and very German-influenced term Industrie 4.0 and the fourth industrial revolution. The Industrial Internet refers on the one hand to the entire product lifecycle, from product development, to process planning, to production and up to service, as well as, on the other hand, consumer and investment goods and services. The actual revolution is the development, production and marketing of innovative, networked products, production systems and services based on new, internet-based technologies and the continual miniaturization and cost reduction of electronic components. A typical example is a contact lens with an integrated chip, sensor and antenna that measures a person's glucose levels and, either via the internet or BTLE (Bluetooth low energy) forwards the data to an implanted insulin pump. This revolution, however, would have to first take place in the brains of everyone participating in a product lifecycle. During this process, only complete rethinking and lateral thinking can lead to success. We must ask ourselves: Are our accepted and important successes in optimization and systemization of the product creation process (PCP), especially in the realm of variant and adaptive constructions, still sufficient on their own for the innovative power of our economy, and are our hierarchical organization structures adequate for creative products, production systems and services, or do we need small and dynamic innovation cells? Are our engineering processes and IT solutions agile and interdisciplinary enough, and are our vertical discipline-oriented, industrial as well as academic training concepts prepared for the future?

[1]Industrial Internet Insights Report, GE and Accenture, 2015.

[2]Deutsche Bank Research, 05/2014 and Market Foresights, Future Management Group AG, 02/2015.

9.2 Demands to a Modern Product Development Process

In addition to the worldwide networking of development, production and sales, especially the extent of the original functions and thus complexity of the products under development[3] will continue to rapidly rise. Today, technical products are already increasingly becoming multidisciplinary systems that are developed by several engineering disciplines. Virtualization, integration and multidisciplinarity between the realms of mechanics, electrical and electronic systems, software and service as well as overlapping cooperation between individual phases of the product lifecycle are becoming the basis of a modern development process. The increasing integration of information and communication technologies into products and the linkage to services is causing a paradigm change. There is talk of smart engineering [1], meaning new methods, processes and IT toolchains, e.g. system lifecycle management [2], for the product creation process (PCP). The so-called revolution aims at the development, production and marketing of innovative, comprehensively networked products, product systems and services which correspond to the core elements of the industrial internet centered on new internet-based technologies [3]. However, the PCP is subject to crucial changes, and not only because of the industrial internet. Figure 9.1 shows the relationships between the megatrends for the PCP. Multiple networking and interdependencies of the individual trends is problematic. A major challenge in the coming years will be to reasonably assume and implement these trends and to guarantee their social acceptance.

Such a comprehensively networked system development requires rethinking today's familiar engineering development methods, for instance for construction, processes, IT solutions and organizational forms [4, 5]. Electronics, software and services are making up an increasingly large portion of products. Construction and design methods in all disciplines—that is, mechanical construction, electronic construction and electronic development, as well as software engineering—must all be put to the test, their suitability with regard to the modern approach of the industrial internet verified, and ultimately transformed into a common, integrated and interdisciplinary method and process approach. According to the assessment of queried companies, IT and automation technology will continue to gain in importance, especially with regard to competitive capability [2, 6–8]. The influences result from altered marketing conditions and consumer patterns, from new demands to "smart" products and systems and from the customer's perspective [9]. In addition, an increase in system complexity results, on the one hand, due to a considerably stronger degree of globalization and personalization of products through derivative and varietal diversity, and, on the other hand, from the constant increase in electronic components and the related embedded software. Today, only

[3]In the following, the author will only refer to "products," as he believes that production systems are also products.

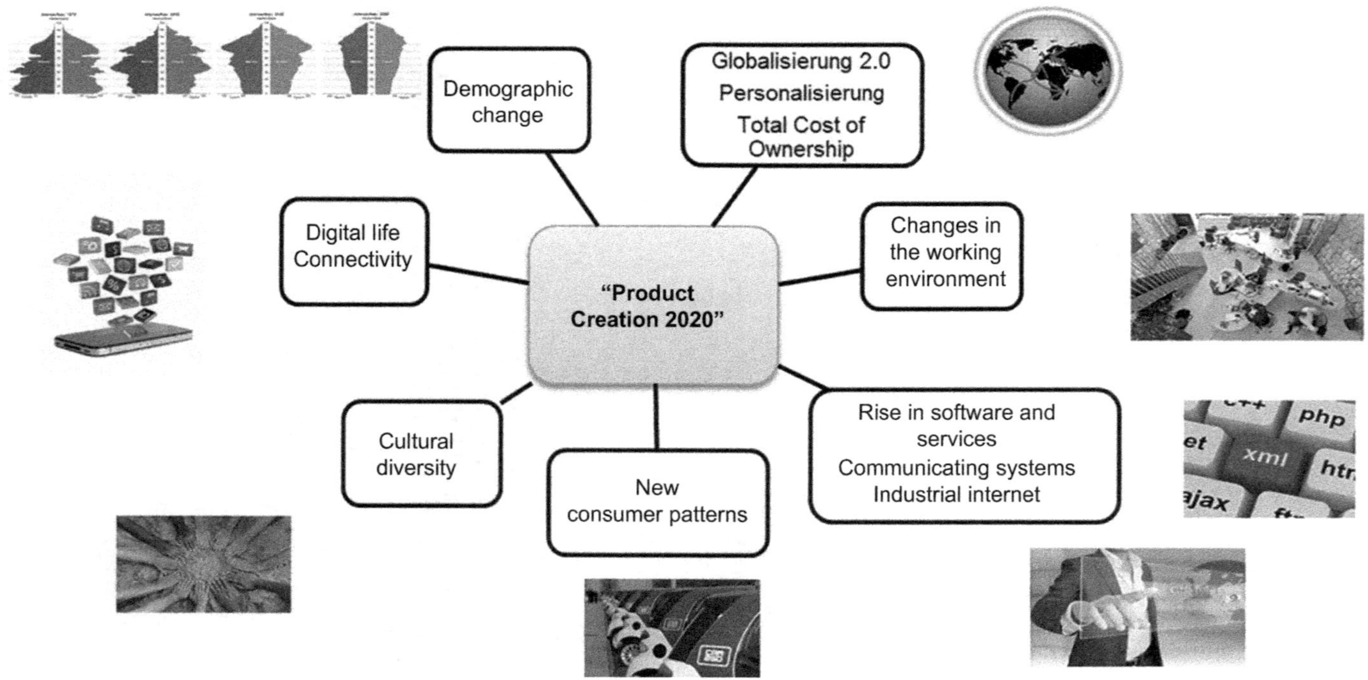

Fig. 9.1 Megatrends for the product creation process (PCP). (Eigner)

one percent of the physical world is networked. With the internet protocol IPv6, in future, 430 sextillion internet addresses will be available (that's 430 with 36 zeroes). By 2020, then, around 37 billion "things" and services will be connected to the internet (→ Digital life, Connectivity).

9.3 Industrial Internet

The industrial internet is leading to networked systems communicating with each other and services based on them [6]. Through reciprocal networking and influence, the functional extent of current mechatronic systems can be significantly expanded. When they communicate with one another, we speak of "cyber-physical systems (CPS)" or "cybertronic systems (CTS)" [2, 10]. In contrast to CPSs, CTSs are more strongly based in engineering and represent a further development of mechatronic systems in the direction of intelligence and communicability. They can communicate and cooperate with other product systems in open networks, and connect to each other to form "intelligent," partly autonomous, self-adjusting systems. However, there is currently still a lack of methods, processes and integrated IT tools to develop and manage the information of such systems. Building on model-based development, research is being done on the methods of multidisciplinary and integrated development of CTSs that contain both products as well as production systems [2, 10, 11]. In order to improve the system and process quality for manufacturing companies, service-oriented, scalable (cloud) platform concepts for predictive quality data analysis could aid in creating intelligent, application-specific feedback loops in quality management, for example. In the future, software will enable a number of new functions and further increase the functional complexity of products, while on the other hand, through a shift in variance from hardware to software, partially reducing the developmental and manufacturing complexity. A central production control system can be transformed into a decentral, self-organizing process [10, 12]; the result: autonomous, smart machines.

Nowadays, full-service concepts (see Fig. 9.2) cannot be sufficiently implemented to their full extent, because they are coupled with a high degree of insecurity and risk. The reason for this is a lack of information and transparency about the overall system during operation or use at the customer site (e.g. regarding component wear). By using and intelligently assessing field data, including the deduction and utilization of defined status information, communicable product systems can be used to eliminate these insecurities and better assess risks. In addition, new possibilities emerge for individualizing service products related to investment goods. Similarly, generating and offering customer- or machine-specific, full-service concepts will be possible, in order to ensure the highest degree of availability, better resource planning, more precise determination of replacement part potential and for the automated triggering of service processes [11].

Crucial to the design of the industrial internet with the Internet of Things and Services are explicit technologies with sensors and actuators as well as embedded intelligence. Only with these features is it possible for products to detect

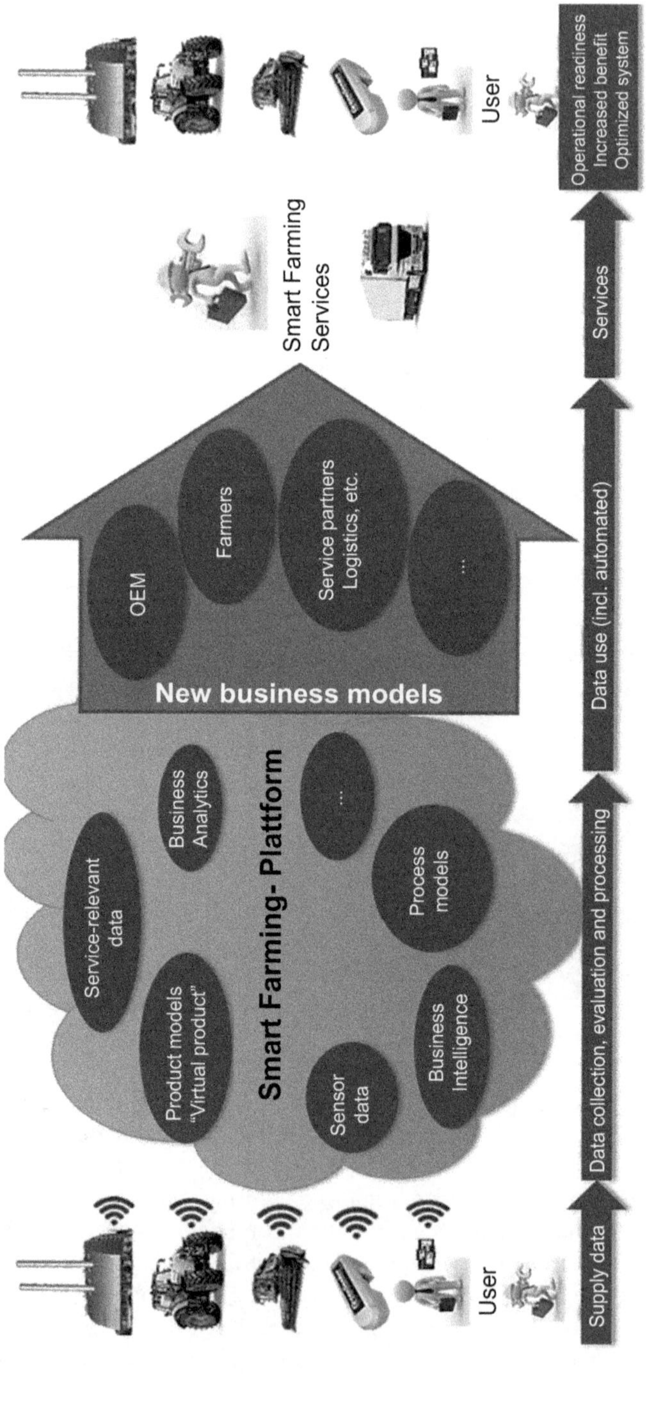

Fig. 9.2 Full-service concept using the example of smart farming. (Eigner)

their environment and interact with it. Wireless communication, such as broadband cellular telephony or RFID (radio frequency identification) is also vital. Consequently, the semantic description of services and abilities is important, as it ensures the interaction of product components and machines in an intelligent way. "Smart production" and "plug and produce" enable machines to automatically detect their environment and be able to connect and interact with other machines. Thus, an exchange of information, for example concerning orders, utilized capacity and optimal manufacturing parameters, can take place. A central element for this function is the construction of a specific (also cloud-based) backbone concept that helps on an administrative level to keep the information complexity of a product system (big data) manageable over its entire lifecycle. Figure 9.3 shows a typical example of how consumer goods as well as investment goods, based on an embedded active sensor/actuator and intelligent data processing (→ Business analytics), form the basis of service-oriented business models.

To sum up, smart systems open up a whole new era of product innovations and business model changes with great social, societal, economic and ecological significance. They are based on the increasing intelligence of modern, communicable components through internet-capable and inexpensive sensors and actuators, and a new connectivity made possible by the internet. Key technologies on this tier include sensor/actuator technology, intelligent hardware, communications technology and embedded systems. They are used to construct an internet-capable system and service platform, enabling aggregation, fusion, intelligent evaluation, optimized control and regulation and graphic visualization. The basis of this tier is composed of software technology (business analytics, cloud computing, big data, security, safety, context-sensitive systems, etc.), theoretical system and mathematic modeling, and analysis and simulation processes. The next level up develops new service-oriented business models and operating optimizations (Internet of Services) as well as the networking of participating partners and components/systems (business intelligence). The tiers cited rely on new, common and interdisciplinary engineering methods, processes and IT tools. Moving from bottom to top, the tiers are increasingly application-oriented, and their services are directed at the respective application field, such as smart farming, smart energy, smart products, smart factories and smart buildings. The five levels and the application fields form a complex competence matrix and serve as the reference model (see Fig. 9.4) of 17 scientists of the University of Kaiserslautern, who have come together to form the initiative Center for Smart Systems Engineering. Only with this breadth of expertise from five departments (mechanical and process engineering, economics, information technology, electrical engineering and construction engineering) can the challenges of the industrial internet be met.

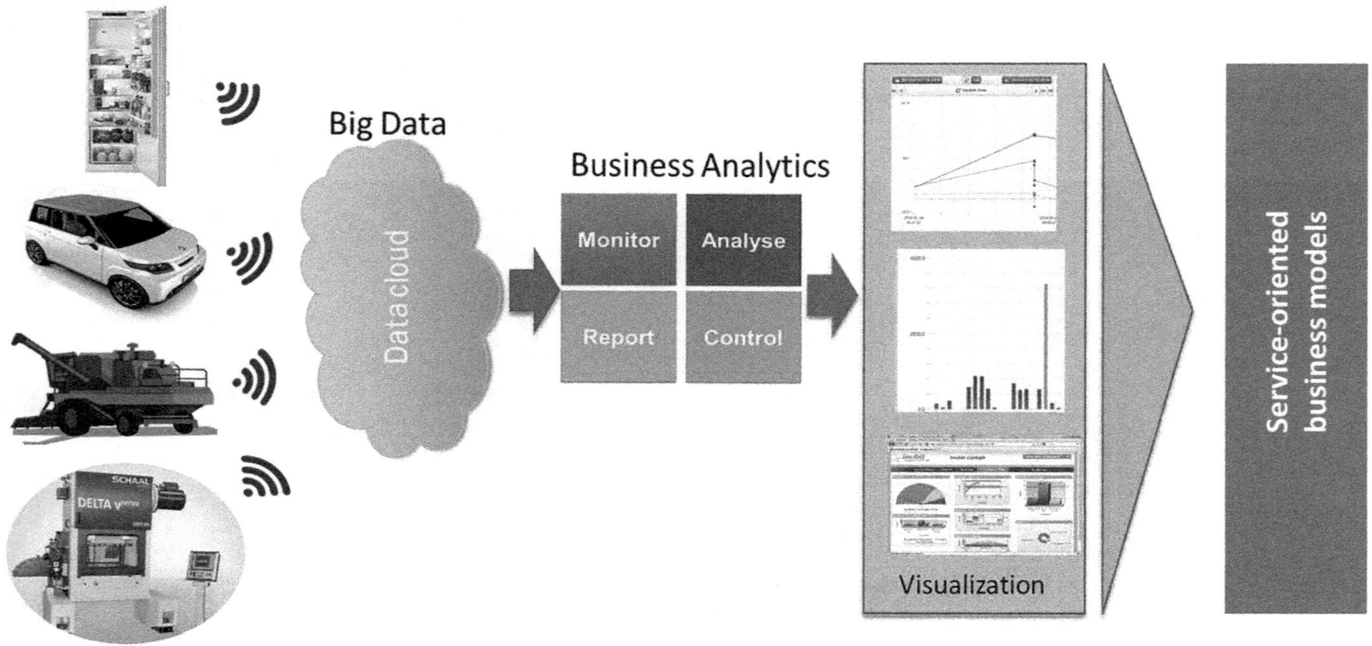

Fig. 9.3 Basic structure of service-oriented business models. (Eigner)

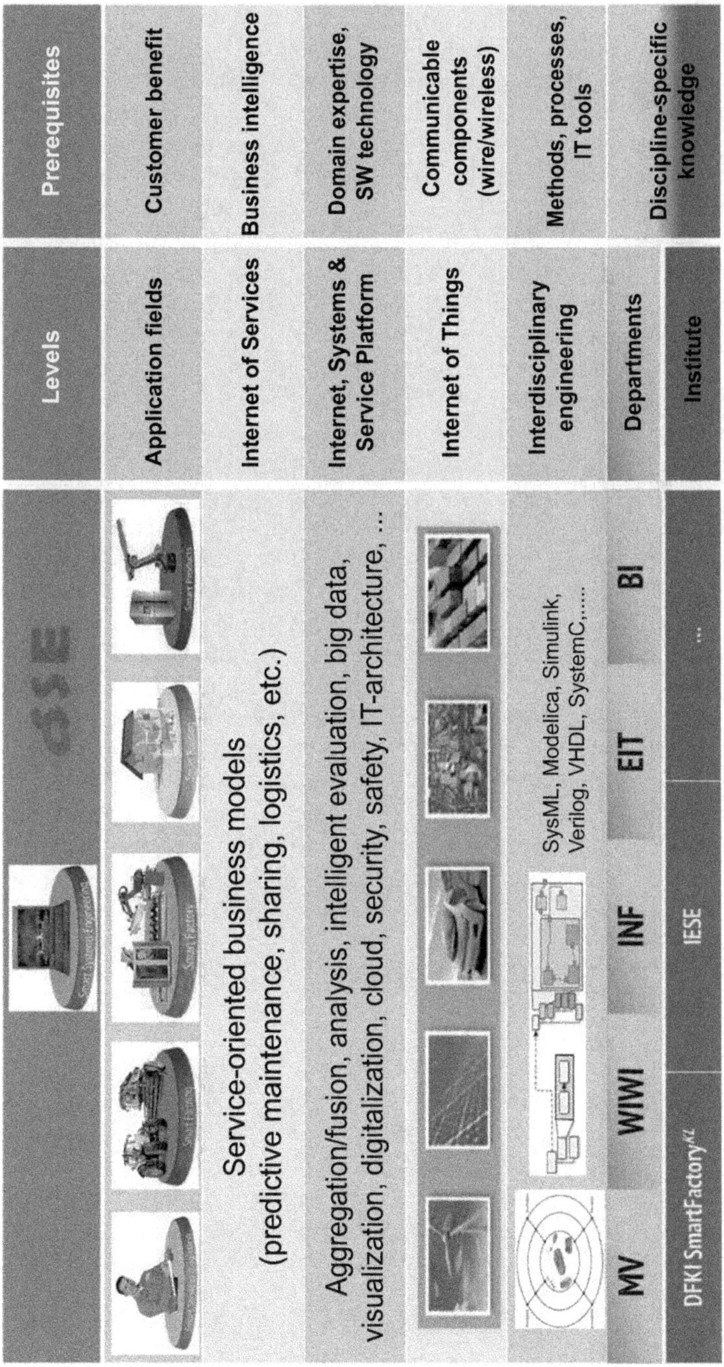

Fig. 9.4 Reference model Center for Smart Systems Engineering of the TU Kaiserslautern. (TU Kaiserslautern)

9.4 From PLM to SysLM

The complexity within a product lifecycle management strategy (PLM) has already reached a very high level, and the increase in complexity of product systems and their development will continue to accelerate [8, 13–15]. To master this complexity and ensure the fulfillment of new demands, there must be traceability over the entire lifecycle in the form of a closed process chain. Currently, traceability in common PLM solutions is often limited to the linking of product requirements and the elements on the bills of materials (BOM) [16]. System lifecycle management (SysLM) [8] has been expanded as the subsequent step of PLM, and has been suggested as a key concept for the transparent description of complex, smart products within the context of the industrial internet (Fig. 9.5; [17]). Two research projects being funded by the German Federal Ministry of Education and Research (BMBF) (→ mecPro^2 and InnoServPro) support these efforts.

System lifecycle management does not provide smart product and production systems, but, on an administrative level, can provide the right information at the right time and in the right context, in order to support construction processes [18]. System lifecycle management (SysLM) is general information management, which augments product lifecycle management (PLM) by adding an explicit view of previous (→ upstream) and subsequent (→ downstream) development phases under consideration of all disciplines, including services. The concept is based on the direct and also indirect integration of various authoring systems along the entire lifecycle of a product or system. System lifecycle management solutions, as the technical and administrative backbone, are responsible for product and system models and engineering processes, especially data exchange along the supply chain, release and change management, as well as configuration management.

The points cited represent a series of demands to SysLM solutions that must be expanded for the support of an industrial internet-capable product creation process.

9.5 Demands to SysLM Solutions

9.5.1 Interdisciplinarity

Demands to SysLM solutions are based on the engineering tasks along the entire *product lifecycle*, meaning from the early phase of determining requirements, through product development, product planning and production, operating business including service and replacement parts supply right up to recycling, spanning all *disciplines* (→ mechanics, electrical/electronic systems, software and services) and providing organization and technical system support beyond a company's area limits (Fig. 9.6).

Vital to a SysLM solution is a reasonable integration of the various authoring systems along the product lifecycle and the various disciplines. These especially include the early conceptional PCP phase (see Sect. 9.5.5) and CAD and CAE applications for mechanical, electrical and electronic construction, as well as for

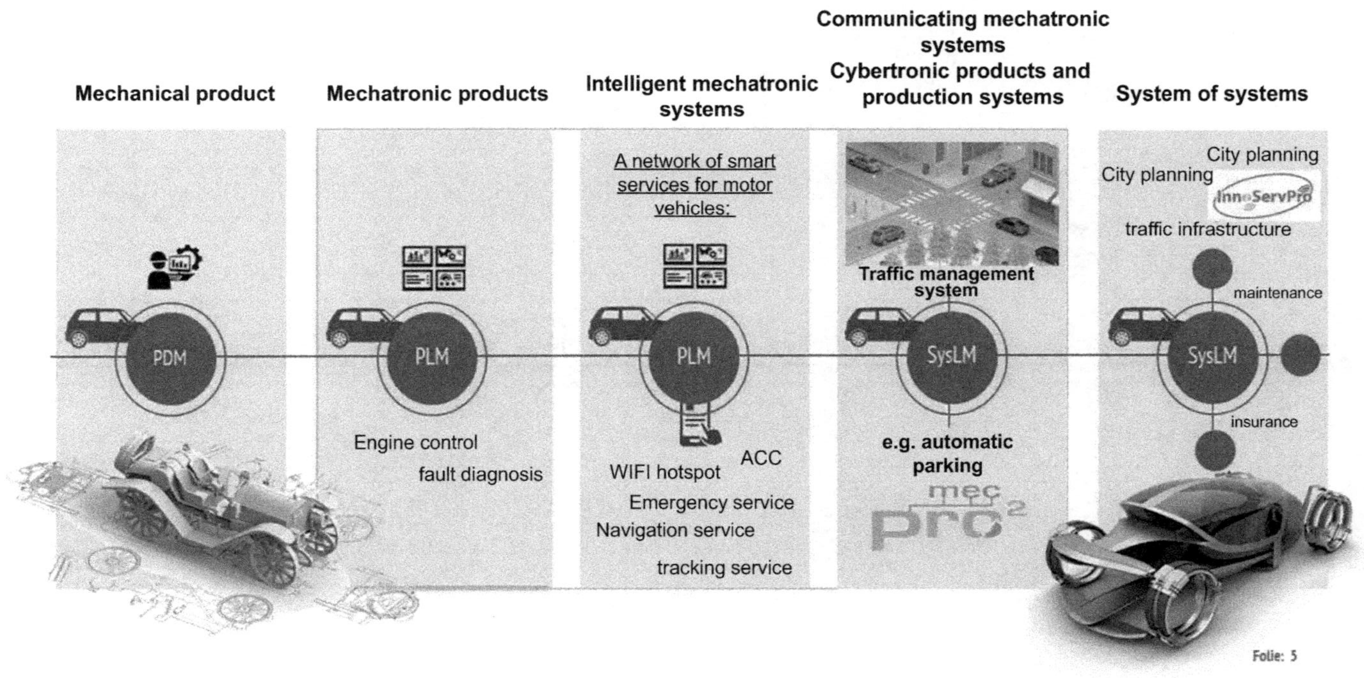

Fig. 9.5 System lifecycle management as a key concept for the detailed description of complex, smart product systems within the context of the industrial internet. (Based on Eigner [6]; Eigner et al. [12]; Eigner and Geissen [17]; © Lehrstuhl für Virtuelle Projektentwicklung (VPE) (Department of Virtual Project Development), 2016)

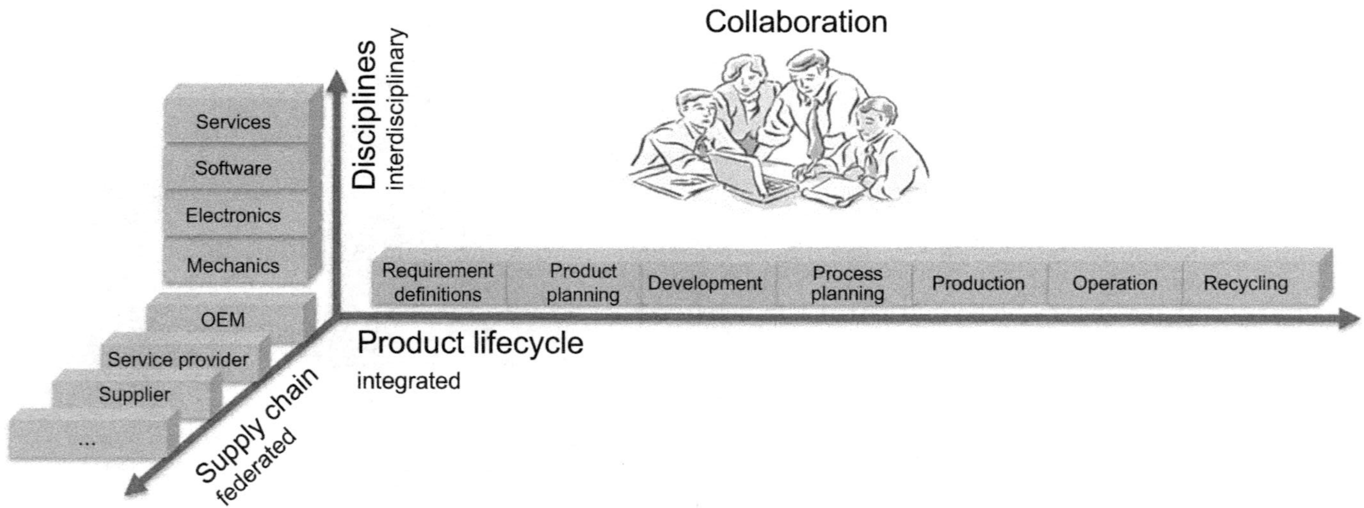

Fig. 9.6 Interdisciplinary, integrated and federated product lifecycle. (Eigner et al. [16])

software development (→ CASE). It is especially important to consider the diversity of the development processes for mechanics, electronics and software. Yet their integration will not stop at the end of the PCP process, but rather, the trend is clearly moving toward integrating SysLM solutions into the subsequent areas of the product lifecycle. Such areas include production planning and service support (see Sect. 9.5.6).

Overview
What interdisciplinarity means for SysLM:

- Coverage of the entire product lifecycle through the provision of integration interfaces for all phases
- Coverage of especially the early development phase through interdisciplinary development methods (model based systems engineering, MBSE)
- Coverage of production planning and production to enable related production and factory planning with the aid of consistent product models
- Integration of all disciplines through the provision of suitable CA interfaces for mechanics, electrical/electronic systems and software development
- Integration into the four-tier architecture of the VDA, in order to implement an infrastructure for IT integration
- Open interfaces and the use of standards (OSLC, ReqIF, AP233, AP242, SysML, etc.).

9.5.2 Digitalization

Modern development of complex technical products and production systems includes the interplay of various disciplines in mechanical and electronic construction as well as software development along the product lifecycle and through the supply chain (see Sect. 9.5.1). Digitalization, that is, the complete description of a product in digital models, represents a suitable approach to bring these disciplines together in early development phases. A subset of this concept is model-based systems engineering (MBSE) (see Sect. 9.5.4). For this, engineers and designing engineers consistently work with digital models in the early, conceptional phases of product development. This consistency of digital models along the product lifecycle and partly across the disciplines (Sect. 9.7) allows the networking of all development results. The conceptional product description basically consists of functional, logical and performance elements which comprise either hierarchical or network-type structures. In this way, a bridge can be built between demands and detailed construction on the SysLM level. Likewise, a system break between development/construction and production planning and production can be overcome. The prerequisite for this is a stronger integration of the functions of a digital factory and manufacturing execution systems (→ MES). ERP systems in this scenario play more of an executing role (see Sect. 9.5.8) (Fig. 9.7).

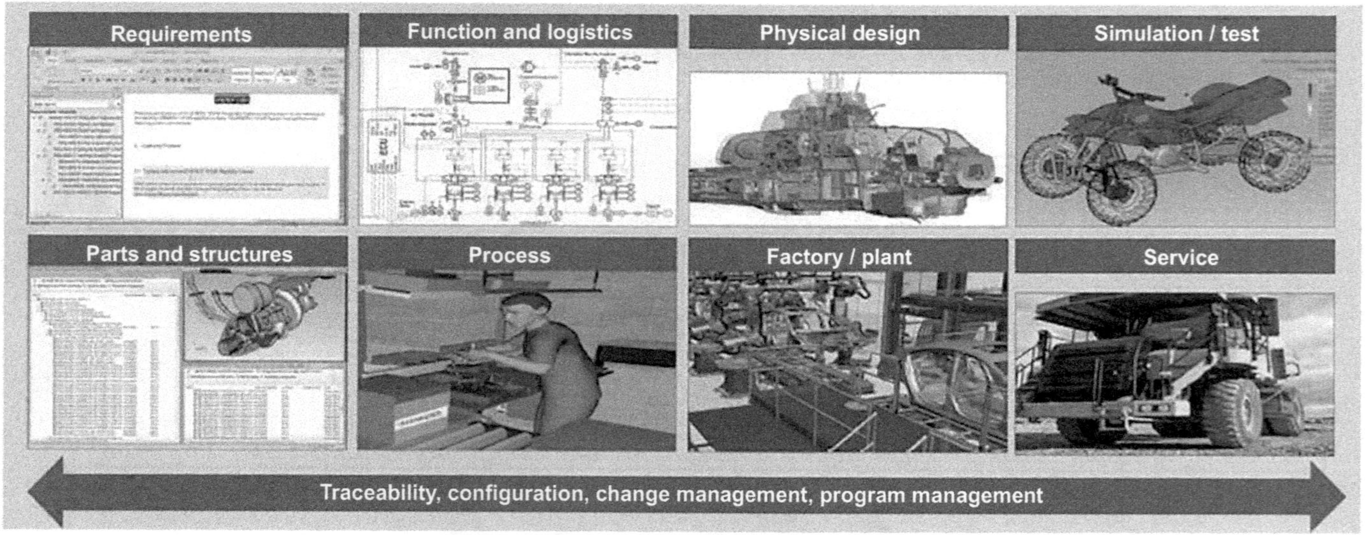

Fig. 9.7 Increasing digitalization of the product development process. *Source* SIEMENS Digital Factory Division

While, in the 1980s, product descriptions were still focused on documentation, in the meanwhile—partially due to the increased introduction of CAD in mechanical and electronic systems—BOM-oriented, hierarchical models (→ BOM = bill of materials) are prevailing, parallel to a geometric description. Today, these measures are not sufficient in the face of the increasing importance of mechatronics and cybertronics; they must be augmented by linear (software) and network-type structuring methods (MBSE) (Fig. 9.8).

The hardware—both mechanical as well as electric/electronic—is described at the uppermost administrative tier via hierarchical bills of materials. In the electrical/electronic system, CAD systems generate network-type schematics and layout plans which are converted to hierarchical BOMs right on the TDM (team data management) level. However, instantiation takes place at any rate on this tier, since mounting positions are managed with it (see Sect. 9.5.3). In software development, there are parallel strings (→ Trunks), branching (→ Branch) and merging (→ Merge). Configuration is achieved in software development by linking the physical files which are labeled with their revision and version (→ Baseline). Figure 9.9 depicts these relationships in the phase of concrete product development as a digital SysLM model. There are two things to watch out for: firstly, the conception and implementation of interdisciplinary release, change and configuration processes, and secondly, their integration in an operating system architecture according to the four-tier approach of the VDA (see Sect. 9.5.8).

Overview
What digitalization means for SysLM:

- Coverage of the entire product lifecycle through the provision of digital models for each individual phase
- Coverage of both interdisciplinary and, in subsequent phases, discipline-dependent models
- Coverage especially in the early development phase by interdisciplinary development methods (model based systems engineering, MBSE)
- Coverage of production planning, production and after sales/service
- Existence of integration interfaces for all phases
- Open interfaces and the use of standards (OSLC, ReqIF, AP233, AP242, SysML, etc.)

9.5.3 Instantiation

Instantiation of a digital model is vital for several reasons. In complex products and systems, for instance, in the realms of plant engineering, shipbuilding and aircraft construction, several installed components must be traceable and individually identifiable. The components of a certain type, such as Pump 4711 D, are installed in a frigate in several positions, perhaps with several other parameters,

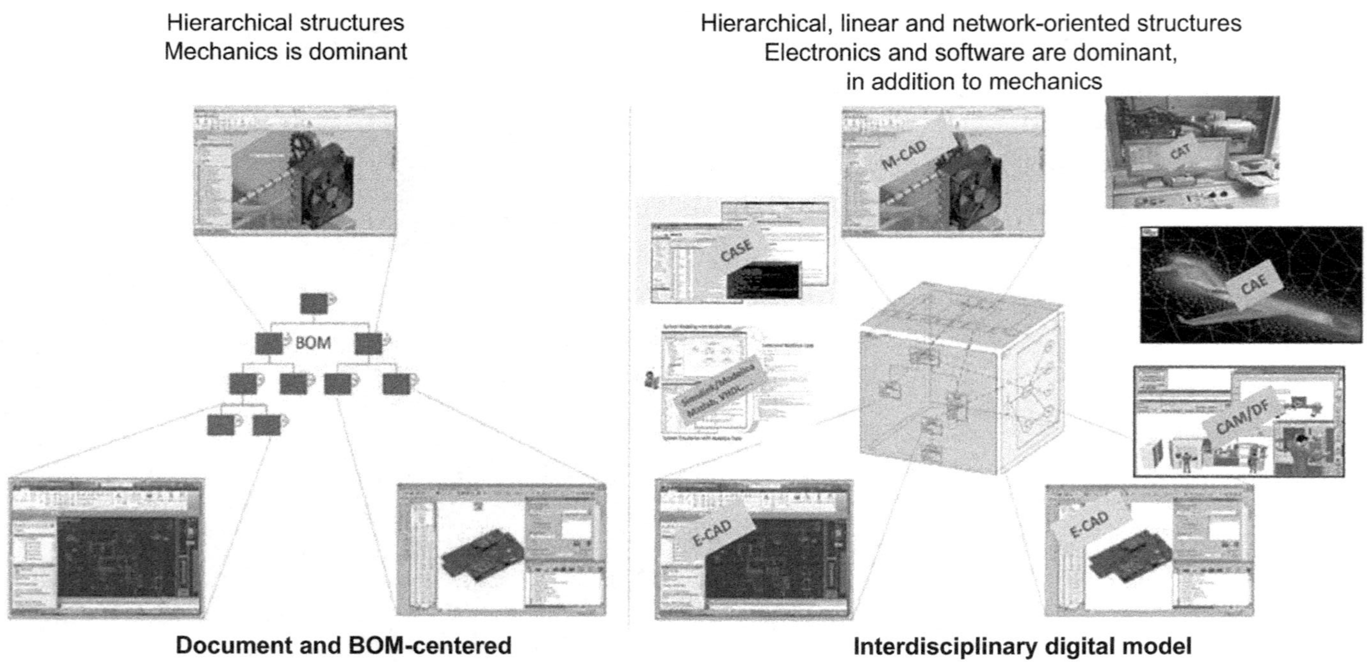

Fig. 9.8 From a description based on documents and bills of materials to a model-based digital description. (Based on Pfenning et al. [19])

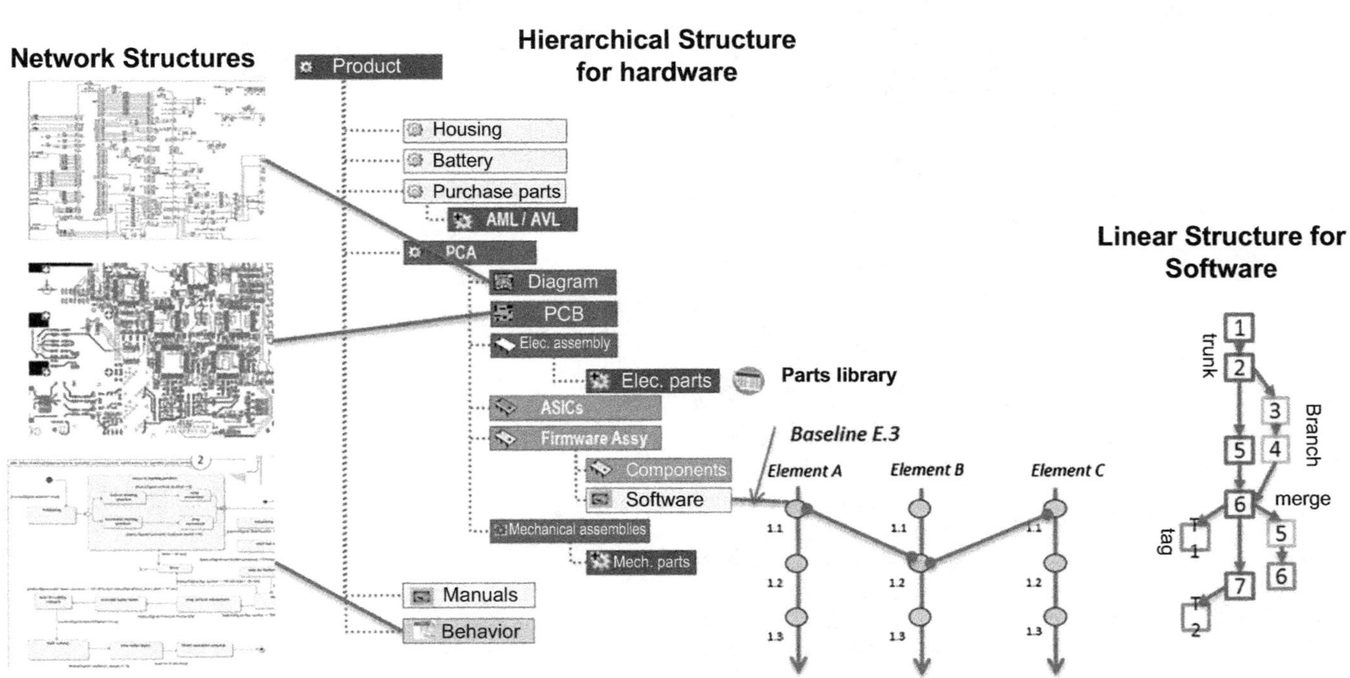

Fig. 9.9 Integration of MCAD, ECAD, SW (Case) in a SysLM backbone in the form of an interdisciplinary digital product model consisting of hierarchical, network-type and linear structures. (Eigner)

e.g. maintenance data. The various instances are definitively identified by a serial number, in addition to the item number and revision/version. Important components are individually tracked. Every part thus receives a serial number in addition to an item number, with which a seamless documentation of the individual component is possible. The context-specific identification of all pumps of a ship is performed by allocating the respective instances (item number, revision/version, seral number) to the serial number of the ship. This relationship is depicted in Fig. 9.10

Instantiation through serial numbers is sufficient in most cases, but only when the installment location is not of interest. For products manufactured in large volumes, only one serial number, if any, is supplied on the highest tier. In electronics, instantiation is usually accomplished using position indicators, because the position of the respective component is relevant to the assembly process. Thus, it is typical in the schematic and layout diagrams and in the bill of materials to additionally identify identical components of equal value by position indicators (for example, capacitors with the same capacity each have an identification number, a revision/version, a part name and the installation position C1, C2, C3, etc.).

Due to the industrial internet, new demands, especially based on the definition of service-oriented business models, have cropped up which require an instantiation within the context of the installation position and product. These values, delivered by sensors, can only be interpreted within this context (Fig. 9.11). Thus, a definitive allocation to an IP address and the contextual connection between individual sensors and the machine tool is also ensured.

Overview

What instantiation means for SysLM:

- The digital system model must possess application-specific type and instance plans
- Typical possibilities include serial numbers and/or position indicators

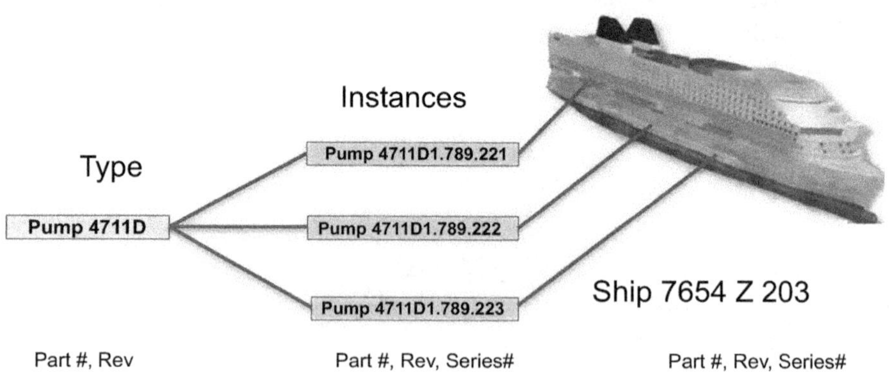

Fig. 9.10 Relationship between type and instance, and differentiation by serial numbers. (Eigner)

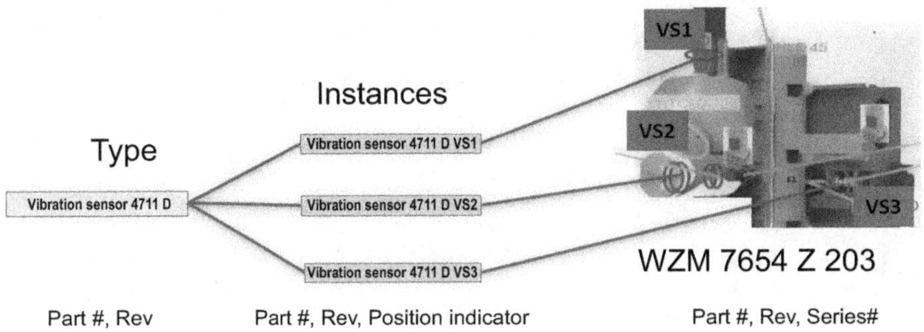

Fig. 9.11 Relationship between type and instance and differentiation via position indicators

- A further attribution or linkage with data sets must be possible, e.g. for maintenance-related and operational information
- Definitive allocation of product, component, sensor and IP address. Only through this context can a definitive allocation, identification and evaluation of sensor values occur.

9.5.4 Collaboration

Interdisciplinary product development ultimately leads to an increase in globalization within the value creation chain, both within the OEMs as well as between OEMs and their suppliers, thus also leading to more complex, networked task organization and processes (See Fig. 9.12). This means that product data and typical engineering processes are distributed throughout the entire supply chain. The demand for interdisciplinary communication between all participants along various cultural areas and time zones is becoming ever more important. In addition, the internet-based integration of customers in the form of an engineering collaboration platform must be part of a SysLM solution.

The Wikipedia definition of "collaborate" on the German version of the site calls it "a recursive process in which two or more persons or organizations work together in a PCP work phase toward a common goal." On the SysLM level, communication between the stakeholders of a PCP facilitates collaboration. With a common vault, all designers can work on the same construction objects. Access logistics ensure that the correct employee can see and, if necessary, edit information at the right time and place and in the permissible subset. SysLM offers a number of tools with which companies can collaborate internally and externally. To some extent, simplified communications mechanisms are offered from the realm of social media.

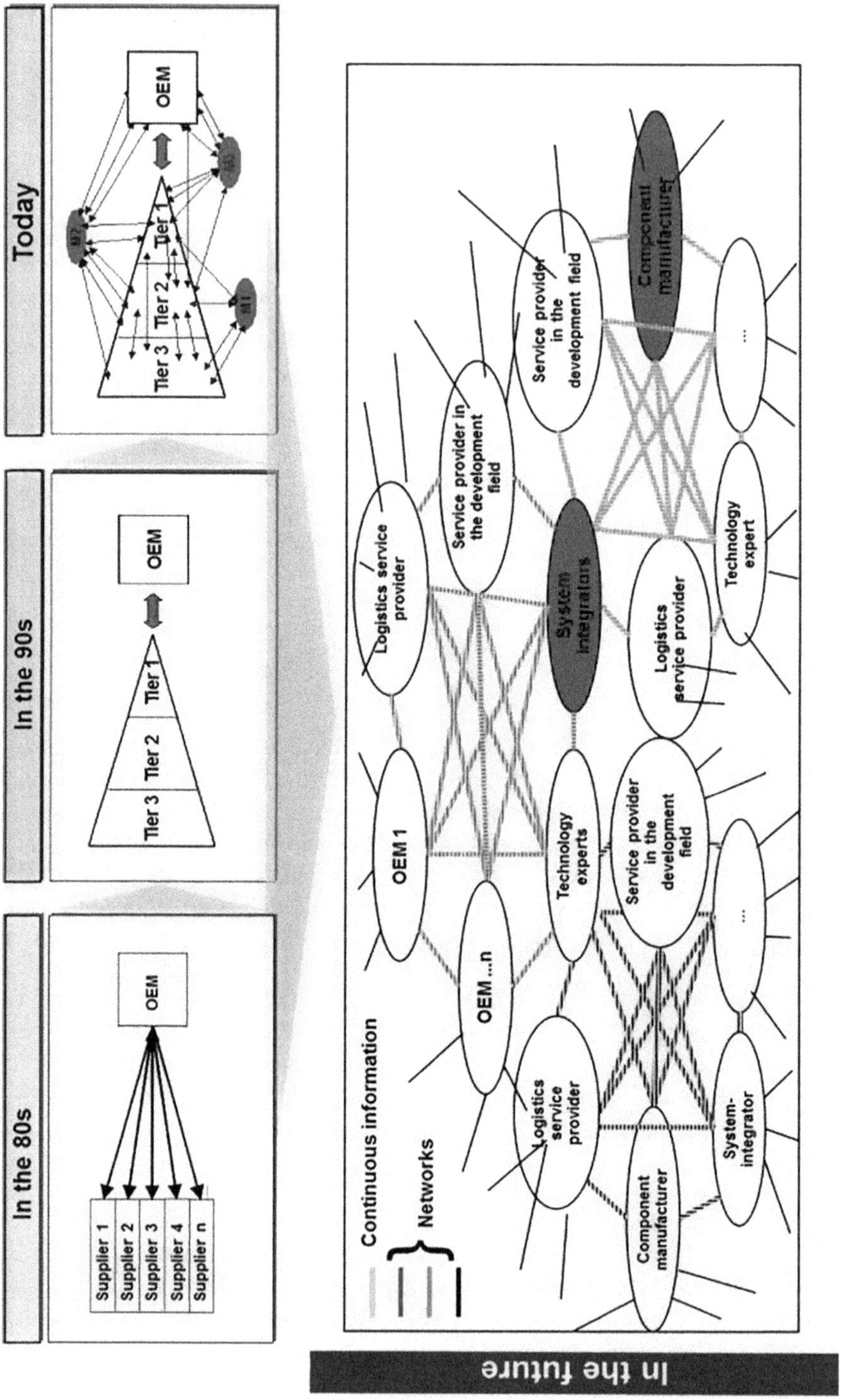

Fig. 9.12 Supply chain in automobile manufacturing. (Source: Dr. Göschel, Magna)

Overview
What collaboration means for SysLM:

- The provision of a virtual construction and information exchange platform
- The provision of suitable visualization methods based on lightweight formats (JT, TIFF, PDF, etc.)
- Solving of access problems and thus guaranteed protection of the intellectual property of various organizations and persons participating in the PDP
- Common vault system allowing common data access
- Communication structure similar to social media systems

9.5.5 Early-Phase Integration of the Product Lifecycle (→ Upstream Process)

Industrial internet-compatible products and the accompanying engineering processes require an increasing emphasis on early phases of the PCP. Together with the necessary interdisciplinarity, model based systems engineering (MBSE) results in a new approach to product development that offers optimal prerequisites for developing more complex mechatronic and cybertronic products. This, in turn, results in new model elements which, on the one hand, are administered and, on the other, are subject to engineering processes. These include specifications, functions, behavior and logical system blocks, among others. The problem with the integration of components during the development process can be tackled at the earliest stage possible through the use of such modeling languages, by defining the correlations between system specifications, functions, behavior and structure. The consistent, model-based development in virtual production is of central importance and thus also a significant challenge to the optimization of the PCP for mechatronic and especially cybertronic products and systems. The methods of model-based systems engineering can contribute to the description of an interdisciplinary product in an abstract way. The German standard VDI 2206 defines a systematic approach for the development of mechatronic systems. The focus lies in the left wing of the 'V' and expands it with the tools of model-based systems engineering. In the research project mecPro[2], funded by the BMBF, the approaches to the software platform for embedded systems (→ SPES) have been joined with the construction methods of mechanics (VDI 2221), resulting in an expanded V model [20] (Fig. 9.13).

Three tiers of digital modeling can be identified (Fig. 9.14):

- **Modeling and specifications:**

A system is described with qualitative models. They contain specification, functional, behavioral or logical system structures. The models are descriptive and cannot be simulated. Graphical editors for description languages such as the SysML (systems modeling language) can serve as authoring tools.

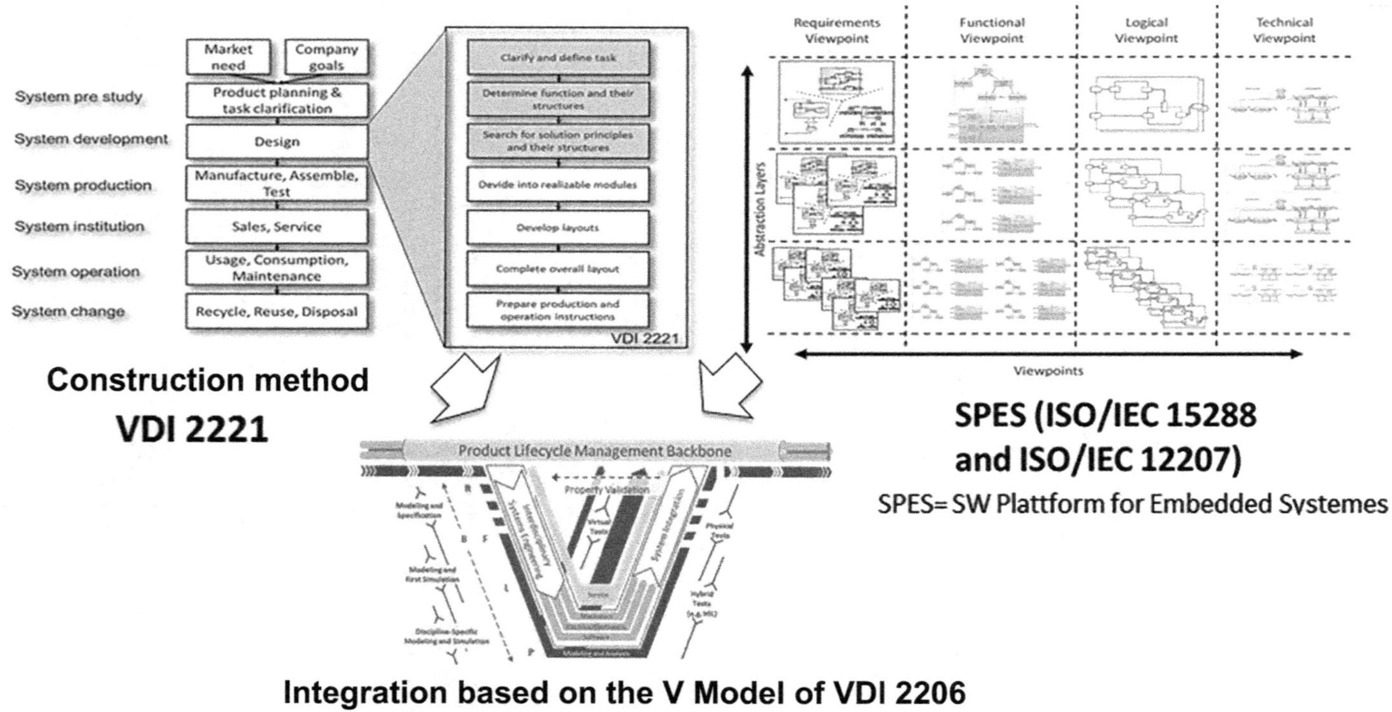

Fig. 9.13 Joining of SPES with VDI 2221 to form an expanded V model. (mecPro[2] [20]; Gilz and Eigner [21])

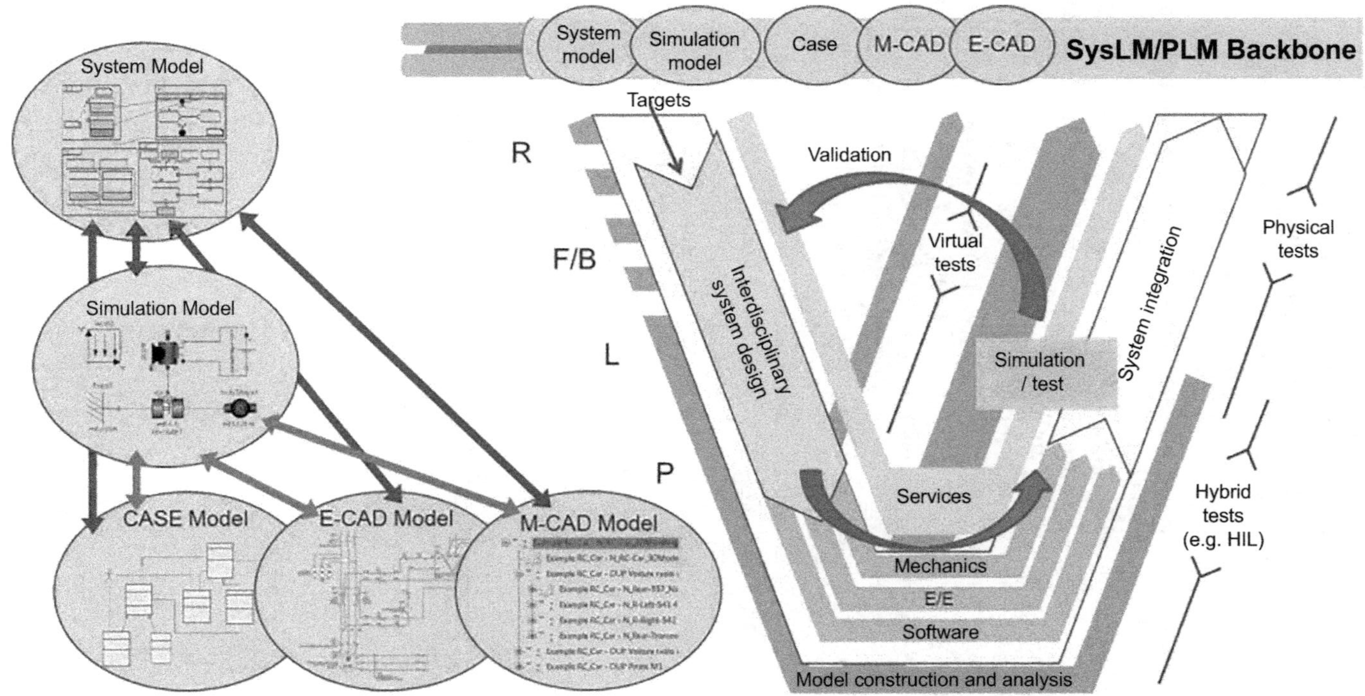

Fig. 9.14 V model for model-based systems engineering (MBSE) with a SysLM backbone. (Eigner)

- **Modeling and initial simulation and validation:**

On this tier, usually quantitative, simulatable models are generated, such as multi-physical simulation models involving several disciplines. Simulation editors such as Modelica, Matlab/Simulink or, in electronics, VDHL, Verilog or SystemC serve as authoring tools.

- **Discipline-specific modeling and detailed simulation and validation:**

On this level, geometric and CAE models, for instance, are generated which have a very discipline-specific character. CAD systems or discipline-specific calculation and simulation software serve as authoring tools.

Based on initial simulations and the functional description, the discipline-specific development begins, which addresses the physical elements of the system, such as hardware parts or software code (identified by P in Fig. 9.15). Here is where CAx processes generally take place in virtual product development. From this level on, modern PLM solutions are positioned. The major requirements to an SysLM include mapping new artefacts to support specifications, function, behavior and logical system elements and the subsequent engineering processes (→ Release, change and configuration management) (Fig. 9.15). Parallel to the SysLM philosophy, a few providers originally coming from a CASE (computer aided software engineering) application and also due to their favorable application management systems and purchased MBSE tools, have defined a new application area: ALM = application lifecycle management (→ IBM and PTC/MKS).

Similar to the integration of CAD to PLM, in the Department of Virtual Product Development (VPE)[4] at the TU Kaiserslautern, the commands of a conventional PLM system were integrated into the command structure of a SysML (systems modeling language) authoring system and vice versa. Through the linkage with the constructive master data and bills of materials contained in the original PLM scope of work, the consistent integration of specifications, functions, logical blocks and the product development bill of materials (BOM) was achieved. This integration became possible with relatively little effort through the modern service-based architecture (SOA), the openness of the interfaces and the simplicity of customizing via an approach of the participating systems hinging on a model-based repository.

Overview
What early-phase integration means for SysLM:

- Provision of an expanded product model containing specifications, functions, behavioral and logical elements
- Provision of integration interfaces for SysML and the simulation systems in the early phase (Simulink, Matlab, Modelica, VHDL, Verilog, SystemC, etc.)

[4]VPE *Lehrstuhl für Virtuelle Produktentwicklung* (Department of Virtual Product Development).

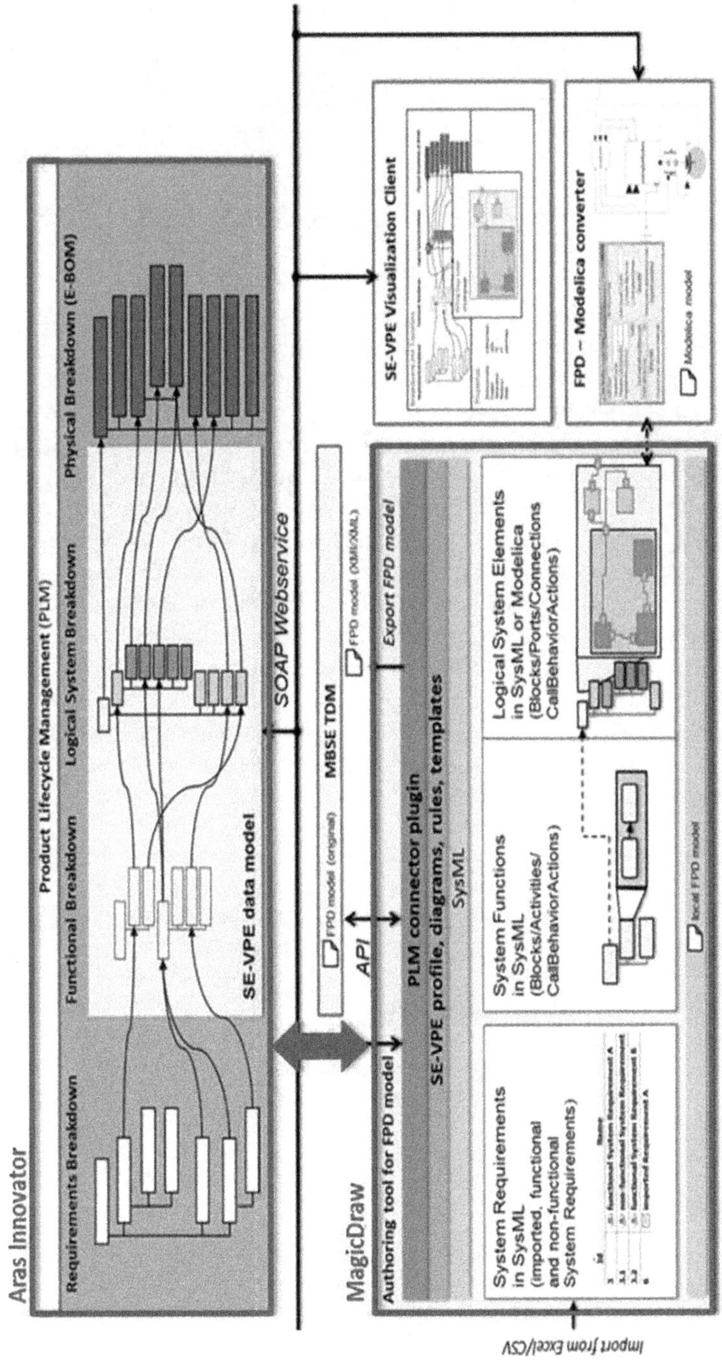

Fig. 9.15 Interplay between authoring systems, TDM and PLM/SysLM backbone. (Gilz and Eigner [21])

- Implementation of suitable engineering processes for the new artefacts
- Easy conformation of the SysLM system, when possible, through configuration, to integrate new objects and relationships
- OSLC- and ReqIF-capability of participating systems

9.5.6 Late-Phase Integration of the Product Lifecycle (→ Downstream Process)

Modern approaches of internet-based services based on communicating products often stem from mass data evaluation in the production and operation phases. This represents an extension of the SysLM solutions right up to the service area. Currently, isolated and non-integrated service lifecycle management systems (SLMs) have also established themselves for this realm. An extension according to a SysLM solution that is based on common master and structural data would be prudent. In this context, SysLM means not only an extension to the early phase, but also to the late phase of the product lifecycle. Figure 9.16 uses the example of a product equipped with internet-capable sensors and actuators to show which feedback loops are relevant. For the optimization of the PCP, it is interesting to know which components and systems lead to qualitative or functional problems. In the service department, a direct optimization of the maintenance and replacement part supply can take place.

This type of feedback loop requires the type and instances concepts introduced in Sect. 9.5.3. Then, service-oriented evaluations are possible for any component (Fig. 9.17).

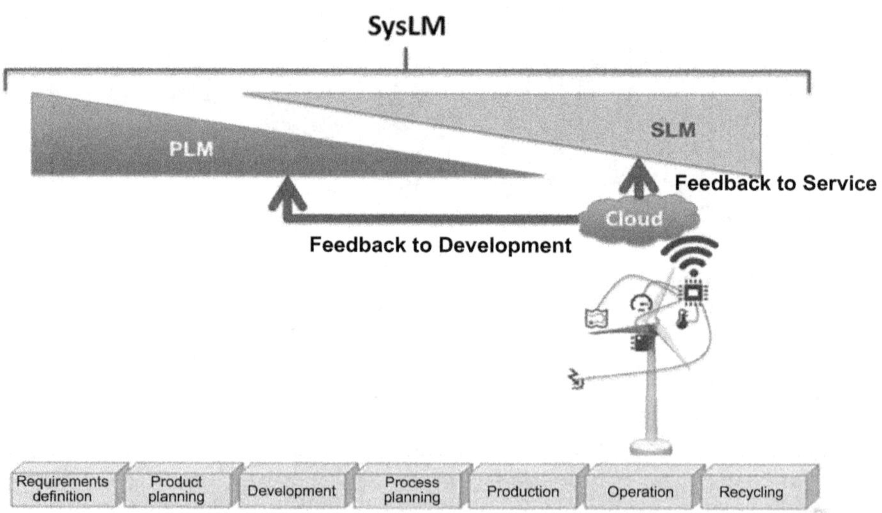

Fig. 9.16 Internet-capable products can send service-oriented information to the development and service departments. (Eigner)

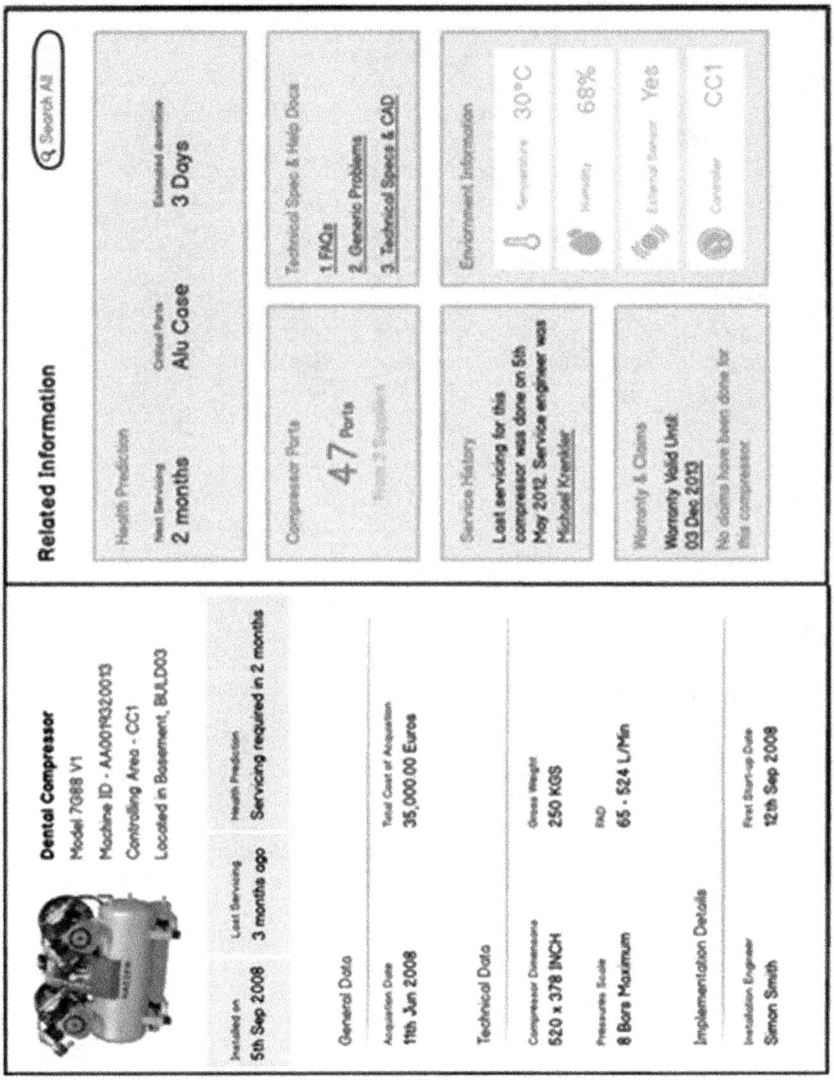

Fig. 9.17 Example of a service-oriented, permanently updated component report. (Graphical material: SAP)

It is obvious that all information linked to SysLM, including 3D graphics, bills of materials and maintenance plans can be displayed with this data sheet. Thus, the service department always has an updated overview of the static and dynamic information regarding the product and its relevant components.

Overview
What late-phase integration means for SysLM:

- Support of the integration of process planning systems and digital factory systems
- Provision especially of functions of service lifecycle management (SLM) and integration in an SLM solution based on common product data
- Provision of solutions which enable communication with the sensors and actuators of internet-capable products
- Additional functions such as cloud integration, business analytics and data mining must be integrated
- Graphical interfaces that show the overall relationships between static and dynamic information.

9.5.7 Visualization

Through all of the previously mentioned requirements to SysLM, such as interdisciplinarity, instantiation, federation and integration over the entire product lifecycle, the digital product model has reached a level of complexity that can hardly be mastered by engineers in daily processing. Acceptance problems are the consequence. Especially typical engineering processes, such as release-, change- and configuration management require a high degree of transparency regarding which objects are influenced by such a process. Graphs are very suitable for visualizing complex structures (Fig. 9.18). Of course, this assumes that an allocation of various application and administration systems have been established via links (see Sect. 9.5.8, Figs. 9.21 and 9.22). The documents linked with nodes must be displayed in conventional "lightweight" formats (→ TIFF, PDF, JT, etc.).

Overview
What a simple and transparent visualization means for SysLM:

- Integration of graph-oriented visualization tools
- Open and documented interfaces, data formats and standards
- Change and configuration management that is as harmonious as possible (prerequisite: all object classes in all application systems must allow revision, version and validity areas (→ effectivity).
- Linking of various application systems (→ ALM, PLM, SLM, MES, ERP) through model-based, semantic networks

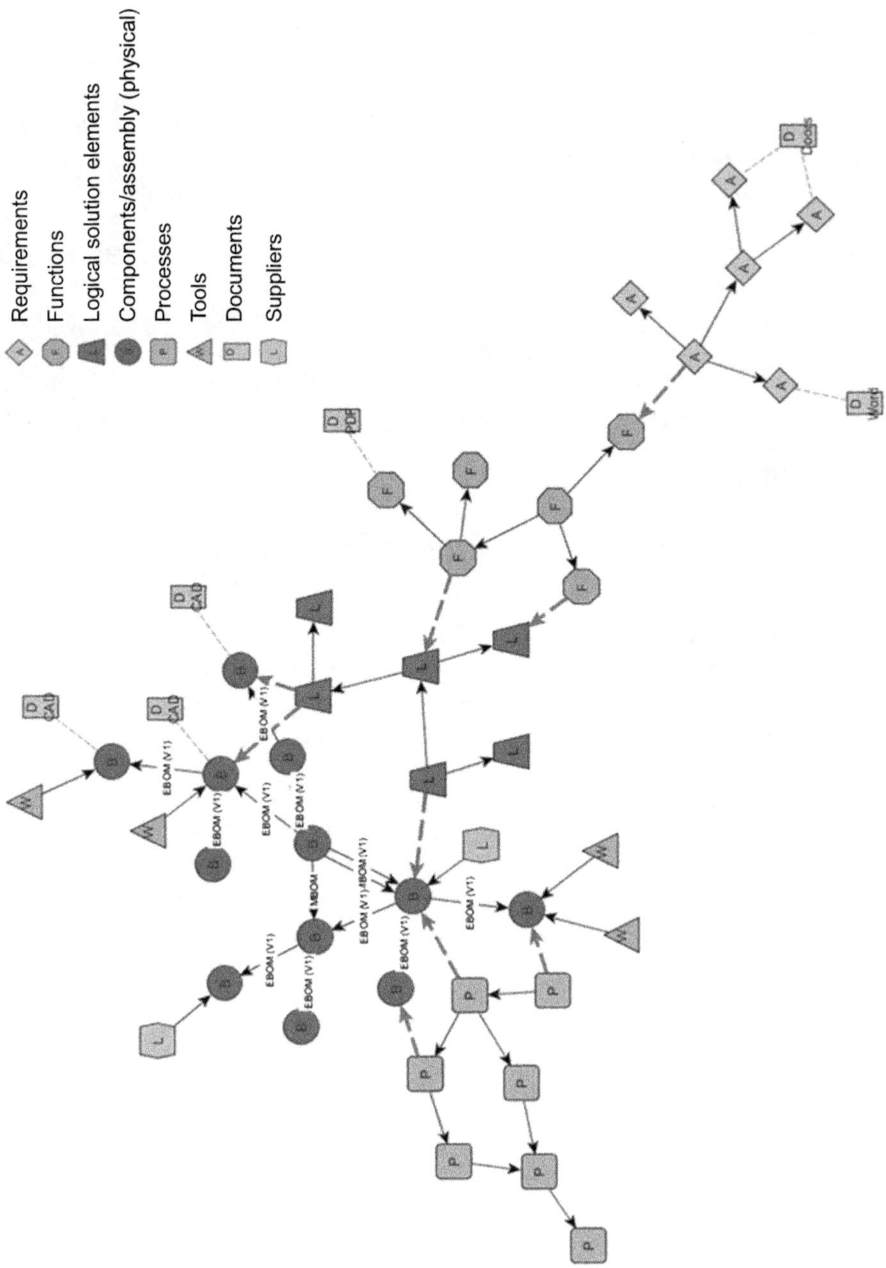

Fig. 9.18 Graphic-based example of a product model linked over the entire product lifecycle. (Ernst [22])

9.5.8 Embedding in an Operational IT Architecture

An interdisciplinary and integrated PCP that supports the development of products and production systems suited to the industrial internet is based on a number of authoring systems in the various phases of the product lifecycle and in various disciplines. They must be embedded in a common product and process backbone via a suitable architecture spanning one or, depending on the complexity, two hierarchy levels. These concepts are identified through the four tiers determined by a working group of the German Association of the Automotive Industry (VDA):

- **Authoring systems** (MBSE, MCAD, ECAD, CASE, CAP, CAM, Office) and calculation and simulation systems
- **Team data management** (TDM), an administrative tier which manages authoring system-related information directly allocated to the authoring systems. This tier generally manages the native formats of the authoring systems. If authoring systems are structured too simply, this tier can also be omitted, which is then called direct coupling.
- **SysLM/PLM backbone**, the central PCP level, which contains the interdisciplinary product structure with all of its accompanying documentation—generally in neutral formats. This forms the basis for developmental change and configuration management. This is the actual SysLM solution tier, which can be supplemented by ALM and SLM.
- **PPC (production planning and control) backbone**, which, in the case of global distribution, usually consists of several local instances and frequently, various adapted PPC systems. Today, the logistics and production-related portion of change and configuration management is implemented on this level.

Figures 9.19 and 9.20 represent example approaches of a possible IT architecture with the goal of integrated release and change management (→ Engineering release/change management ERM/ECM) and the configuration management based on it. This takes into account that, in recent years, a new IT solution combination has appeared. The typical CASE tool providers have supplemented their solutions to include requirements management (RM) and MBSE tools, and call it ALM (application lifecycle management). ALM, then, is either implemented on the TDM tier or the backbone tier. However, a much more frequent case is that these three functions in a company have been historically selected according to the "best in breed" method and now must be integrated via a SysLM backbone. This is identical to the positioning of SLM in the late product lifecycle phase.

The TDM level serves as an intermediate layer for a number of authoring systems to be integrated, which manages authoring system-related information, such as native RM, MBSE, CA and CAE files. Only that product data absolutely necessary for the engineering processes reach the PLM backbone in this way. Visualization on this level works with neutral formats like TIFF, JT and PDF.

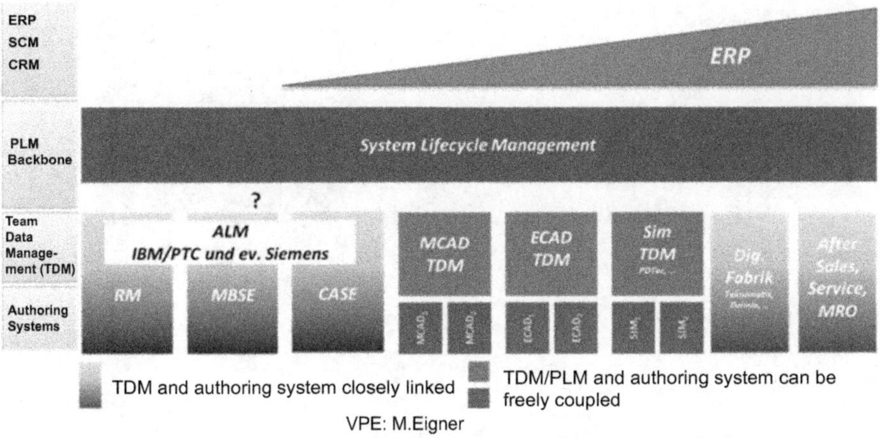

Fig. 9.19 Architecture with dominant SysLM system, ALM and SLM on the TDM tier or RM, MBSE and CASE individually integrated. (Eigner)

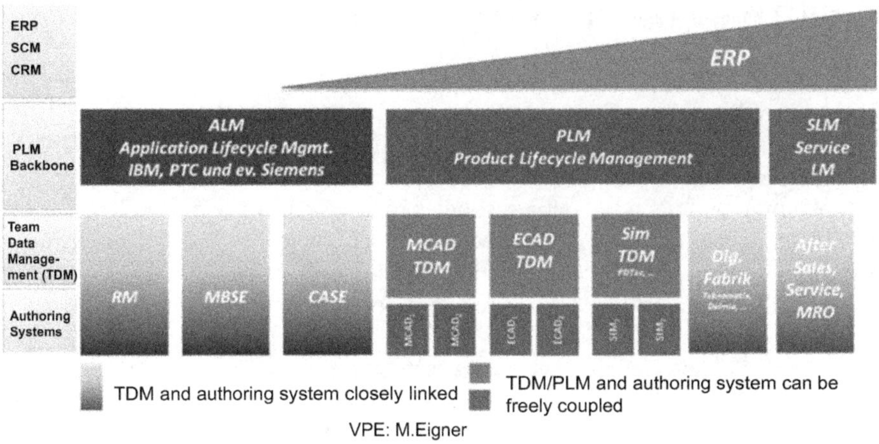

Fig. 9.20 Architecture, ALM, SLM and PLM together form the SysLM backbone. (Eigner)

The main problem with this architecture often lies in the coordination of information and processes between the design chain, determined by SysLM, and the supply chain, determined by PPC. What is more, PPC systems do not possess the necessary flexible design options for either company-specific adaption of the product or the process model, and thus often base common process design on the lowest common denominator rather than on the optimum. As an alternative, a more or less evolutionary solution is available, involving outsourcing process control to a superordinate system, e.g. one based on SharePoint (Fig. 9.21). The project

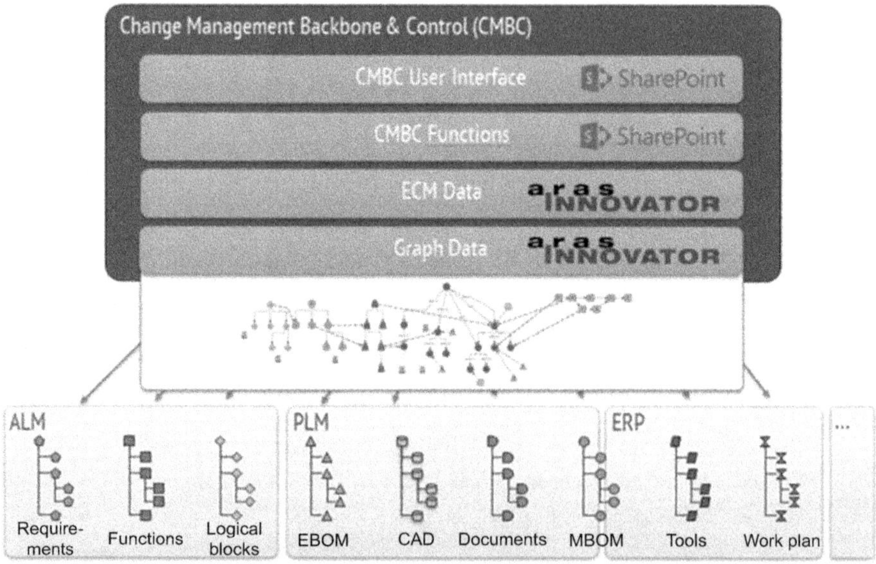

Fig. 9.21 Change management in SharePoint with the aid of a conventional repository. (Eigner)

was achieved in cooperation with the companies ILC and ARAS. Without consistent engineering processes via the design and supply chain, all integration attempts remain piecemeal. A more revolutionary solution would be to also couple production planning with its production resources to the SysLM backbone. This requires an efficient integration of digital factory systems and the MES (manufacturing execution system). In this scenario, ERP would be more likely to take on the role of an executing system. This would make it possible to implement all engineering processes on one common level.

Generally, when defining the IT infrastructure, one must keep in mind that, through the Internet of Things and the associated connection of several subsystems, an immense volume of data and numbers of interfaces can accrue. SysLM providers face the challenge of optimizing their SW technologies to meet this requirement. In the Department of Virtual Project Development (VPE), work is being done on ideas that no longer see the SysLM backbone as a monolithic total system with a physical data silo, but rather as a model-based repository based on a semantic network. Data remains in its applications, including TDM, and is linked via OSLC.[5] These solutions are based on experiences gained in the SharePoint project (Fig. 9.22). Any mix of solutions with a persistent, physical data management of basic data and linked data in the other application areas can also be implemented. This architecture, of course, offers the optimal prerequisites for the visualization of structures according to Fig. 9.18.

[5]OSLC = Open services for lifecycle collaboration.

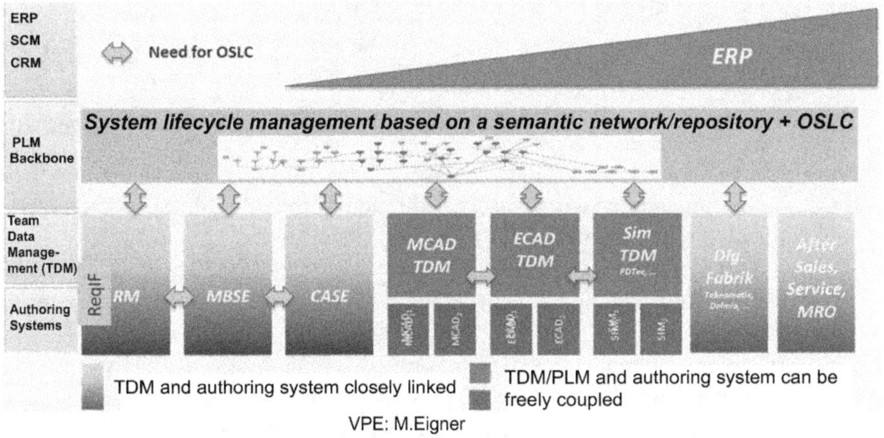

Fig. 9.22 Research plans of SysLM based on a model-based, semantic network and OSLC. (Eigner)

Overview
What embedding in an open, operative IT structure means for SysLM:

- Selection of a basic architecture type
- Open and stable interfaces
- Open and documented data formats and standards
- Highly harmonious change and configuration management (prerequisite: all object classes must allow revision and version as well as validity areas) (→ effectivity)
- Simple customizing, if possible through configuration and not programming
- Upward compatibility of customizing
- In the future, no monolithic silos, but rather model-based, semantic networks
- The goal of the architecture should be to execute engineering processes in a comprehensive, not fragmentary, manner on a single level

9.5.9 New Technologies

Modern SysLM/PLM solutions already employ SOAP and Rest-based web services. For the future, further modern IT technologies must be utilized:

- Model-based semantic network (MSN)
- In-memory databases and grid computing (IMSBM)
- Cloud computing

- Big data
- Security/safety
- New methods of interaction and presentation (usability)
- Strict implementation of relevant standards

Thoughts on MSN have been noted in Sect. 9.5.8. Only on the basis of this technology can fundamental progress on the reduction of the total cost of ownership be achieved through reduced customizing and upgrade costs.

The main idea of the IMDBM concept is to store the entire data stock of a company in main memory in the form of so-called in-memory databases or memory-resistant databases.

Grid computing involves an infrastructure for the common use of autonomous computing power. The vision of grid technology consists of obtaining computing power from the network, much like electric current is obtained from a power outlet connected to a power grid. The target is a comprehensive functional scope and increased networking of IT resources within the framework of cloud computing. In this process, the user must no longer individually run computer processes or applications, but can store these IT processes in a cloud (→ Cloud). This technology is accompanied by ever more inexpensive offers from service providers.

The increased use of IT solutions in industry is leading to increasingly large data stocks, which are collected along the entire product lifecycle. The challenge in processing and in the intelligent analysis of such large volumes of data in an industrial context is often referred to in the simplified term "big data." The main idea behind it is to intelligently evaluate these "data treasure chests" using intelligent algorithms and processes (such as data mining or business analytics) and to also make the results available to SysLM in an application-friendly form. Providers are also already offering the operation of a SysLM/PLM solution in the cloud.

According to Kaspersky Lab, in 2014 there were approximately 13,000 cases per month of computers with automatic process control systems becoming infected. The data in these critical systems needs to be highly accessible and absolutely secure. Yet, with an increasing networking of IT and products on the Internet of Things (think Industrie 4.0), the challenges regarding security are also growing. For Industrie 4.0, security of the underlying IT systems is an absolute prerequisite. Safety primarily concerns physical safety and worker protection in operating a machine or production process. There are safety standards and guidelines for the construction and operation of such systems, such as the German standard DIN EN ISO 13849, including principles for design [23].

Ease of use is largely influenced by the handling of the PLM system by the user (→ Usability). Usability profits from new interaction options between humans and computers. The natural interfaces of humans with their environment (language, gestures, touch, sight, hearing, etc.) were ignored by software developers for decades. Trends such as Bring your own Device (BYOD) and Choose your own Device (CYOD) will considerably influence the use of devices.

Discussions on standards have already begun in several places, as they are an absolute prerequisite for integration, considering the large number of old systems

Fig. 9.23 Overview of relevant standards for the implementation of the industrial internet. (Eigner)

which have developed over time. Figure 9.23 provides an overview of standards necessary for an IT architecture suitable for the industrial internet.

Conclusion

In the year 2030, intelligent systems and other services, networked via the internet, will encompass all industries, and will have replaced conventional, mechanical and mechatronic products. The developments in this sector will continue to progress at breakneck speed, in the scientific as well as the practical environment. Just which of the development trends will prevail in the future and be met by users with widespread acceptance will become evident in the coming years. However, we can already confirm that interest in further functions and applications for further SysLM solutions is continually growing and an effective organization of the lifecycle of the systems is absolutely essential. System lifecycle management (SysLM) is being established and expanded as the next step from PLM and is considered to be a key concept for a detailed strategy based on the "industrial internet" approach. We must use this unique opportunity; let us rethink and think outside the box; let us tear down barriers, and let's start now …

References

References Used

1. Anderl, R., Eigner, M., Sendler, U., & Stark, R. (Eds.). (2012). *Smart Engineering—Interdisziplinäre Produktentstehung, acatech DISKUSSION* (1st ed.). Berlin: Springer Vieweg.

2. Eigner, M., Roubanov, D., & Zafirov, R. (Eds.). (2014). *Modellbasierte Virtuelle Produktentwicklung* (1st ed.). Berlin: Springer.
3. Eigner, M., Faißt, K.-G., Apostolov, H., & Schäfer, P. (2015). Kurzer Begriff und Nutzen des System Lifecycle Management—im Kontext von Industrial Internet mit Industrie 4.0 und Internet der Dinge und Dienste. *ZWF Zeitschrift für wirtschaftlichen Fabrikbetrieb, 110*(7–8), 475–478.
4. Ehrlernspiel, K., & Meerkamm, H. (2015). Integration versus Spezialisierung—Von der Notwendigkeit einer ganzheitlichen Konstruktionsforschung und Lehre an Universitäten und Hochschulen. *Konstruktion—Zeitschrift für Produktentwicklung und Ingenieur-Werkstoffe, 6*(3), 3.
5. Eigner, M., Schuh, G., Baessler, E., Stolz, M., Steinhilper, R., Janusz-Renault, G., et al. (2009). Management des Produktlebenslaufs. In H. Bullinger, D. Spath, H. Warnecke, & E. Westkämper (Eds.), *Handbuch Unternehmensorganisation—Strategien, Planung, Umsetzung* (3rd ed., pp. 223–315). Berlin: Springer.
6. Eigner, M. (2015). Industrie 4.0—nur Produktionsautomatisierung oder doch mehr? *Konstruktion—Zeitschrift für Produktentwicklung und Ingenieur-Werkstoffe, 6*(3), 3.
7. Stark, R., Kim, M., Damerau, T., Neumeyer, S., & Vorsatz, T. (2015). Notwendige Voraussetzungen für die Realisierung von Industrie 4.0—Ein Beitrag aus der Sicht der Industriellen Informationstechnik. *ZWF Zeitschrift für wirtschaftlichen Fabrikbetrieb, 110*(3), 134–141.
8. Sendler, U. (Ed.). (2013). *Industrie 4.0—Beherrschung der industriellen Komplexität mit SysLM* (pp. 1–20). Berlin: Springer.
9. Porter, M., & Heppelmann, J. (2014). Wie smarte Produkte den Wettbewerb verändern. *Harvard-Business-Manager—das Wissen der Besten, 36*(12), 34–60.
10. Aurich, J., & Meissner, H. (2014). Entwicklung cybertronischer Produktionssysteme—Vorgehen für einen integrierten Entwicklungsprozess cybertronischer Produkte und Produktionssysteme. *ZWF Zeitschrift für wirtschaftlichen Fabrikbetrieb, 109*(1–2), 70–73.
11. Aurich, J., & Gülsüm, M. (2015). Produkt-Service-Systeme für Werkzeugmaschinenhersteller. *ZWF Zeitschrift für wirtschaftlichen Fabrikbetrieb, 110*(4), 177–181.
12. Eigner, M., Apostolov, H., Dickopf, T., Schäfer, P., & Faißt, K.-G. (2014). System Lifecycle Management—am Beispiel einer nachhaltigen Produktentwicklung nach Methoden des Model-Based Systems Engineering. *ZWF Zeitschrift für wirtschaftlichen Fabrikbetrieb, 109*(11), 0947–0085.
13. Fischer, J. (2015). Licht ins Dunkle—PLM verstehen heißt Lebenszykluseffekte (er)kennen. *ZWF Zeitschrift für wirtschaftlichen Fabrikbetrieb, 110*(1–2), 36–39.
14. Terzi, S., Bouras, A., Dutta, D., Garetti, M., & Kiritsis, D. (2010). Product lifecycle management—From its history to its new role. *International Journal of Product Lifecycle Management, 4*(4), 360–389.
15. Eigner, M., von Hauff, M., & Schäfer, P. (2011). Sustainable product lifecycle management. In J. Hesselbach & C. Herrmann (Eds.), *Glocalized Solutions for Sustainability in Manufacturing* (pp. 501–506). Berlin: Springer.
16. Eigner, M., & Stelzer, R. (2009). *Product Lifecycle Management—Ein Leitfaden für Product Development und Life Cycle Management* (2nd ed.). Berlin: Springer.
17. Eigner, M., & Geissen, M. (2015). System Lifecycle Management—am Beispiel einer nachhaltigen Produktentwicklung. In Smart Engineering—ProSTEP iViP Symposium 2015, Stuttgart, May 05–06, 2015. Böblingen: Kessler Druck, p. 48.
18. Paredis, C. (2012). Why model-based systems engineering?—Benefits and payoffs. In 4th PLM Future Conference, Mannheim.
19. Pfenning, M., & Muggeo, C. (2015). Die Rolle von MBSE und PLM im Industrial Internet. In S. Schulze & C. Muggeo (Eds.), *Tag des Systems Engineering* (pp. 279–287). Munich: Hanser.
20. mecPro^2 Projektunterlagen. www.mecpro.de. Accessed May 12 2016.

21. Gilz, T., & Eigner, M. (2013). Ansatz zur integrierten Verwendung von SysML Modellen in PLM zur Beschreibung der funktionalen Produktarchitektur. In M. Maurer & S.-O. Schulze (Eds.), *Tag des Systems Engineering* (pp. 293–302). Munich: Hanser.
22. Ernst, J. (2016). Phasen- und System-übergreifendes Werkzeug zu Management technischer Änderungen. doctoral dissertation submitted at the Department of Virtual Project Development (VPE), TU Kaiserslautern.
23. Mauerer, J. (2015). Safety und Security: Sicherheit bei vernetzten Industrieanlagen. Computer Woche, Oct. 1, 2015.

Further Reading

24. Eigner, M. (2013). Modellbasierte Virtuelle Produktentwicklung auf einer Plattform für System Lifecycle Management. In U. Sendler (Ed.), *Industrie 4.0—Beherrschung der industriellen Komplexität mit SysLM* (pp. 91–110). Berlin: Springer.
25. Annunziata, M., & Evans, P. (2012). *Industrial internet—Pushing the boundaries of minds and machines*. Fairfield: GE General Electric.
26. Annunziata, M., & Evans, P. (2013). *Industrial Internet—Eine europäische Perspektive: Neue Horizonte für Minds and Machines*. Fairfield: GE General Electric.
27. Tschöpe, S., Aronska, K., & Nyhuis, P. (2015). Was ist eigentlich Industrie 4.0?—Eine quantitative Datenbankanalyse liefert einen Einblick. *ZWF Zeitschrift für wirtschaftlichen Fabrikbetrie, 110*(3), 145–149.
28. Weyer, S., & Fischer, S. (2015). Gemeinschaftsprojekt Industrie 4.0—Fortschritt im Netzwerk. *ZWF Zeitschrift für wirtschaftlichen Fabrikbetrieb, 110*(1–2), 0947–0085.
29. Bauer, W., Herkommer, O., & Schlund, S. (2015). Die Digitalisierung der Wertschöpfung kommt in deutschen Unternehmen an—Industrie 4.0 wird unsere Arbeit verändern. *ZWF Zeitschrift für wirtschaftlichen Fabrikbetrieb, 110*(1–2), 68–73.

Industrie 4.0—Digital Redesign of Product Creation and Production in Berlin as an Industrial Location

10

Challenges and Solutions for Digital Transformation and Innovation

Rainer Stark, Thomas Damerau and Kai Lindow

Abstract

At the end of 2015, approximately 449 research and implementation projects in Germany were dedicated to the topic of Industrie 4.0. The great challenges, on the one hand, are to transform existing partial solutions, new findings and results into comprehensive and standardized application, while, on the other hand, identifying "white spots" and diligently continuing to research them. This chapter presents innovative Industrie 4.0 projects for the real and digital factory and product management from the Production Technology Center (PTZ) in Berlin, and offers a research map for the allocation of its own activities. A stage model is used to illustrate how the implementation and operationalization of information management required in the future can be mastered. The future-oriented concept of the information factory serves to demonstrate how, with the aid of the digital twin and smart data, gains in the efficiency and effectivity of product creation and production can be achieved.

10.1 Industrie 4.0—More Than just Smart Production

As multifaceted as the term "Industrie 4.0" itself is, so, too, is the research environment surrounding the topic very diverse. Currently, the research community is in a diffusion process, meaning that, all over Germany, new findings and results

R. Stark (✉) · T. Damerau
Virtual Product Creation Sector, Fraunhofer Institute for Production Systems and Design Technology (IPK), Berlin, Germany

K. Lindow
Department of Industrial Information Technology, Technical University of Berlin, Faculty V—Mechanical Engineering and Transport Systems, Institute of Machine Tools and Factory Management (IWF), Berlin, Germany

U. Sendler (ed.), *The Internet of Things*,
https://doi.org/10.1007/978-3-662-54904-9_10

emerge every day within the wide research and application spectrum. At the end of 2015, approximately 449 research and implementation projects [1] throughout Germany were dedicated to the topic of Industrie 4.0. The great challenges include, on the one hand, transforming existing partial solutions, new findings and results into a comprehensive and standardized application, while, on the other hand, identifying "white spots" and diligently continuing to research them. The interdisciplinary character of Industrie 4.0 research, as well as the fundamental vision of complete digital networking throughout all value creation processes, make it necessary to collect and consolidate the resulting inventions and innovations. In the process, it is important to overcome the barriers between the mentality of the stakeholders and those in communication, and offer a practical set of instruments which enable a quick, thematic localization of individual activities, in order to identify crosslinks and future collaboration. Using the example of the Production Technology Center (PTZ) in Berlin, we will demonstrate how this can be achieved with the aid of a two-dimensional Industrie 4.0 research map.

The PTZ, serving as a double institute of the Fraunhofer Institute for Production Systems and Design Technology (IPK) and the Institute for Machine Tools and Factory Management (IWF) of the Technical University of Berlin, with more than 400 employees, represents the pivotal Industrie 4.0 pacesetter in the German capital city. Through close cooperation with industry, in a continual circuit between basic research and application orientation, solutions have been found here since 1979 in a wide spectrum, from the factory of the future to virtual product creation to medical technology. Four of the current 17 Industrie 4.0 projects in the city alone call the PTZ home, and a few are portrayed in the following.

10.2 Projects at the Production Technology Center in Berlin

To start, we will describe a few selected Industrie 4.0 research and development projects, including their Industrie 4.0 core solution elements, currently running at the Fraunhofer Institute for Production Systems and Design Technology (IPK) and the Institute for Machine Tools and Factory Management (IWF) of the Technical University of Berlin and locate them on a research map.

10.2.1 IWEPRO—Intelligent Self-Organizing Workshop Production [2]

In large-batch production runs, such as in the automotive industry, production lines are primarily employed which are geared toward specific components. However, due to the wealth of variants, such rigid production systems are reaching their limits, especially with regard to continual reactivity, capacity utilization and delivery dependability. In workshop production having decentral control, even reaching self-organizing, product-controlled manufacturing with a situative instead of a rigid allocation of operations and manufacturing resources, industry sees the potential to make manufacturing more flexible on the whole, as well as more robust and reactive toward unplanned events. Intelligent, cooperating subsystems and components in the sense of cyber-physical production systems (CPPS) and the integration of workshop personnel with their experience-based knowledge, offer a promising approach.

Manufacturing enterprises consequently expect an optimization of their production processes, especially in the realms of small lots and varying products requiring individual passes through production. Intelligent, self-organizing workshop production will offer a higher degree of flexibility in adaptively controlling the course of processing and dynamically reacting to unplanned events.

The goal is to develop solutions with which it will be possible for networked products, production machines, transportation systems and manufacturing resources to exchange order and production information among themselves and cooperate with the workers in a task- and situation-oriented manner. Such "smart" workshop production enables foresighted planning and goal-oriented allocation for pending production orders. The focus is on the synchronization of central and decentral control and monitoring functions through the connection of the virtual information and communication world with the real objects, the integration of workshop employees for planning, control and monitoring tasks in a cyber-physical production system and methodical support for the participatory design and implementation of such solutions. It is necessary for the staff working with this system to be sufficiently prepared for their new task, which requires a high degree of flexibility.

Starting with the boundary conditions in a delimited manufacturing area, the scenario for future workshop production is conceived and modeled with intelligent, communicating components. The interplay of decentral, distributed production control with the system components and the performance of the overall system are examined using simulations. In this project, tools for modeling and simulation are being generated, as are an adaptive production management system, a suitable communication infrastructure, a knowledge-based, self-learning workshop control system, autonomous, decentral software agents, an interoperable machine tool as well as intelligent equipment. This development work is accompanied by sociological job research, in order to involve the management as well as production employees in the user-friendly design process right from the start, integrate them seamlessly as participants in the production system and prepare qualification perspectives.

In this process, a migration concept is being developed which includes gradational, decentral intelligence and the networking of subsystems. This incorporates comprehensive technology, business process and qualification in the form of an expandable shell model with products, machines, tools, equipment and transportation systems. The testing and validation of the new self-organizing shop manufacturing system with the integration of shop employees is done in an application scenario for parts production with high versatility in automotive engineering.

The expected results will also be able to be used by other system providers and industrial sectors for the manufacture of high quality, versatile products, for example in the metalworking industry with their supplier companies, in mechanical engineering, automotive engineering or medical technology. The solutions for self-organizing shop manufacturing offer the potential for broad transfer, especially to small and medium-size manufacturing shops.

10.2.2 VC-SHP—Virtual Commissioning with Smart Hybrid Prototyping [3]

Virtual reality (VR) is excellent as a medium for coordination in interdisciplinary teams. All participating disciplines can benefit from its strong visual expressiveness, as well as from the navigation options, spatial searches, work step planning and creative support. Economic advantages, such as the reduction of changes through early product visualization and product testing, resulting from the use of VR in industrial development processes, are empirically documented.

For large-scale manufacturing companies, tools and methods of digital factory planning are also part of the state of the art. For instance, they use virtual commissioning (VC), also in combination with VR methods, to visually check ascertainable characteristics. Task- and function-oriented interactions, on the other hand, cannot yet be achieved using VR, due to a lack of interaction technology.

The challenges of using these virtual technologies lie in the occurrence of data discontinuity events, the export of production system CAD data to VR as well as VC tools, which, to date, have interfered with widespread use of these virtual technologies. A lack of consistency also exists, for example in forwarding kinematic information or metadata from PDM systems to the processing systems of VR and VC.

Within the context of the joint project "Virtual Commissioning with Smart Hybrid Prototyping—Modular Systems for the tangible Validation of VC-SHP Systems" a modular system is thus being developed with which small and medium-scale plant manufacturers and suppliers can quickly and easily generate functional prototypes of manufacturing systems with virtual technology. These hybrid prototypes are to be capable of being functionally tested and improved during the conceptual stage by all parties involved in the development process—constructors, workers, customers, managers, production and plant planners, even before they are manufactured and assembled. Subsequent users should also be able to be more deeply involved in the development of manufacturing systems and processes than was previously possible.

The goal of the joint project is to cultivate an interactive development environment for virtual plant prototypes in which the interplay of mechanics, electrical systems and software can be functionally tested and the developers of the various domains can use a central model as the discussion basis for their collaboration. The development process is supported by the SHP module. In addition to providing the domain-specific partial models for automation technology components (mCAD, eCAD, behavior models), it also provides partial models for haptic interaction and enables testing of control elements of a plant in coordination with the customer and future operators, at an early stage in the development process. A further demand of the project is to consider and secure the control of requirements and influences of Industrie 4.0 in the development process of plants. In order to plan a networked production system in the early development phases, behavior models of the plant and surrounding production IT systems are used to validate system controls. In addition, a method is being developed to transfer virtual control to real control which, after extensive testing, can be confidently connected to the real systems.

10.2.3 PICASSO—Cloud-Based Control [4–6]

In the realm of robotics and complex automation systems, each individual machine has its own closed, so-called monolithic control. The processing power in them is rarely used under normal operation. However, if, for example, complex algorithms need to be calculated for process optimization, the capacity of conventional control systems will not suffice. A scaling or adapting of processing power to the algorithms being calculated is currently not possible. This means that the integration of functions for production systems with cyber-physical systems cannot be achieved. In the case of smartphones, solutions already exist in which, for instance, computationally intensive speech recognition algorithms are not calculated on the smartphone, but in the cloud.

The goal of the research project pICASSO is thus the provision of a scalable control platform for cyber-physical systems in industrial production. It offers scalable processing power that is automatically made available depending on the complexity of the algorithms. The monolithic control technology is broken up and relocated to the cloud. When doing so, the strict requirements of production engineering, such as real-time capability, accessibility and security, must continue to be observed. Furthermore, scalability and mutability improve while costs are reduced, for instance, by saving on parts for the control hardware.

A server-capable control platform is being developed for cloud-based industrial control platforms in cyber-physical systems which calculates control functions on a hardware-independent basis. To do so, previous control functions are modularized and expanded to include cloud-computing mechanisms, such as central data processing. For the connection of remaining local actuators and sensors to the control platform, suitable communication mechanisms are analyzed and expanded. Based on that, added value services to increase production efficiency, such as simulation and visualization of complex production processes for human interaction, are being examined. The safety aspects regarding sensitive data and the protection of operating personnel are taken into consideration over the course of the entire project.

The project results are demonstrated on robots and production plants that are controlled via the cloud. Dissemination of the results is taking place as an open-source project. This control platform can also be employed in other sectors, such as the pharmaceutical industry, which requires uninterrupted documentation of process steps. It offers a basis for self-organized production with the opportunity to create innovative business models (e.g. the app concept).

10.2.4 MetamoFAB—Metamorphosis into an Intelligent and Networked Factory [7, 8]

The successful manufacturing enterprises of tomorrow place their trust in efficient, result-oriented communication and cooperation along the entire value creation chain. The introduction of cyber-physical systems (CPS) in companies can increase the mutability of production conditions and contribute to an increase in the flexibility of production and logistics. All process-related stakeholders, such as people, machines, workpieces and information technology, must be involved. To do so, it is necessary to prepare companies for the paradigm change to Industrie 4.0 through an introductory process. Only with a clear CPS implementation strategy can a company of today develop into a smart production company of tomorrow without the susceptibility of disturbances in business operations.

The goal of the research project MetamoFAB is to enable the metamorphosis of existing factories into intelligent and networked factories. According to the vision of CPS, significant increases in productivity and flexibility can thus be achieved. The three application scenarios "Production of Automation Technology," "Semiconductor Manufacture" and "Manufacture of Electrotechnical Components," as well as the definition of related requirements and realization paths form the basis of the planned metamorphosis into a CPS factory.

One of the planned solutions is the definition of suitable rules for decision processes in networked systems with decentral intelligence. For this, a decision model is being developed under consideration of all involved stakeholders in a networked factory structure. Using this model, rules for coordination procedures with varying planning horizons and optimization goals, for example for the production planning process, are derived. The qualification of people, who will increasingly take on the role of flexible problem solvers, and the generation of decision capability from the technical side, are supported by the development of new networked and flexible organization structures for CPS factories of the future. Through parallel real-time mapping and the calculation of possible decision options, the behavior of all elements capable of making decisions according to the developed rules are virtually validated. Methods and tools for the planning of the transformation process are developed under the explicit consideration of step-by-step realization in real application environments.

The overall result of the project are methods and tools for the planning, support and execution of the metamorphosis of existing factories into intelligent and networked factories in the sense of the future-oriented project *Industrie 4.0*. The usability of the procedures and tools in MetamoFAB are tested and, upon successful validation, demonstrated in the real application environments of the industry partners. In order to ensure the transfer to industry, multi-application and multi-industry procedures and necessary qualification processes are developed for the planning, support and execution of the transformation into a future CPS factory. They offer German production enterprises considerable support in increasing the efficiency of their existing factories through the use of CPS systems.

10.2.5 Allocation of Projects at the Production Technology Center Berlin

A brief description of just four research projects alone underscores the fact that Industrie 4.0 must cover a much wider spectrum than smart production. This applies to addressing the lifecycle phases as well as to the thematic spectrum of the technologies, from the purely digital, interpersonal and human-with-machine interactions, up to strategic embedding and business model development. The research map of Industrie 4.0 (see Fig. 10.1) displays these differentiation characteristics and allocates them in a 3 × 4 matrix. On the y-axis, the projects and activities are organized according to their relationship to the lifecycle phases of product and service development, systems and factory development, operative production and use and service in the field. The x-axis shows content-based allocation in the realms of technology, collaboration and strategy. Figure 10.1 allocates the projects at the Production Technology Center accordingly.

Figure 10.1 demonstrates how multi-level research of the topic of Industrie 4.0 can be successful on the horizontal as well as vertical levels. Project results enable

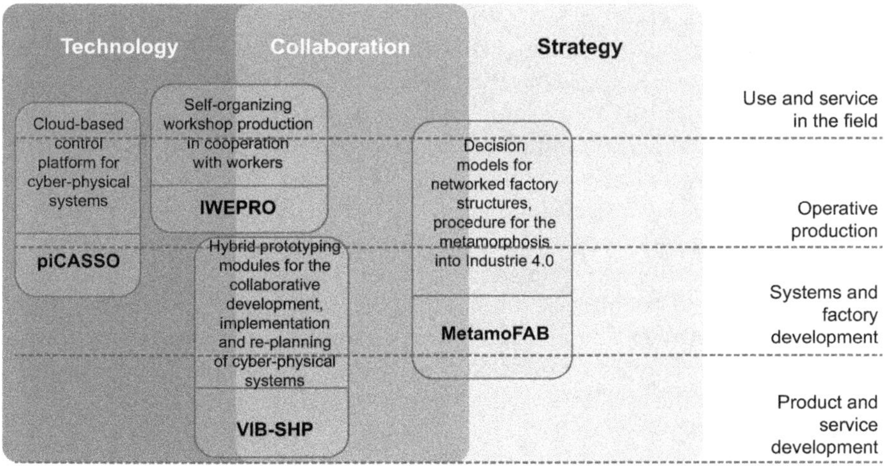

Fig. 10.1 Industrie 4.0 research map, allocation of selected Industrie 4.0 projects at the Production Technology Center Berlin. (IPK)

developing and manufacturing enterprises to gradually equip themselves for Industrie 4.0. In order to intensify the comprehensive embedding of the presented and other activities relating to the topic of digital transformation, the Berlin Fraunhofer Institutes FOKUS, IZM, HHI and IPK have joined to form a digital networking performance center. In the future, the application areas and trending topics of mobility, city of the future, medical technology, health, energy, critical infrastructures, production and Industrie 4.0 will be researched in Berlin in an integrated manner. The joint goal of the institutes is to process solutions for the challenges of digital networking with regard to security, robustness, speed and quality of information and communication networks and the use of generated information. The question as to how information can be used in a profitable way over the entire process and value creation chain, from the initial product idea to recycling, is being researched at the Fraunhofer Institute for Production Systems and Design Technology (IPK) under the heading "Service Engineering": because it is clear that information and its interpretation will be experienced as the crystallization point for digital innovations, new services and business models, a new understanding of the world and thus as the trailblazer for a completely new way of experiencing product development.

10.3 Industrial Information Technology as the Metronome of Industrie 4.0

The fourth industrial revolution is largely characterized by the increasing digitalization and networking of products in their production and utilization contexts. Accordingly, value creation chains and business models will change in the future. Consciousness of this phenomenon has already formed in industry and research, as is shown by various studies (see also pwc: *Industrie 4.0—Chancen und Herausforderungen der vierten industriellen Revolution*). In most companies, a consciousness of great change already exists on a strategic level, which has developed in some areas but not yet collectively. However, this does not automatically mean that companies are ready to act on it. One major contribution to being capable to act is provided by industrial information technology (IIT). Industrial information technology deals with the further development of digital solutions for the improvement and expansion of engineering activities in the entire course of virtual product manufacturing, i.e. from the product idea through product development up to the planning and procedural safeguarding of production, as well as during factory operation and, increasingly, also during the operation of products in the field. In the course of expanded digitalization and networking, product and production intelligence must be increasingly heightened. This brings with it new challenges and potential to industrial information technology. Future topics in IIT are seen as being between intelligent products and production, but also between smart products with their environment and infrastructure.

The primary goal of Industrie 4.0 in the context of industrial information technology is the seamless integration of the real and virtual worlds. Significant elements of the virtual word include simulation, planning and explanatory models (also: descriptive models), which Industrie 4.0 engineers will have to use more often in the operation of plants and production systems and of products in the field for successful control. Explanatory models are used to virtually and digitally map the real world. Existing situations, such as real production processes, can be virtually mapped and improvements added to the procedures, such as the optimization of resource efficiency. In planning models, on the other hand, a virtual world is initially generated, which subsequently is to be realized. The goal of industrial information technology is to integrate both planning and explanatory models with each other. This will lead to a symbiosis of real and digital factory and product operation. In an ideal situation, the real factory can be controlled from the virtual factory planning or real product services can be performed with the aid of OT services, based on the planning models of integrated product-service systems. In the course of Industrie 4.0, this is planned to be integrated not only vertically, but also horizontally. While horizontal integration refers to the digital continuity of lifecycle and value stream levels in RAMI, vertical integration refers to the hierarchy levels (see Fig. 10.2). It is important to note that the depiction of the lifecycle, based in the design of IEC 62890, is very simplified, and does not do justice to the actual complexity of the lifecycles of technical systems. The differentiation according to "type" and "instance" indicates that a product is first virtually created (type) and subsequently realized in production as a real system (instance).

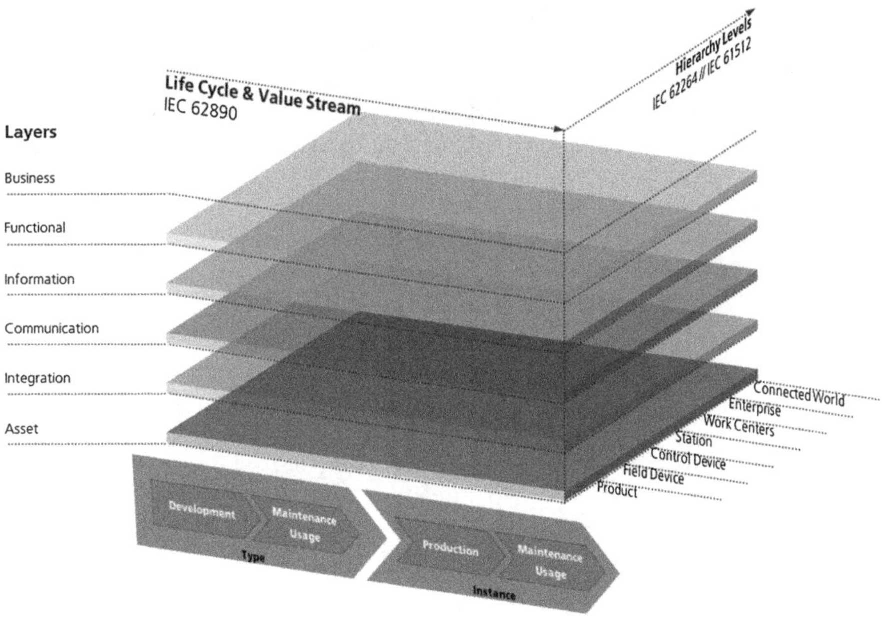

Fig. 10.2 The reference architecture model RAMI 4.0 of the *Plattform Industrie 4.0*. (www.zvei.org [9]; Plattform Industrie 4.0)

Under consideration of the various layers, the problem of interoperability between previously existing partial solutions needs to be solved for the future.

With the aid of digital/virtual models, simulations of vertical and/or horizontal value chain networks can be created, in order to enable tough decisions to be made (for example: using digital/virtual planning models, decisions can be made regarding resource and information flow in a current or future factory). It is important to connect different models with each other, in order to enable resolute decisions via PPR (product process resource).

From this, the following research topics have developed for information management in Industrie 4.0:

- Digital continuity of engineering over the entire value creation chain: integration of the real and virtual worlds
  - Development of an application-capable, data-driven modeling theory for vertical and horizontal integration
  - Development of a generally-valid meta planning model for horizontal integration for companies
- Digital continuity of engineering across the entire value creation chain: systems engineering
  - Development of methods and information technology tools for the integrative development of mechatronic products in relation to their interaction with other technical systems or the environment
  - Development of an engineering process chain for the integrative development of product, process and production systems
- Industrie 4.0 platform with reference architectures and distributed service-oriented architecture
  - Development of a reference architecture for the new "digital model worlds of the future" beyond today's partial architectures "PLM," "ERP," "SCM," "Digital Factory/Digital Manufacturing," "Shop Floor IT," and "Service Portals" for the determination of the interoperability of software products and services, as well as other solutions from various manufacturers. Within this context, the initiative "Industrial Data Space" [10] is worth mentioning, having the goal of providing reference architecture for the supply chain.
  - Development of a general deployment and migration strategy from the current IT construction in engineering to the future system world of "digital working worlds."

Through performing research on these topics, engineers hope to become capable of cooperatively conceiving and validating Industrie 4.0 solutions, as well as adapting them to running operations.

10.4 Information Factories—the New Digital Workbenches

Information technology, as a significant solution source for digital transformation, today provides technologies for generating data in development, production and the utilization phase in previously unknown dimensions. For instance, a modern CNC machine already produces 30 TB of data per year, while a factory generates 2 EB of log data annually, and on a domestic flight with a Boeing 737, 240 TB of data are generated. The networking of all realms of life in the Internet of Everything will accelerate this immense data growth even more. For instance, experts estimate that the global data stock will increase by almost five times its current size by 2020, from 8.6 to more than 40 zettabytes [11]. In order to be able to consolidate these huge amounts of data (big data) into value-creation-relevant information conceivable to people, smart data algorithms are already being employed. In the dynamic systems of Industrie 4.0, however, the question is raised as to who requires what information when and in what quality, and which data can deliver new findings in what combination.

Thus, a challenge, previously not comprehensive enough, is to plan information logistics ahead, from development to the product lifecycle end and to implement it as an integral component of product creation and manufacturing operation. The ability to structure, secure and control information flow in an economically and technically optimal way is a measure for the successful implementation of the vision of an intelligent Industrie 4.0 system. Beyond the existing methodical and technological gap, further factors must be taken into consideration. For instance, as digitalization has led to a geographical leveling out of where performance and new stakeholders are situated, the coexistence of standards hinder the development of comprehensive information logistics. In addition, a solution must also take into account the fact that each enterprise is following its own migration path toward Industrie 4.0.

Based on the classic meaning of a factory, the business sector Virtual Product Creation of the Fraunhofer IPK, in close cooperation with the department of Industrial Information Technology at the TU Berlin, is researching and developing the **Information Factory**—an alliance of several different "digital workbenches," whose commodity is information as a production factor. The Information Factory is a platform that implements comprehensive IT concepts in support of the development, production and utilization of cyber-physical products and production facilities within the context of intelligent and self-organized production sites or field use. Regarding the use of intelligent algorithms, the Information Factory provides functions with which circumstances in product development, production and utilization can be visualized, analyzed and optimized. Thus, the Information Factory supplies the fundamental data processing architecture that connects relevant data sources and enables bearers of knowledge (product knowledge of development engineers, market knowledge of corporate executives, data analysis knowledge of data scientists or third parties) to reach cooperative decisions and design intelligent information logistics. The Information Factory is considered to be an operator environment for intelligent, networked products and production facilities.

Definition of the Information Factory
The Information Factory refers to the vertical and horizontal interconnection of the whole of all necessary information systems (PLM, ERP, SCM, IoT, etc.) and expertise for the operator platforms of the future. Along the product lifecycle, the Information Factory serves as an integrated operation environment for the information-driven development, production and operation of products, production facilities and services.

- For this purpose, the Information Factory combines existing data (both unstructured and structured) and intelligences (control and behavior logistics) of technical systems (mechatronic, cybertronic) using smart data approaches to form higher-quality, value-creating information.
- The processing of (smart) data into information and continuative decisions (intelligences) is conducted in the Information Factory centrally (such as with the aid of a cloud-based, back-end server) as well as decentrally at the sites of local information processing (fog and edge computing).
- Within the fully-networked Industrie 4.0, the Information Factory enables the analysis, control and alteration of technical systems and accompanying processes in the sense of an increasing degree of autonomy.

Figure 10.3 shows a diagram of how information-based interaction of value-creation participants or information logistics will function between the instances of the Information Factory via a secured cloud. Beyond classic, multi-company collaboration, the Information Factory also enables new forms of collaboration through the integration of any third party (such as data scientists, freelancers or scientists from complementary knowledge domains) using the app principle.

Individual instances of the Information Factory communicate via a secured corporate cloud and connect third-party providers and their expertise via apps to value creation and information processing.

Within the context of research, initially, three exemplary application scenarios will be realized, using the example of the Lot Size 1 of the production demo cell "Smart Factory 4.0." This is a testing and validation environment for the Information Factory and digital twin methods. The application scenario of virtual commissioning achieves the validation of the re-configuration of processes within the demo cell and the adaption of control programs in the virtual room. At a consistent quality level, however, quick re-planning and cost and time savings can also be achieved through the parallelization of plant and control development. A second application scenario, process-accompanying simulation, shows the potential embedded in the implementation of digital twins using the Information Factory. The array of variants is countered with what is now known in manufacturing as batching, that is, the systematic processing of stacks of similar tasks. Using the Information Factory, however, a real production of a lot size of 1 is made possible.

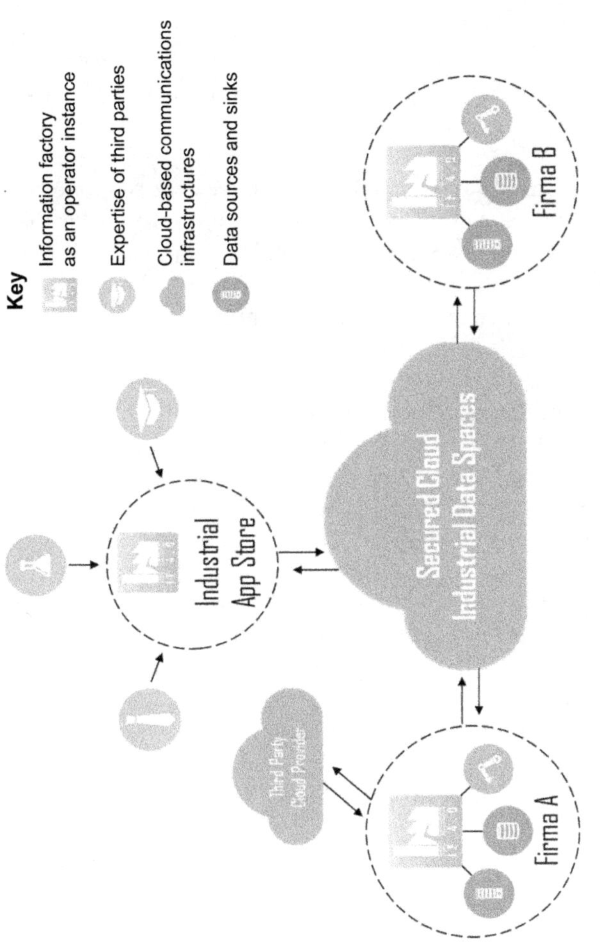

Fig. 10.3 Schematic depiction of the use of Information Factories. (IPK)

Starting from component geometry and product definition, cyber-physical production systems simulate ad hoc production processes and implement the optimal process. As a result, planning efforts can be reduced by decreasing the necessary planning depth, costs and time are cut down, thus making the manufacture of lot size 1 considerably more economical. The third application scenario, business intelligence, addresses the use of smart data. With Industrie 4.0, information logistics is changing. The introduction of new sensors and actuators has led to the breakdown of the automation pyramid, meaning that cascading data aggregation is no longer necessary. Distributed intelligences are networked and new data sources and data sinks must be served. Turning away from traditional information logistics makes it necessary to have solutions at the ready which enable plant operators to make well-founded decisions and intervene to influence control. Using a web-based information dashboard, relevant data from the participating information and communications systems can be combined and consolidated to information within the context of product and domain know-how. In turn, the user is then able to gain intuitive access to functions such as data mining, data analytics and visual analytics—in short, smart data. Web and industry standards such as POC UA, Node.js and COAP are used for this purpose. The information dashboard improves the quality of analysis and decision-making and helps to save money and time in operative production and engineering.

Implementing the Information Factory, and respectively, the application cases presented, is based on the concept of the digital twin. The goal of a digital twin is to create a convergence between the real product in its context and its virtual map. With regard to RAMI 4.0, this means that, for every "type," not only a real but also a virtual, bidirectionally coupled "instance" must exist. Bidirectional coupling enables changes to the virtual model (such as software alterations for the interactive behavior of a robot with its environment) to be assumed by the product, on the one hand, and on the other, data from the product can be fed back into the virtual model and the processes of product lifecycle management, in order to be able to offer predictive maintenance services, for instance. A digital twin is required to secure physical processes in the virtual realm, for one, as well as to control and coordinate dynamic interactions of the CPS in real usage. Digital twins can be seen as the next evolutionary step in the development moving from a DMU to an FMU and up to the virtual prototypes. Since such a digital twin is continually fed with information from the Internet of Things, we call it a "living digital twin."

The concept of the Information Factory, the living digital twin and the application scenarios described, however, cannot at this time be converted ad hoc to industrial application. This is due to the fact that, especially from an information technology point of view, prerequisites such as the networking of information from development and planning only partly exist. In addition, data stemming from the domains of development, planning, work preparation and production exist in differing, heterogenous formats and thus cannot be directly used for the Information Factory. In order to meet this challenge and allow for a gradual migration, the "Industrie 4.0" step model has been developed (see Fig. 10.4).

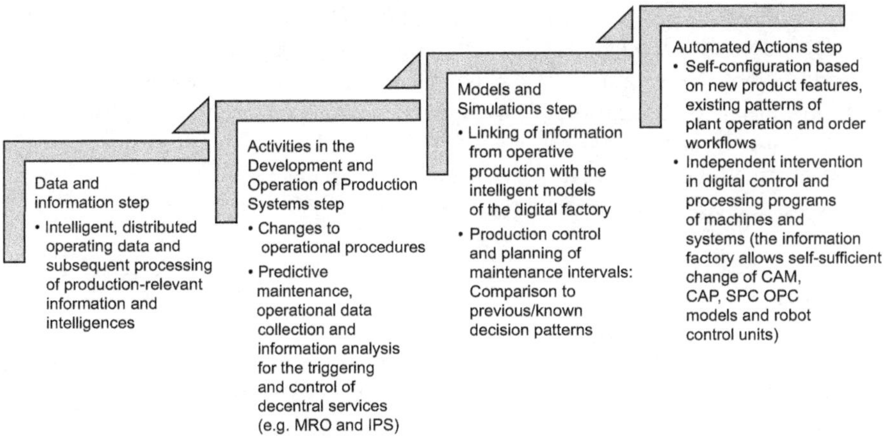

Fig. 10.4 "Industrie 4.0" step model for the implementation and operationalization of information management on the way to the Information Factory. (IPK)

Starting with the step "Data and Information," an intelligent, distributed operational and machine data collection must be implemented as a prerequisite to the product-relevant processing of contained information and intelligences. Based on this, in the second step, "Activities in the Development and Operation of Production Systems," information-driven changes to operational processes and the control of services are possible, such as in the realm of predictive maintenance. In addition, Step 2 enables product development to develop optimal hybrid performance bundles. Once the decentral activities have been defined and achieved, the "Models and Simulations Step" can be reached. Decentral services can be used to obtain information on operative production and link it with intelligent models of the Digital Factory, for instance, intelligent simulation or optimization models of maintenance planning or production control. In this step, known or successfully achieved decision patterns should also be taken into consideration, in order to enable a self-learning factory. The last step, the "Automated Actions Step," is not only intended to influence the planning of processes, but also change and optimize those processes. This makes autonomous reconfiguration possible, based on new product characteristics, existing patterns and workflows.

The Information Factory serves the implementation of the steps presented throughout the entire lifecycle. It enables information extraction and aggregation, and makes knowledge regarding the control of product lifecycles available. The fascinating question is in what way this knowledge will be made available and utilized. Similar to the Web 2.0, information factories have the potential to disruptively alter development, production and operation. The increasing convergence of reality and virtuality, tendencies toward the democratization of product creation and development (the open source and maker scene) and the monetary valuation of the information capital (infonomics) are cultivating a moment which can have a great influence on the development of Germany as an industrial location. No matter where this development leads, it is vital to develop new capabilities now, in order to be able to react to the ever-increasing pace of global changes. The digital workbench that is the information factory is seen as an enabler innovation, with which to successfully participate in a global redistribution of value creation shares in an information-based way. The necessary components, IT services and intelligences are already in development and being tested.

References

1. Förderkatalog. (2014). German Federal Ministry of Education and Research: Hightech Strategie, German Federal Ministry for Economic Affairs and Energy: Autonomik für Industrie 4.0.
2. www.projekt-iwepro.de. Accessed May 12 2016.
3. www.ipk.fraunhofer.de. Accessed May 12 2016.
4. www.ipk.fraunhofer.de. Accessed May 12 2016.
5. www.produktionsforschung.de. Accessed May 12 2016.
6. www.projekt-picasso.de. Accessed May 12 2016.
7. www.produktionsforschung.de. Accessed May 12 2016.
8. www.metamofab.de. Accessed May 12 2016.
9. Industrie 4.0: Das Referenzarchitekturmodell Industrie 4.0 (RAMI 4.0). www.zvei.org. Accessed May 12 2016.
10. http://www.fraunhofer.de/de/forschung/fraunhofer-initiativen/industrial-data-space.html. Accessed May 12 2016.
11. IDC (2012). *The Digtal Universe in 2020.*

Part III

Articles from Industry

Industrie 4.0 is an initiative attempting to turn a vision into reality. Consequently, there is a great deal of theory in this book, and as realistic as the articles from research in the previous chapters are, their ideas have been only limitedly applied to industrial reality as of yet. But the big question is: How quickly and favorably can the visions, ideas and theories be implemented in industrial processes, the organization of enterprises and the reality of factories and their networks? That is why the topic of Industrie 4.0 would be incomplete without a few concrete examples from practical situations. The following five chapters provide exactly that: concrete examples from very different areas and with very different positions on Industrie 4.0. Among them are large corporations, as well as small and midsize enterprises; companies from the areas of discrete manufacturing, automation and process industry, but also from the IT realm; components manufacturers are represented, as are suppliers of comprehensive solutions and cloud platforms. The chapters are presented in the alphabetical order of the respective company names.

Christopher Ganz is the Group Service R&D manager at ABB. In his article, he not only explains how processes and products change in the wake of progressing digitalization. He also demonstrates that, for an international corporation such as ABB, *Industrie 4.0* is only one initiative of several, including the Industrial Internet Consortium and other platforms, in which ABB participates. He emphasizes the firm's special approach reflected in the company's motto "The Internet of Things, Services and People." Not only is the focus on new technologies, networking and the autonomous decision-making of intelligent, developed machines and devices, but also and especially people, for whom data-based services are ultimately being developed.

Dr. Roman Dumitrescu, the manager for Strategy, Research and Development at it's OWL, not only represents just one company. it's OWL is the nationally recognized cluster "Intelligent Technical Systems OstWestfalenLippe," in which many firms of the region, primarily SMEs, have come together to jointly find their road into the digital future in close cooperation with various research institutes. His chapter shows not only the approach of this unique collaboration, but, using practical examples from work done by the cluster, also describes how this particular organization is contributing to an enormous spread of the basis for Industrie 4.0 ideas.

Dr. Tanja Rückert is the Executive Vice President at SAP, responsible for product development for the Internet of Things and Industrie 4.0. Among the IT powerhouses, SAP is one of the most important representatives with headquarters in Germany. It is active in leading positions both in the *Plattform Industrie 4.0* and the IIC. The products of SAP for IT support in moving toward the Internet of Things have already been productively employed by several companies – whether in the realms of predictive maintenance or intelligent logistics. Also, SAP's IoT platform is considered as one of the reference architectures for Industrie 4.0.

At the time this book was completed, Anton Sebastian Huber served as the CEO of the Digital Factory Division at Siemens AG. The transformation of the automation company to an enterprise offering top solutions for industry software around the world in the form of its Digital Enterprise Software Suite is closely tied with his efforts spanning several years. In recent years, Siemens was not only on the board of directors at the *Plattform Industrie 4.0*, but also invested a great deal itself in the integration of its own software solutions to support a consistent digital value creation chain. Today, Siemens also offers MindSphere, an industrial cloud platform.

Dr. Stefan Michels, head of the Standards and Technology Development division at Weidmüller, is one of the pioneers at the aforementioned cluster it's OWL. In several projects, his firm, with its own concepts and innovations, serves as a positive example for the large number of small and midsize industrial enterprises which, in connection with larger corporations, have secured globally leading positions for Germany in the manufacturing industry. This chapter shows that, in the next step of industrial development as well, focus must also be placed on this part of industry.

Of course, as is the case for the articles on research: In these five chapters, excellent examples have been collected which are only representative for the several hundred projects which in the meantime have been initiated. It is also largely a matter of coincidence as to which companies ultimately have the time and interest to publicly present their position and strategy in a book.

This editor is thus all the more thankful for the following articles. They prove that the engine is now in motion – and that we can already discern what course must be set.

11 The Internet of Things, Services and People

Christopher Ganz

Abstract

ABB (Asea Brown Boveri) is an energy and automation engineering corporation based in Zurich. In 1988, it resulted from the fusion of the Swedish ASEA company and the Swiss firm BBC. ABB employs approximately 140,000 persons worldwide in 100 countries, and comprises more than 330 consolidated subsidiaries. Its range includes products and solutions for power generation, transfer and distribution, systems and services for power companies, motors, drives and industrial automation as well as systems for the automation and optimization of industrial processes. ABB is a typical investment goods manufacturer with products, systems and services for the manufacturing and process industry. ABB was represented by the head of the research center in Ladenburg, Dr. Christian Zeidler, in the German working group *Industrie 4.0* by acatech and the research union, whose results were submitted to the German government in April of 2013 in the form of "implementation recommendations." Soon after the foundation of the Industrial Internet Consortium, ABB became a member of its committee. Both of these initiatives represent the most significant externally visible efforts for enterprises with regard to the next stage of industrial development, and are thus treated at the executive level. In several other initiatives in various countries and regions of the world, ABB is also active in cooperation with the respective local organizations.

In the year 2014, the corporation formulated the slogan "Internet of Things, Services and People (IoTSP)" for its position within the context of its next-level strategy. It is intended to express that, in the further development of industry, not only the utilization of the internet for products and services is important, but also

C. Ganz (✉)
ABB Technology Ltd, Affolternstrasse 44, 8050 Zurich, Switzerland
E-Mail: christopher.ganz@ch.abb.com

U. Sendler (ed.), *The Internet of Things*,
https://doi.org/10.1007/978-3-662-54904-9_11

that especially in this step, people are the focus. According to ABB, the Internet of Things is no more or no less than a means to an end. That end is the optimization, flexibilization and increase in productivity of industrial processes and the use of advanced services for the benefit of people.

11.1 Now We Know How to Do It

In the last few years, in which the discussion on the further development of industry, especially sparked by the initiative *Industrie 4.0*, but also through the Industrial Internet Consortium, has been conducted with a great breadth, spanning all social areas, not much has actually changed. We don't see that industry—by which we mean the discrete manufacturing as well as the process industry—has actually already taken a significant step in the much-discussed direction of the vision of Industrie 4.0. Yet the discussion has nevertheless been very influential. We now know a lot better what we are talking about. We know better which challenges lay ahead of us. And we know where the people with the right solutions are in our own company and outside of it.

However, it is not the case that the discussion itself first set this development into motion. My own initial slides on this topic are a few years older than that. ABB had already developed its "Aspect Object" technology at the beginning of the millennium, in connection with the development of the process control system 800xA. The Aspect Object technology basically alludes to what is now called the cyber-physical system. In 2001, there was a whitepaper entitled "Aspect Object technology—Industrial^{IT} Solutions from ABB." If you look at the illustrations in a report on the subject from 2010, it is immediately reminiscent of similar ones now be found in the reference architectures of *Industrie 4.0* and the Industrial Internet Consortium (see Fig. 11.1).

To that extent, discussions taking place in the initiative as well as the reference architectures defined in them for the digital factory or an individual Industrie 4.0 component are nothing really new to ABB. Yet, it would have been amazing if, on the contrary, something completely different had come out of it than what resulted from our market and customer-oriented research and development.

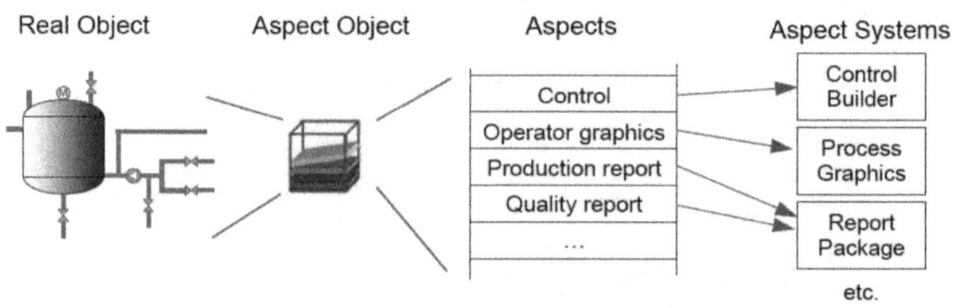

Fig. 11.1 ABB's Aspect Object system of 2001. (Whitepaper ABB 2010, p. 3)

When the term 'Industrie 4.0' was coined a few years ago, nobody except the members of the working group *Industrie 4.0* really knew what that meant. For a long time, there was not even an official definition of the term. All of the other terms closely associated with it were also unclear and ambiguous. Big data, smart data, smart factory, smart service, the Internet of Things and Services—all of these expressions were not self-explanatory. Everyone seemed to understand them slightly differently. Members of the working group from the IT industry saw the expressions and terminology from a different perspective than members from the realm of investment goods manufacturing. There were no differentiations, nor was there a common understanding of how the individual terms were related to each other or overlapped. The past few years have been characterized by creating clarity and forming a platform of common understanding.

Today, there is an officially recognized definition of Industrie 4.0, the *Industrie 4.0* implementation recommendations were replaced in the spring of 2015 by a clearly-formulated implementation strategy and initial results from the various working groups now exist. The image has become clearer, reachable goals have been defined more recognizably, if not tangibly. Nobody is asking any more whether it is all just hype. On the contrary, all participants in industry want to know what they can do to be successful in the next phase of the industrial revolution—of which meanwhile everyone knows that, in reality, it is more of a rapid continued development of the technological evolution.

Industry has discussed how its world will look in the future. At the same time, it investigated which paths lead there, which technologies and methods and which tools they need to successfully follow those paths. Today, we can say: There is agreement on where we want to go from here. We also know what we need, and that we have or can create the means with which to do so. Now we know how to do it. And, like ABB, many have already begun to implement this knowledge in practical measures.

Industrie 4.0 is kind of like the moon landing in the 1960s: The goal was clear, the technology required for reaching the goal was developed step by step and component by component, but it took a while, twenty years to be exact, until the first person set foot on the moon. The development of Industrie 4.0 is taking a similar route: We know what it means, we know what we need to have and do. Yet just how it will really turn out will only be seen in several years.

For us at ABB, Industrie 4.0, as well as the industrial internet, are core elements for our comprehensive understanding of the Internet of Things, Services and People. The networking of software-controlled devices and systems via the internet enables the range of systems and services that help people in industry to complete their tasks faster, more flexibly, efficiently and better than before. We know how we will achieve this. The technology exists, and the cloud as a technical element plays a significant role. The Internet of Things is technology, and technology is the means to the end. That end purpose includes advanced services with which the technology can be utilized. The next step after networking and digesting the technical elements is the implementation of advanced service products. They will be created in the coming years, and will become the center of discussion.

11.2 The "Intelligence" of Machines

In the discussion surrounding the role of the internet, the fact often gets ignored that the actual heart of the development, including of Industrie 4.0, is the software—the gigantic advances than have been made by digitalization and that are still being made. Technological development—for instance in the cloud—has brought virtually limitless storage capacity. Processing power and the development of algorithms have been increased so enormously that processes can be calculated and consequently precisely planned and optimized which, just a few years ago, were completely impossible.

In the chemical industry, several processes run relatively slowly. Previously, we would spend twelve hours performing measurements at our customer locations which were then evaluated. ABB had a model of the process that effectively supplied the target data. This target data was compared with the actual data, and the calculated result provided the ammunition for optimizing the process.

Then, in the realm of drive systems and components, the optimization of the control system, which runs in one-second cycles, could be undertaken with the aid of software. It initially took several minutes until reliable results could be obtained which allowed adjustments to the control system. Today, highly-complex processes can be calculated in fractions of seconds, enabling, for instance, the virtually infinitely variable and imperceptible driving of a motor using software in such a way that the motor operates with the highest possible efficiency and the lowest consumption of resources.

It is this digitalization in the devices and machines that allows them to appear "intelligent," because they seem to switch and optimize their own operation magically or based on their own "thinking," and they do it with more precision than a human could. However, in truth, it is the intelligence of the programmers that enables the machines to work like that. They have written the software such that exactly those things happen that they have observed as being optimal under given and predictable conditions. The machines only run the logical program, which nowadays is supplied with data by a number of sensors, and can react to that data.

Of course, humans can continue furthering this development. There are research projects in which extremely complex procedures are broken down into their smallest individual aspects and functions. So-called software agents are then programmed which individually only treat a single aspect and have a single, tiny task to complete. Then, the software agents are interconnected to obtain the overall task. The development of a swarm intelligence is being studied here, not unlike that of creatures of the most varied of species.

However, this type of research is still far from being applied to industrial processes. And any doubts about whether it will ever be safe enough to use for industrial processes are completely valid. Currently in industry, a deterministic way of thinking is so prevalent that the actual autonomy of machines—or even larger systems and entire factories—seems practically unthinkable. This is not to say that things will remain this way. Most of what we use today on a daily basis and consider self-evident was purely science fiction just twenty years ago.

Just how big the difference is between programmed and actual intelligent machines can be seen in a short anecdote: Our robot YuMi (Fig. 11.2) can work together with people without the need of a cage enclosure. It notices if, for example, a person comes too close, and then it slows down or stops its movements. The safety function of previous industrial robots consisted of the robot automatically switching off if someone opened the cage. In contrast, YuMi seems fairly "intelligent." In reality, though, it is equipped with sensitive sensors that interpret any deviation from the norm—such as in terms of acceleration per second—as a malfunction and switch the robot to a safe mode for safety reasons.

When ABB announced in a press release in 2015 that this robot can speak "six languages," one daily newspaper asked to conduct an interview with YuMi as the "employee of the month." Just because the robot comes with programming software, operating instructions and a user manual in six languages does not mean it has a speech recognition system, can understand natural language or even speak itself. Now you can tell YuMi in human language what you want, but it will not understand a single word or react to you. However, it would be technically possible. One could equip the robot with an advanced speech recognition system similar to those in cars or smartphones, and teach it the meaning of individual words and how to react to them. Intelligence and digital function are not one and the same.

Yet the digitalization of products and processes has currently reached a level which opens up very many possibilities to enable machines and factories to function better, and ABB is using these possibilities in its products and services. Naturally, we are also working on the future outlined above by investing in companies that study "artificial intelligence" systems.

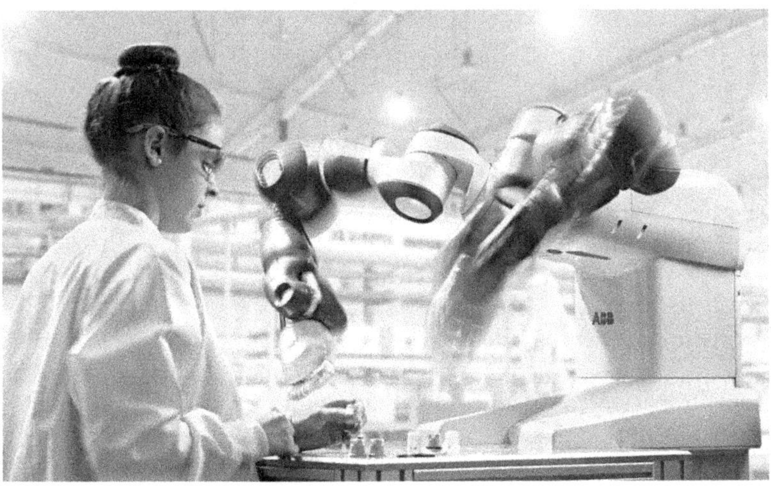

Fig. 11.2 The robot YuMi, suitable for working together with people. (Photo ABB)

11.3 Shifting System Barriers

The YuMi example shows us something else: The cyber-physical systems are shifting their barriers ever further outward. YuMi does not operate within a cage, but rather in almost any place; one could envision it as a repair robot on a robot line in running operation, for instance. It is capable of interacting with its environment, with people, other robots and machines. Such a removal of system barriers is true for more and more products today, and is a significant element of Industrie 4.0 and the Internet of Things, Services and People.

A car no longer merely knows the tire surface as the interface between itself and the street and the car body as its interface with the environment. It is connected via the internet and other services with the environment, but also with other vehicles, with people and services all over the world. That is why manufacturers can now ponder services stemming from this network and integrate them into their cars. The same is also true for the investment goods industry.

The difference emerging as a result of shifting boundaries can be explained using the example of the optimal operation of ship engines. Cruise and container ships, tankers, large yachts and offshore installation vessels are highly complex systems. The bridge on a modern ship has long since become a place that is not only where the rudder is controlled and the engine is started or stopped. They have become control rooms such as those in power plants, furnished with monitors depicting the status of several motors and drives on board. Today, all active components of a system on such a ship can be equipped with sensors, and the crew on the bridge can find out specific information concerning the status of these components—that is basically the Internet (or, more fittingly, Intranet) of Things, and nothing more.

If we look at a single ship, we see that, through software and sensors alone, a large degree of operating optimization can be achieved which previously did not exist. The exact position of the bow in the water, and information regarding the strength and direction of current and wind, enable a continual adjustment of the engine speed in such a way that it results in a considerable reduction of fuel consumption. There are countless other possibilities for optimization that have become achievable. For example, a part of the ABB software called Octopus is used on cruise ships to largely prevent seasickness in passengers through the corresponding optimization of ship control.

Octopus is a module of the comprehensive and very extensive Automation and Advisory Suite (see Fig. 11.3), which ABB offers for the shipping industry. Yet it is only with the integration of data streams of a ship to the internet that creates new opportunities which stretch far beyond the optimization of a single ship control process: especially with regard to repair during a malfunction at sea and concerning the overall planning of ship or fleet operation.

A disturbance in a drive of a large ship crossing the ocean represents a safety risk, and can cost a lot of time and money if, for example, the ship has to cut its speed in half and continue on at that speed for days until the malfunction is repaired in a port. If, however, all data from the engine is accessible, if it can be

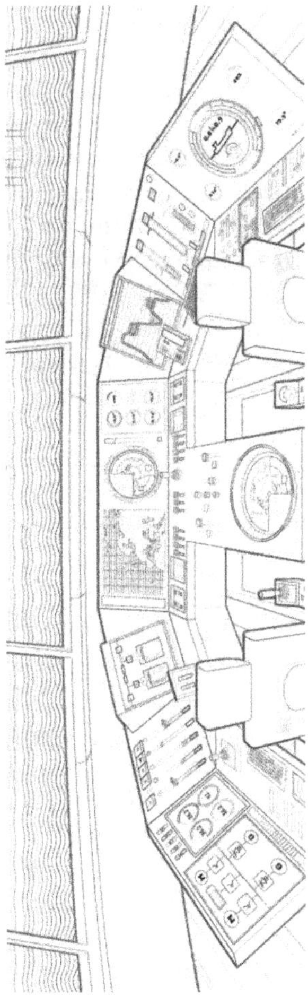

Fig. 11.3 Model of the ABB Advisory System. *Source* ABB

linked to the models of normal operation, and if, based on such information and with the competence of a remote specialist, the cause of the malfunction and the necessary repair measures can be determined, then the Internet of Things, Services and People can take action: Using an internet connection, the shipping company can now give a service specialist from any part of the world access to the ship via software to look at the ship and its control systems and quickly come up with a solution.

With internet access, the shipping company now also has access at all times to information which can optimize planning the tour of individual ships or an entire fleet. As with the networking of cars, with the exception of ocean weather service information, the current data pertaining to the remaining fleet and perhaps also partner fleets are also accessed. Not only the current and the weather are used to steer an individual ship; the shipping company now has an eye on every ship in the fleet in relation to the overall weather situation or political circumstances.

The wide angle of the internet and the shifting of boundaries of the shipping system across the world's oceans enable services to be offered that previously were not possible. The fact that this offer by ABB is not only technically possible, but also gives operators immediate, enumerable advantages, is evident in the fact that more than 400 ships have already optimized their systems with this IoTSP solution.

11.4 Data Enables Integrated Operations

The boundaries of the processes in companies and the borders between manufacturer and customer are also not remaining as hard and clear as before the discussion of Industrie 4.0. Digitalization and networking have led to the function of a product and the completing of tasks becoming more and more the focus, whereby the individual product loses relative significance. This initially happens on the customer side, but naturally leads to fundamental changes on the manufacturer side—otherwise the vision of a comprehensive optimization of value creation chains through IoTSP cannot become a reality.

For example, today within ABB, there is a clear distinction between the divisions: The division of Process Automation is responsible for the development and construction of complete systems; the Discrete Automation and Motion division offers products which are partially marketed separately, and partially also built into systems, such as motors and drives. Both divisions have their own distribution and service channels.

If a customer, such as from the mining industry, had previously had a problem with one part of a process because something did not go as expected, that customer would call ABB. The Swiss mining specialist had a look at the problem and determined that it most likely was not caused by the process itself, but by a drive or motor. Thus, a specialist from another division had to be consulted, who may, in turn, have needed another specialist. All parties had their information about their subarea on their PCs or departmental servers and had to discuss with each other how to handle the problem. Customers, however, are not interested in such internal connections. They only want to know that their process can be back up and running quickly.

Nowadays, all information pertaining to the entire system—in our example, a mine—and all devices and components installed in that mine can be stored in the cloud. No matter in which division the customer call first originated, any ABB specialist can immediately access all relevant data. The function of the system is the deciding factor. The complete digitalization of the entire system and its devices offers all data required to solve a problem in any location, even using a smartphone. And based on that data, the manufacturer's expertise about the process and the devices lead to the solution.

Yet the availability of data is not only important to servicing malfunctions. In a mine in which 20 processes were previously monitored and controlled from 20 monitors, now an integrated asset management system allows all processes to be collected on a single user interface, to be combined, comprehensively displayed and all relevant data continually evaluated (see Fig. 11.4).

The boundaries between the processes, corporate divisions and employed products are becoming blurred, because they are no longer needed to the same degree with complete digitalization. This has led ABB to undertake internal changes as well. Requirements to service employees are not decreasing, but on the contrary, are expanding considerably. ABB needs specialists who are proficient in more than one area. They must be able to deal with an overview of the entire system and know what to do with the data. Our organization will also keep changing in that regard. Restructuring will be the rule, not the exception.

11.5 Data Scientists and Process Knowledge

When data is collected and analyzed, it is not necessarily a task requiring big data analytics. We are talking here about advanced analytics. ABB has been using advanced analytics for a long time now; even if a large amount of data must be processed very quickly, to date, we have been very able to do so using conventional solutions.

At Twitter, they talk of big data when 15,000 tweets per second are processed. In our systems, 30,000 measurement values and more per second are not unusual. This is because we approach the evaluation with the knowledge of the process and the data model.

Big data solutions are especially important where correlations between data are sought to make informed conclusions. Everyone is familiar with offers appearing on retail sites immediately after entering a search that say something like: "People searching for this product were also interested in the following products." For this, data sets must be evaluated which are initially not related to each other. Big data analysis supplies the relationships and thus make this data an element of the business transaction.

Fig. 11.4 A look at the control center 800xA. (Photo: ABB)

In industry, we have the opposite case. The manufacturer of a system programmed and built by that manufacturer's engineers has a digital model of the system and the process. He or she knows exactly how the system behaves during specific points in the process, and which measurement data is supplied in normal operation. The relationship between the data of systems, machines and processes is well known. When analyzing this data, our specialists know very well what they are looking for and what is to be deemed irregular.

Data scientists at ABB Research have repeatedly told us that they could help us develop completely new ideas with big data analytics. So, we tried it out. We gave them data from thousands of robots. Except for very few and insignificant results, our analyses only showed what we knew all along: what movements the robot arm makes at which times, or what force it applies for which action. In our devices, there is not one signal that we are not familiar with and whose relationship to other signals is unknown. That is why big data analysis is no great advantage here. The same can be said for the figures coming from ABB Sales. The finding that all customers first purchase the system and only then, in a second step, the maintenance, was no surprise to us.

It is possible that useful applications for big data analytics exist for the investment goods industry provided we collect more and more data from our devices in operation and store them in the cloud. However, such applications must occur in close cooperation between those people with the process knowledge and data scientists. They have to find out where new solutions might lurk once the familiar analysis of known models is factored out. But, for the time being, our main attention will remain focused on advanced analytics.

11.6 Cyber Security Is an Executive Task

A dramatic change has taken place in recent years with regard to data security, and not only in connection with Industrie 4.0. The rapid development of digitalization and especially internet connectivity and the use of the cloud has attracted remarkably increased attention to the topic. Systems are becoming ever more complex, and connections between devices and between devices and people are increasing without hindrance, and thus, of course, potential dangers are also on the rise (Fig. 11.5).

In the past, when we spoke of data security, we were referring, for instance, to a system that was self-enclosed. Today, this is only partially true, because there are increasingly more connections to the outside world. Yet something completely different has been added: When we relocate data from machines, robots or systems to the cloud and analyze them, we are immediately confronted with the problem of privacy. While this customer data does not pose a threat to the system itself, it can be used against the customer, which is why we need to take this issue just as seriously.

Fig. 11.5 Image from an ABB video on cyber security. (Internet video ABB)

In recent years, ABB has invested a great deal in this realm; not only in products and systems which serve security purposes, such as the Cyber Security Monitoring Services. That is not the decisive factor. Moreover, it is the consciousness of all involved parties of the significance of this question for the entire company. For example, roadshows have been conducted at all of our large sites, in order to inform and enlighten employees. ABB is also active in several committees and events in this regard.

In the meantime, there are responsible persons throughout the corporation for cyber security, and ABB has a Cyber Security Team. The CEO himself issued instructions to all employees regarding what tests are to be conducted, who must be immediately informed, and how to deal with certain problem situations. For the IT industry, of course, these are well-known topics. But for industry, with the comprehensive digitalization of companies, they are now just as important.

The most important element of this issue are the security processes that have been introduced and are being expanded. They pertain not only to access methods, passwords and authentication, but also include things such as a comprehensive checklist for all development units, and a principle conduction of tests for typical hacker attacks. And for the software that ABB has integrated into its devices, very special measures are part of these processes.

Today, if a product manager suggests postponing the release of a product due to cyber security or the respective risk, no member of the cyber security team would even dream of rejecting it. Attitudes have fundamentally changed in this regard. After all, the data is not only one part of the whole. Increasingly, data is becoming the most important capital of industry, upon whose security and proper employment successful business will increasingly depend in the future.

11.7 Customer Data

The more frequently visions of the Internet of Things, Services and People are achieved, the clearer it becomes that it will be of great benefit to ABB as well as its customers. We can already claim this to be true, because we already have extensive experience with initial services that are based on machine data.

A couple of years ago, nobody was talking about data from this perspective. Data did not yet play a role in the relationship to customers. This has changed extremely quickly, even though the extent of development of our cloud services is not completely finished. Initial pilot trials have shown us that we can greatly raise potential for our customers.

For instance, in India, we have set up a service center for industrial robots. There, data from about 5000 robots around the world is collected on a permanent basis—of a total of 250,000 installed ABB robots (Fig. 11.6). Every thirty minutes, the servers receive the data from all connected units. In this way, we can more quickly determine if there is or will be a problem in one of the systems, and we can immediately inform the local service team to find a solution. What is more, we can use this massive collection of data to come to conclusions which are much more valuable than those previously garnered from the data of individual systems. This results in a variety of services for our customers, ranging from the optimization of running operation to preventive maintenance.

Of course, customers must agree to the use of their data, because the data of their products and systems belongs to them. At ABB, there are no buts about it. However, we have determined that, in contrast to some concerns, many customers have a positive attitude toward our collecting and evaluating data from their devices for such extra service, because, generally, the data itself is not interesting at all. There are only a few exceptional cases in which customers decidedly say: The data from the pumps in our system are strictly confidential, as conclusions

Fig. 11.6 ABB robot. (Photo ABB)

about our processes or even our recipes may be obtained from it. But generally, customers enjoy great advantages when we collect and evaluate device data—with our knowledge and analysis models—because it makes their processes better, safer and more efficient.

The example with the robot data also shows that the Internet of Things, Services and People works best on a global level: a service center in India—or, in the future, in the cloud—and local specialists, who search for a solution, either in the cloud or on site. A redundant operation of such services would not even be possible in any part of the world. And, by the way, the quote from the CEO of ABB, Ulrich Spiesshofer, printed in the *Frankfurter Allgemeine* newspaper on October 8, 2015, rings true:

> The age of closed systems has passed anyway. In the end, differing standards will prevail that harmonize with each other.

That is why ABB is also striving for closer cooperation between the German initiative *Industrie 4.0* with the Industrial Internet Consortium, established in the USA.

Data will be what will also drive the business of industry in the future. However, whether or not this will result in several new business models is questionable. Business models aimed at the time-based use of machine power are, first of all, not new, but rather have already been employed in several industries and branches of business for years. Secondly, we are not really dealing with new business models, but ones that have simply changed their means of financing: leasing instead of buying.

Such models work well when they deal with standard products that are used in a pre-fabricated form. It does not matter whether the product is hardware or software. In the investment goods industry, however, customers generally gain their competitive advantage precisely from the company-specific configuration of the machines or systems, and not from the simple use of a standard, of an "off-the-rack" system. That is why, in this industry, most likely only a few individual cases of such new business models, as it were, will be observed. Yet ABB has put out all its feelers in this area, too, and will investigate every opportunity that comes up.

11.8 Step by Step to the IoTSP

The Internet of Things, Services and People did not just crop up from one day to the next. It is being created in a continual process of change which includes the digitalization of products, processes and services mentioned above.

It is especially important in this context to see that customers are not given an ultimatum to either also proceed in this direction and invest accordingly in the newest products, that is, in machines, systems, motors, etc., or to remain at the old level, unable to participate in the next developments of the industry. As fundamental as the changes are that we are experiencing at this moment and that we are helping to shape, it is just as vital, especially in the investment goods industry, that an investment does not turn out to be a mistake.

In all of the newer devices, it is already the case that a large portion of the integrated software allows an upgrade in functionality of the machines or systems by installing updated software. Just as the software in a car will soon be able to update itself while the vehicle is in operation, so, too, will machines be able to update their own software.

While ABB on the one hand is researching, developing and working with such products, engineers are also on the lookout for possibilities to raise the quality of older machines and systems through sensors, actuators and software, such that they can be integrated into the new world of industry.

And naturally, software systems such as the Automation and Advisory Suite mentioned can bring the advantages of the IoTSP to factories by driving and optimizing hardware that is already installed.

The next step in industrial development will require a holistic approach, the comprehensive instruction and advanced training of employees and the use of modern technologies with digitalization and internet connectivity on all levels of industry. ABB sees itself as well-equipped for this next step. It is a primary objective of ABB to contribute to this development and assist its customers in also re-inventing their enterprises—step by step, and under no circumstances spanning the entire value creation chain all at once.

Utilizing Opportunities for the Industrial Location

12

Roman Dumitrescu

Abstract

In East-Westphalia-Lippe, a cluster of industrial enterprises and research institutes was formed to make it´s OWL, which researches technologies that are required for intelligent products and production processes and implements those technologies in joint projects in actual situations. These projects and the management of it's OWL are supported by the Federal Republic of Germany and the state of North Rhine Westphalia. In this chapter, the cluster is presented, as well as important contributions from its work and especially practical projects of its members which best illustrate the opportunities of the network for all involved.

12.1 A Cluster for SMEs

The technology network it's OWL—Intelligent Technical Systems of OstWestfalenLippe—was honored in a top cluster contest by the Federal Ministry for Education and Research, and is considered to be one of the largest initiatives in Germany for Industrie 4.0. it's OWL connects leaders on the global market and leaders in technology in the realms of machine engineering, the electric and electronic industry and the automotive supply industry. Together with regional research institutes, it is working on 47 projects focused on new technologies for intelligent products and production systems.

A total of 33 of these projects pertain to innovative product developments which are led by member companies in cooperation with research institutions

R. Dumitrescu (✉)
it's OWL, Zukunftsmeile 1, 33102 Paderborn, Germany
E-Mail: roman.dumitrescu@ipt.fraunhofer.de

U. Sendler (ed.), *The Internet of Things*,
https://doi.org/10.1007/978-3-662-54904-9_12

right up to market introduction. Five projects are cross-sectional projects, in which regional technical colleges combine individual areas of expertise on a variety of topics and provide them to the network. There are nine sustainability measures which make sure that the cluster's attained progress can be secured beyond the cluster's subsidy period, which ends at the close of 2017.

Technology transfer plays a significant role, enabling even small and midsize enterprises, possessing insufficient if any of their own resources, to utilize the new technologies. Just how important this aspect is, can be seen by the great number of corresponding transfer projects that have been initiated here in the meantime: 73 have already been completed, and a further 100 will be implemented by the end of 2017.

Besides the member companies, colleges and transfer partners, about 100 other companies have joined as supporting members. They want to participate in the results of the research at the forefront.

In 2014, initial results, concrete technologies and solutions were already presented, using best-practice examples, in the brochure "*Auf dem Weg zu Industrie 4.0*" ("On the Way to Industrie 4.0"). In a second publication, the Cluster dealt with a series of suggestions for architecture models for Industrie 4.0, now available, presented the perspectives of several companies and made recommendations. The focus of the third brochure is the successful technology transfer to small and medium-sized enterprises.

From the perspective of it's OWL, the initiative *Industrie 4.0* and the debate it has unleashed about the future of industry in a digitized society and economy offers great opportunities for Germany as an industrial location. If these opportunities are understood and used correctly, the location can also secure a significant spot in the future as a technological leader on the global market.

Of course, the digitalization of industry brings risks with it that must be taken seriously. People will not automatically profit from it, the conditions necessary on the levels of society, education and training, and especially corporate management, will not crop up by themselves.

It is good that German politics has recognized the significance of further industrial development at the highest level and has made Industrie 4.0 the core of its high-tech strategy. Nevertheless, Industrie 4.0 is not all politics. And not all wishes that Industrie 4.0 has produced for politics have been taken on, much less fulfilled.

it's OWL not only wants to supply technical and technological contributions. Especially for small and midsize enterprises, so important to Germany as an industrial location, the network, whose members mostly come from SMEs, will develop paths on the way from the status quo to Industrie 4.0. This process includes two topics that are steadily gaining in interest: the effects on the working world and the search for and establishment of new business models.

12.2 Strategy Development in the Network

Industrie 4.0 is a topic based on the technical level of employed systems. How must machines communication with each other and with people? Which IT structure and which applications are necessary for such communication? Before an enterprise can answer such questions, however, a few other tasks have to be completed.

These systems are intended to control processes. Not every company thoroughly analyzed and defined its processes in the past. And if they have, then these processes are ones which were used in decades gone by. In any case, they will have to be redefined for Industrie 4.0. How must a drive be developed and produced for use in a networked production plant? What needs to be taken into consideration at various points in the process? Who is involved?

The entire industrial process landscape is being put to the test with Industrie 4.0. Yet, to redefine value creation chain processes and correctly link them to each other, an enterprise needs a strategy; it must know what goal is to be achieved. Are we dealing with the same product lines as before? Will the business model change? Will new business models develop alongside the old ones? Will the company become a software or service provider that uses its products as the basis of such activity? For many firms in industry, especially the smaller ones, it is not a matter of course to pose such questions. The product has to sell itself and turn a profit. Often, that must suffice.

It is even more difficult, armed with a broad vision and knowledge of market and technological developments and other trends, to go about finding a fitting and, especially, successful strategy. Generally, it is the larger companies with sufficient capital and thus human resources at their disposal which can professionally design their innovation management.

Foresight, strategy development, process definition—those are the prerequisites to then take the next step toward Industrie 4.0. it's OWL sees part of its tasks in assisting members by accompanying them along these steps, which most cannot tackle on their own. In this process, digitalization and networking in initial projects have already served as pathfinders for another kind of industry than we have previously known. Instead of seeing other enterprises as competitors, contractors or suppliers, an atmosphere of cooperation has set in, which will most likely envelop all of industry: Because no single firm can meet the demands of the market with their own products and on their own power, networks, platforms and ecosystems are being established which, a decade ago, would have only been seen very rarely and under special circumstances.

One example for such networking was a study conducted by it's OWL in 2015, in which several member companies of varying sizes participated. It resulted in the second brochure of the cluster: "*Auf dem Weg zu Industrie 4.0—Erfolgsfaktor Referenzarchitektur*" ("On the Way to Industrie 4.0—Reference Architecture as the Factor of Success"). Six different models for an Industrie 4.0 architecture were studied and compared. For this purpose, the Heinz Nixdorf Institute and the Fraunhofer project group Mechatronics Design Methods, in cooperation with the cluster partner UNITY AG, surveyed thirteen companies from the realms of machine and systems engineering, automotive and automation engineering, the electronics industry, as well as software and consulting companies all over Germany. The participating enterprises included Atos IT Solutions and Services, Beckhoff Automation, Bender, FASTEC, Gestamp Umformtechnik, Intel Deutschland, Krauss-Maffei Technologies, MODUS Consult, Adam Opel, PHOENIX CONTACT Electronics, SAP, Siemens and Smart Mechatronics. Thus, in addition to the various business fields, they also represented very different company sizes, making it a thoroughly representative group.

Nowadays, industrial processes and products, all levels of a modern company, are controlled using information and communications technology. A depiction of corporate architecture using the automation pyramid that had been so typical for a few decades has become obsolete. It assumes a hierarchical structure and clear dependencies between the individual levels. Up to recently, everything had its place in the hierarchy, from the control level to the shop floor level of input and output signals. However, when sensors emit signals which trigger machine activity, other rules obviously apply. The suggestions for a reference architecture are designed to understand these new rules and structure them such that—in lieu of the automation pyramid—they can be helpful in the redesigning of processes, enterprises and the cooperation of entire networks. From the standpoint of it's OWL, three superordinate aspects need to be considered: vertical integration, horizontal integration and a comprehensive systems engineering (SE).

Vertically, the various levels of a company's IT must be interlinked such that physical and technical processes, including their resources, can be synchronized with business processes across all corporate levels. In a smart factory, corporate structures right up to production are no longer predetermined, but are regenerated from one instance to another, on the basis of data, models, communication and algorithms. To make this possible, ideas for modularization and recycling need to be developed which include clear descriptions, such as of the capabilities and behaviors of system components (see Fig. 12.1).

Horizontally, Industrie 4.0 requires the interlinking of machines, operating resources, products and components, as well as warehouse systems, across corporate borders, to create an efficient value creation network. This requires the consistent integration of the IT systems implemented for the control and management of the respective process steps, from materials acquisition and production to distribution and maintenance. Here, great opportunity exists for new services and business models. However, these networks also require clear rules for cooperation, in order to establish balanced partnership relationships (see Fig. 12.2).

Along with Industrie 4.0 and multidisciplinary technical systems, comprehensive systems engineering—originally employed especially in the aerospace industry—has also made the jump to general machine and systems engineering, and even to components manufacturers. Only when technical systems are developed and produced in relation to the other systems to be networked can the vision of Industrie 4.0 be achieved. Model-based systems engineering (MBSE) appears to be the most powerful tool, since it facilitates communication beyond departmental disciplines. For this to happen, however, considerable requirements must be met,

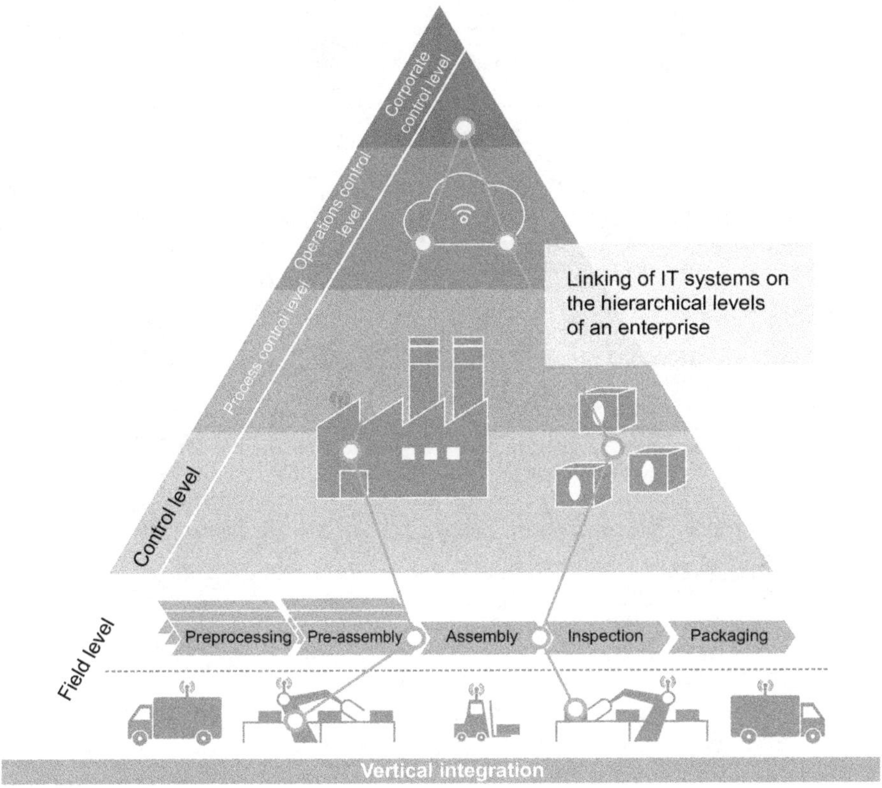

Fig. 12.1 Vertical integration. (it's OWL)

both on the organizational as well as the education and training levels, and regarding IT systems.

The enterprises surveyed agreed to these three superordinate aspects. However, when weighting them, opinions differed greatly. Especially the manufacturing companies placed great importance on vertical integration. The increase in the degree of automation and a rise in production networking are often cited as basic goals of Industrie 4.0. Horizontal integration, or even comprehensive systems engineering, are currently receiving only marginal attention, if any at all.

The reference architectures studied include "CPS (cyber-physical systems) with distributed services" ("*CPS mit verteilten Diensten*"), published by the VDI in 2013; two different proposals (2013 and 2014) of the ZVEI group, "MES as a Central Platform" ("*MES als zentrale Plattform*") and "Central Connection between Office and Shop Floor ("*Zentrale Verbindung zwischen Office und Shop Floor*"); the "IoT Platform" by SAP (2015); the "Reference Architecture Industrie 4.0 RAMI4" by ZVEI and *Plattform Industrie 4.0*, published in April of 2015, and finally, the "Industrial Internet Reference Architecture IIRA," which was published in July of 2015 by the IIC.

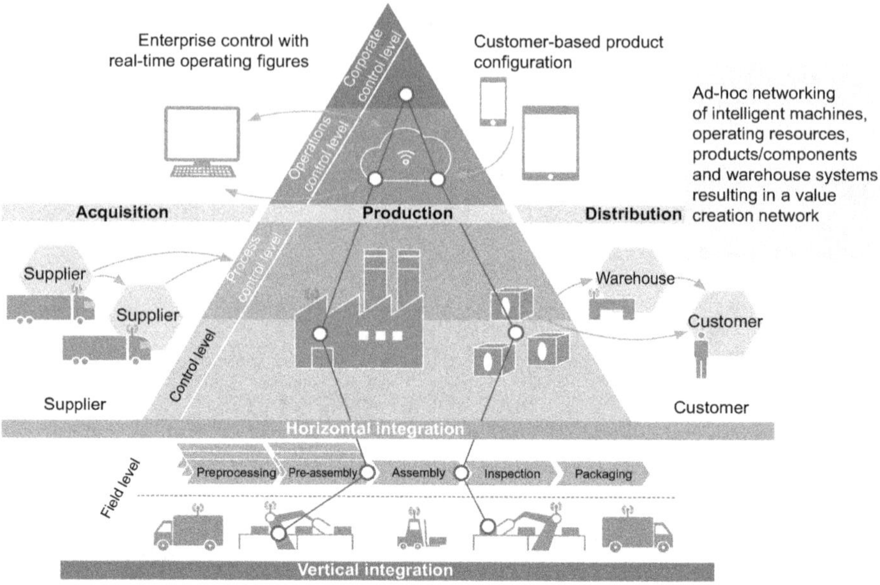

Fig. 12.2 Horizontal integration. (it's OWL)

The partially very scientific models address various perspectives and target groups. Each one cites important aspects and covers a portion of the requirements. This was also confirmed by the surveyed enterprises, which, depending on their industry, were able to identify with the individual models to a greater or lesser extent. Even if an overview of the degree of fulfilment of the models (see Fig. 12.3) regarding requirements to a reference architecture cites the model RAMI4 as the one which fulfills the most requirements, it does not mean that it will prevail. Its suitability for practical industrial situations remains to be seen; only then will companies pay more attention to the topic of reference architecture for Industrie 4.0.

12.3 Successful Projects

it's OWL sees a significant task in accompanying enterprises on their way away from the status quo and building them bridges, so to speak, that they would otherwise not have without the cluster. One important pillar to this bridge are the joint projects in which industrial enterprises cooperate with scientific and research institutions as well as IT companies, in order to address individual aspects of Industrie 4.0 and work on solutions—solutions which may not only pertain to their situation, but can also be employed multiple times or lead to standard services.

Several of the 47 projects mentioned above have already led to presentable results. Not all projects can be highlighted in this chapter, but we will look at a few as an example of where this road can take us.

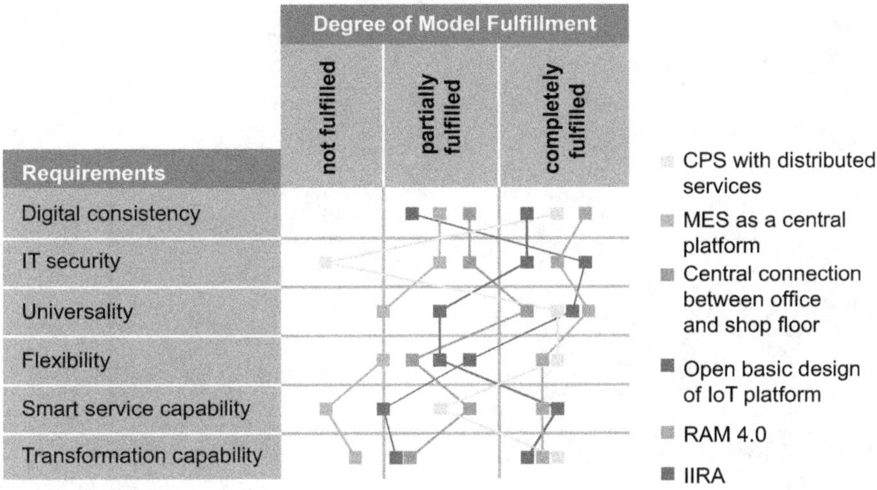

Fig. 12.3 Comparison of reference architectures. (it's OWL)

12.3.1 ScAut

In the project Scientific Automation (itsowl-ScAut), the project partners cover the entire chain, from the product idea to serial applications. Beckhoff plays a leading role, both as a supplier for automation solutions and through the new developments of a Scientific Automation Platform, and cooperates with the University of Paderborn and in cross-sectional projects of the top cluster. Within the context of three pilot projects, the companies IMA Klassmann, Schirmer and Hüttenhölscher are developing and constructing future-oriented, self-optimizing and energy-efficient processing machines. These machines are then used at the place of the associated end user, nobilia, the largest German producer of fitted kitchens, with 580,000 kitchens per year. Companies like nobilia demand quick, high-precision, reliable, sustainability-focused and efficient production processes for the manufacture of Size 1 batches. In order to reduce delivery times, a networking of production along the supplier-customer chain is essential.

The Scientific Automation Platform offers intelligent hardware and software components, a very efficient runtime environment, software tools for interdisciplinary engineering encompassing the product lifecycle, as well as a set of methods for drafting and implementation. Scientific automation refers to the integration of engineering and non-engineering knowledge, such as measurement technology, analysis and evaluation processes and cognition or adaptation to PC-based automation technologies. Data from a production plant is collected, analyzed and evaluated centrally, in order to then initiate the corresponding control processes in real time. For their processing machines, IMA Klassmann, Schirmer and Höttenhölscher are researching scientific automation approaches such as the integration of measurement technology, energy management, condition monitoring and self-optimization. One solution reached jointly during the project by Hüttenhölscher

Fig. 12.4 Beckhoff control system at nobilia. (nobilia)

and Beckhoff for the early detection of drill bit wear is already being successfully tested at nobilia (see Fig. 12.4).

Beckhoff has also been researching scientific automation solutions on a demonstration platform based on two smart factories which communicate and evaluate machine data via the cloud. In the innovation project eXtreme Fast Automation (itsowl-efa), Beckhoff is working in parallel on the real-time application of manycore computers in automation. Control tasks such as sequence control, robotics and scientific automation solutions are to be distributed such that complex and time-consuming calculations can be processed on several cores within short, coordinated cycles. The result is an increase in productivity, as well as energy conservation.

12.3.2 Intelligent Separators

The GEA Westfalia Separator Group in Oelde develops, manufactures and distributes high-performance separators and centrifuges for the dairy, food and beverage industries. The firm is a subsidiary of the GEA Mechanical Equipment Group, which is researching jointly with the Fraunhofer Institute's mechatronics design methods facility (IEM) to develop an intelligent separator (see Fig. 12.5).

For the industrial production of food, dairy products or pharmaceutical products, high demands exist with regard to product quality. Raw products are refined in a multi-step process. In centrifuges—or separators—substances are separated out of a suspension using centrifugal force. For reliable separation, optimal operating conditions regarding temperature, speed and composition of raw products are

Fig. 12.5 Virtual system model at GEA aids in the optimization of the separation process. (GEA)

essential. Frequently, however, these conditions are not achieved, since the centrifuge is integrated into a superordinate, unstable production process. To optimize the process, comprehensive machine and process knowledge is also required, which is also not always on hand. To improve the reliability and efficiency of the separation process, the separators should learn to adapt independently to changing conditions and, to do so, have access to the necessary expert knowledge.

The goal of this innovation project is the development of a virtual system model with which to develop software solutions for intelligent centrifuges. Intelligent sensors and a database are to provide the expert knowledge.

To achieve this goal, operating conditions and procedures are implemented for various raw products. A virtual system model connects them. Based on this foundation, an intelligent sensor system analyzes the operating conditions in the separator and identifies any deviations to the target state. A database supplies the necessary expertise in the form of mathematical rules, which enables an autonomous evaluation of sensor signals. The project makes use of the results of the it's OWL cross-sectional projects in systems engineering, intelligent networking and self-optimization. Using a demonstrator, the sensors and database are validated and integrated into the centrifuges.

This project enables an increase in the reliability and efficiency of the separation process. An increase in efficiency of at least ten percent is expected. The virtual system model forms the basis for the development of intelligent centrifuges and, for instance, for the implementation of remote maintenance. The sensor technology and system of experts can also be transferred to other industries, such as medical engineering.

12.3.3 Intelligent Networking of Agricultural Machines

For the innovation project on the intelligent modification and networking of agricultural machines, the firm Claas Selbstfahrende Erntemaschinen in Harsewinkel (Fig. 12.6) has come together with the University of Applied Sciences for Business (FHDW) in Paderborn.

The acquisition of agricultural machines is coupled with high investments. Many such machines are only used for a short period of time each year. A combine harvester, for example, is used for an average of 22 days per year. Thus, it is important to achieve an optimal harvest result that is fast and efficient. To do so, machine operators must take such factors into consideration as the respective conditions of the field, such as the degree of ripeness of the plants or the condition of the soil. At the same time, the individual processes—harvesting, transportation

Fig. 12.6 Claas agricultural machines in use. (Claas)

and storage—have to be optimally coordinated. Previously, this was all primarily accomplished manually and based on experience, and for the optimal coordination of the individual processes, all participants—the producer, farming contractors and farmers—were involved.

For the project, the various characteristics of a field and the course of the individual processes were analyzed. Then, the demands regarding the optimal employment of the agricultural machines and the intelligent networking of all participants was defined. Based on these values, software was developed for various machines and situations, which could collect and analyze field characteristics and be used for the autonomous adjustment of the machines, taking the systems of the participants into consideration, such as the databases of the producer and the contractors. The project was supported by results from the cross-sectional projects of self-optimization, intelligent networking and systems engineering. The intelligent software was expanded to include simulation techniques, which was tested on herbaceous forage harvesting, and implemented using the example of agricultural machines.

The results of the project allow Claas to use its agricultural machines with 50% more efficiency, which had previously gone untapped. Thus, a considerably more efficient use of resources and a noticeable improvement in the quality of the harvesting process was achieved. Autonomous adjustment also makes it easier on machine operators, since they no longer need to make changes to the harvesting process manually. The software can also be used for other applications, such as for winter services, the operation of construction sites and transportation logistics. In one transfer project of the dike-construction-machine producer topocare, it has already been made available for flood protection measures.

12.3.4 Energy Management in Smart Grids

Four of the partners are working on this project: appliance manufacturer Miele from Gütersloh, Beckhoff Automation, the Fraunhofer project group Mechatronics Design Methods and the University of Paderborn. The goal is to produce intelligent home appliances for intelligent power grids.

Until recently, power in Germany was supplied by few high-capacity power plants. Their electricity production adjusts to fluctuating consumption throughout the day. However, due to a rise in renewable energy, energy production is becoming ever more decentralized, and is harder to control. Excess power production and shortages are possible consequences. In the future, demand must thus adjust to the fluctuating supply. One possibility lies in intelligent power networks, called smart grids, which connect energy producers and consumers while enabling a synchronization of supply and demand. Yet there is still a lack of home appliances that can react to the dynamic conditions in smart grids.

The target of the project is the development of flexible home appliances, using the example of a tumble dryer that reacts to fluctuating power availability and prices and autonomously adapts its processes accordingly. Another project goal is an innovative energy management system for private households. Such a system determines the optimum balance of energy consumption, cost and time—automatically and conveniently for consumers.

To achieve this, the fluctuating conditions of a smart grid are modeled to determine their effects on the operation of household appliances. Intelligent management software based on this model is designed to then enable the optimization of various goals for a variety of appliances in a single-family home. In developing a flexible-procedure dryer that automatically adjusts its operational state to the conditions of the smart grid using automatic control and other technologies, the project draws upon physical models. The appliance, along with the energy management system is designed, tested and constructed using demonstrators. This project, too, utilizes results from the cross-sectional projects in self-optimization, energy efficiency and systems engineering.

The idea is to use the combination of intelligent software with energy-efficient technologies such as heat accumulation to achieve about a 40% decrease in energy consumption, while at the same time raising the level of convenience for the consumer. The results can be transferred to other household appliances and to more complex consumer structures, such as multiple-family homes, right up to industrial factories or office buildings.

12.3.5 Virtual Commissioning of Machine Tools

A typical example of technology transfer projects is the collaboration between Elha Maschinenbau Liemke KG in Hövelhof and the Heinz Nixdorf Institute (HNI) in Paderborn. Elha is a typical, midsize company in East Westphalia, a family-run enterprise with 240 employees which develops and manufactures complex machine tools, from vertical milling centers to rotary processing centers to special purpose machines for the manufacture and processing of high-precision parts, such as large-diameter, anti-friction slewing rings.

Within the context of the cross-sectional project "Systems Engineering", HNI's professional group Control Engineering and Mechatronics worked out the foundations for an optimized design system for machines and systems. Its goal was to provide the machine construction industry with an instrument for the multi-trade development of smart products and production systems.

In the realm of special purpose machinery manufacture, machines are becoming increasingly complex. At the same time, customers want shorter delivery times and especially shorter periods for commissioning—a dilemma that has not been solved in the presence of ever-higher speeds required to run familiar processes. Elha's goal was to virtualize as many commissioning steps as possible, allowing for the fact that special purpose machines, depending on customer wishes, may be equipped with CNC control units from other makers (such as Siemens, Bosch, Beckhoff and Heidenhain).

The project participants jointly analyzed the market for corresponding software, and defined the specifications to the tool to be used. This included a simulation with a realistic control environment, that is, with real machine data, a real-time simulation for early cycle time measurement and simple fault and function simulations. Six products were then put on the short list. They were thoroughly evaluated and compared in an efficiency analysis.

The system which fared the best allowed a simulation in machine-side real time (under one millisecond) and the import of 3D CAD data and SPC configurations. All conventional control and fieldbus systems were able to be used. In addition, dynamic changes to component and parts geometries were possible, in order to be able to optimize the construction during virtual commissioning.

Subsequently, virtual commissioning was tested with that tool using two sample units—a machine tool and a tool construction machine with two different control units. The trial showed that all necessary function logic was programmable and all real functions were able to be mapped. With the aid of test case checklists, faults were identified and eliminated at an early stage. And new approaches emerged for specification- and function-based development: The constructors were able to integrate method elements from systems engineering into the development of virtual commissioning.

The responsible project participants at Elha discovered that more than 80% of commissioning tasks could take place in the office. Previously, this amount had only been about 40%. In addition, constructors could react much more quickly to faults, because production had not yet been completed. The time required for real commissioning at the machine itself was able to be reduced considerably. All of this led to a reduction in the project duration.

At Elha, this project resulted in a few decisions regarding future work: Virtual commissioning is to be achieved for all relevant control units; a study is to be conducted with regard to the extent to which individual machine groups can be commissioned separately and early, and virtual commissioning will be extended to other machine and system types, such as robot-assisted automation and automatic tooling systems. As a general goal, it was stated that 90% of the efforts for commissioning were to be done at the computer, and only the remaining 10% at the machine itself.

12.4 Taking the Lead by Pioneering

As these examples have remarkably shown, Industrie 4.0 is in no way an event in which scientific parameters lead to visions of the future that have no effect on the present. Quite the contrary is true. Every step taken in that direction also means an improvement in the status quo: an increase in efficiency with a simultaneous conservation of resources; the optimization of processes and procedures, and savings in time and thus cash. Those taking part in the industry and research network it's OWL are also taking the lead. At the same time, however, the participants are the first who can utilize the new technologies and results for a jump on the competition, who may believe that they can still wait before implementing the transformation in their enterprises.

Another thing that has become apparent in the projects and the overall work of the cluster is the size of the gap between what is to be achieved at the end of the road and the status quo, where enterprises and researchers find themselves today. Because as important and favorable the results of the first steps have been, it is almost always only individual divisions of a company, single product lines, and a few professional disciplines that are involved. There are individual projects whose targets encompass cross-company networking; however, we cannot yet speak of a truly consistent, vertical integration of information flow anywhere, nor is horizontal integration beyond corporate and national borders in sight—a central aspect of the Internet of Things and Services, and thus of Industrie 4.0 itself.

Previous project results have demonstrated that several improvements are achievable on the short term in the realm of service. It is no coincidence that the previous director of services at GEA has now been appointed to the board of directors. Intelligent technical systems and their networking enable not only the optimization of service, but especially in this area, business models become conceivable and achievable which are innovative and are accompanied by an expansion of business.

Cloud technology has reached a degree of maturity that also makes it realistic for small and midsize enterprises. Gradually, practical experience should be reducing the fear of risks, which still prevails in Germany. Perhaps it's OWL and the many world-famous brands belonging to the cluster can also contribute to fear reduction—because security, of course, has an extremely high priority for the industrial use of the internet, especially when the personal data of end users, such as those in the medical industry, is involved. However, when a household appliance from Miele, to select just one of the many good quality brands, can not only impress people with the reliability of its functionality, including for its autonomous and remote control functions, but also with a guarantee of the highest degree of security, then the general fear of data abuse can be converted into a competitive advantage. Then it might be possible for global consumers to associate the brand name of a German maker not only with engineering precision, but also with upholding data protection and safety regulations based on the highest European criteria.

As mentioned above, the topic of systems engineering has not yet permeated the consciousness of responsible corporate individuals as also being significant for small and midsize machine building enterprises. Even multi-disciplinary, model-based collaboration between various engineering disciplines, which is a component of comprehensive systems engineering, is currently only being pursued in isolated situations. The IT landscape in most companies is still not at the point which allows an uninterrupted linking of systems, from the development phase to the value creation chain. Also, let us not forget that the employees of such companies are the same ones who implemented the most recent phases of automation and digitalization. Specialists in Germany are scarce. This is particularly true for the specialists now needed for Industrie 4.0: those with an eye for the overall system, with the capability to manage networked project teams. Yet the projects organized by it's OWL are also extremely helpful in overcoming the shortage. The specialists and managers participating in the projects learn precisely those skills which will soon become the most important qualifications.

Naturally, it is not enough to learn on the job in practical projects. School education and especially training, instruction and research at institutes of higher learning are targeted at goals which were defined before the knowledge of the requirements for multi-disciplinary system development and Industrie 4.0 came into existence. Now it is up to the national administration, and especially the Federal Ministry of Education and Research (BMBF) and state ministers, to take action. Just as enterprises are networking, just as engineers are collaborating beyond disciplinary borders, just as organizational structures and processes in companies must be realigned, so, too, must the borders of educational disciplines be readjusted.

The few facilities, such as the Heinz Nixdorf Institute, which have long since offered innovative learning and teaching methods for mechatronics and the engineering of networked systems, could serve as models to such an endeavor. The excellence cluster CITEC and the research institute CoR-Lab at the University of Bielefeld are pursuing an interdisciplinary approach to the interactive systems of tomorrow. There, engineers, information scientists, psychologists, linguists, natural scientists and sports scientists are working together on solutions in the realm of human-machine interaction and cognitive robotics, in which robots themselves learn how to carry out work steps intended for them.

New curricula, new professorships, new or newly adapted institutes—all of these need time. In recent years since the initiation of Industrie 4.0, too few political decisions have been made, and too few ways paved. Without politics, it cannot be done.

On the other hand, Industrie 4.0 is not primarily a political topic, but one of industry—in connection with research, within companies and within such networks as it's OWL. Here, partners are jointly developing their own courses of study to qualify specialists. Examples include student camps for schoolchildren, a summer school for master's and PhD candidates and young professionals, and advanced training for engineers with years of vocational experience.

For the Federal Republic of Germany, the effects of it's OWL with regard to supporting small and midsize industries on their way to Industrie 4.0 is so important that it has become a component of the SME 4.0 centers of excellence, adopted and partly established as early as late 2015 by the Federal Ministry for Economic Affairs and Energy (BMWi). Here, too, it's OWL is involved. The SME 4.0 center of excellence in the state of North-Rhine Westphalia represents a bundle consisting of expertise from it's OWL (smart machines), the Ruhr metropolitan area (smart logistics) and the Rhineland (smart production technologies). Their goal is to support small and midsize enterprises in tapping the potential offered by digitalization.

The IoT Paves the Way for a Networked Economy

13

Tanja Rückert

Abstract

In the past two decades, the internet has connected billions of people, significantly more than half of humanity, with one another, placing their communication on a completely new foundation. Now, "things" are being added. They are being equipped with capabilities allowing them to hear, see, feel and "think," which is described in words as "intelligent" and "smart." And they are being networked. According to the estimates of Gartner and McKinsey, by the year 2020, 20 to 25 million devices will be online via their own internet addresses. And, following communication between people, this will also fundamentally change value creation.

Manufacturers can equip their products with sensors, actuators, miniature cameras and other digital components at ever decreasing costs. Software embedded in the products then allows data to be generated, collected and analyzed while those devices are in use. The Internet of Things will make sure that not only an individual product becomes a data supplier in this way, but that products will be able to communicate with each other and with people using their data in a virtually limitless manner.

13.1 Products: Smart and Networked

In the past two decades, the internet has connected billions of people, considerably more than half of humanity, with one another, placing their communication on a completely new foundation. Now, "things" are being added. They are being equipped

T. Rückert (✉)
SAP AG, Dietmar-Hopp-Allee 16, 69190 Walldorf, Germany
E-Mail: tanja.rueckert@sap.com

U. Sendler (ed.), *The Internet of Things*,
https://doi.org/10.1007/978-3-662-54904-9_13

with capabilities allowing them to hear, see, feel and "think," which is described in words as "intelligent" and "smart." And they are being networked. According to the estimates of Gartner and McKinsey, by the year 2020, 20 to 25 million devices will be online via their own internet addresses. And, following communication between people, this will also fundamentally change value creation.

Manufacturers can equip their products with sensors, actuators, miniature cameras and other digital components at ever decreasing costs. Software embedded in the products then allows data to be generated, collected and analyzed while those devices are in use. The Internet of Things will make sure that not only an individual product becomes a data supplier in this way, but that products will be able to communicate with each other and with people using their data in a virtually limitless manner.

A motor vehicle can recognize and share its position. The networking of several cars thus allows an analysis of traffic flow, among other things, and this analysis can be used to make suggestions to change a driver's intended route. This example alone shows that a single producer alone cannot realize the benefits of the Internet of Things. The networking of things also requires the networking of producers and their customers. For instance, European automotive manufacturers established the Car 2 Car Communication Consortium (C2C-CC) several years ago, with the goal of a cooperative, intelligent transportation system. The IoT allows a redesign in the way people move and how they live. Projects for smart cities are researching this around the world.

The Internet of Things is still in its infancy. Yet it is already hard to imagine that there will one day be any branch of industry whose products do not go online. This means that even products of the investment goods industry, such as machines, systems and even factory floors and warehouses, assembly lines and repair workshops will be networked. With an increasing degree of networked machines and people, the borders of industry will also become less and less distinct. This part of the Internet of Things, which pertains to the networking of industrial processes itself, is referred to in Germany as Industrie 4.0. The term 'industrial internet' in the USA additionally focuses on retail, logistics and energy supply.

The McKinsey Global Institute published a study in June of 2015 which "estimates that the IoT has a total potential economic impact of $ 3.9 to $ 11.1 trillion a year by 2025. At the top end, that level of value [...] would be equivalent to about 11% of the world economy."

This coincides with experiences gained by SAP with its customers in recent years. Especially the discrete manufacturing industry, the entire transportation sector—from the aviation industry to fleet management in logistics—and trade are most fervently pressing for solutions with which they can tackle new business models or optimize current business and organize it to be more efficient.

SAP will concentrate on the development of IoT applications and the provision of reusable services in the form of an IoT platform to enable partners, customers and developers to efficiently develop IoT applications. In addition, the comprehensive protection of highly networked IoT applications is also on the agenda, to ensure the secure exchange of data across all phases of network communication.

The focus is on architectures and standards in the realm of IT security to establish secure applications. It must be guaranteed that data only flows between authorized parties, whether at the device, on the server or in the cloud. The further the degree of intelligence reaches, the more autonomous the devices can make decisions and the more important as well as critical data from the internet becomes for business processes in industry, the greater the significance of securing data flow will become. One core element is the encryption of all data as a matter of principle. Even if unauthorized persons gain access to a part of the information, the owner of the data must be 100% sure that this information is neither readable nor usable for the unauthorized party.

13.2 Closing the Data Chain

Digitizing devices and connecting them to the internet is one thing, but it is not enough. With the Internet of Things, computing had entered a new phase. it must deliver solutions in three ways: Data from things must be collected and analyzed such that business processes can be controlled in a rule-based manner under consideration of identified patterns; the management of this data must be organized accordingly, and finally, innovative business ideas are to be developed that are based on the analysis and evaluation of data. All three tasks are to be mastered by an IoT solution which ensures the integration of information and operation technology and represents the control unit of modern system landscapes. All three tasks cannot generally be completed by the producer alone.

It all starts with things: things whose ability to network is a prerequisite, things that can collect and generate data. Manufacturers and users have to decide which data is to be used for what purposes and how and where they are to be analyzed and processed. Based on these decisions, the correct and suitable paths to integration must be employed. There is a difference whether data comes from the same source at regular intervals with a consistently strong network connection or whether highly varying data volumes are sent at unforeseeable times from various places, where things like the interruption and repair of the network connection must be taken into account.

It is of prime importance that data can be integrated in a way that separates important from unimportant data right from the start, for instance, when exceptional data can be differentiated from standard data. One example of this is in digital farming, where, for the digital processing of farm fields, geographical data, as well as data pertaining to the condition of the field to be farmed, is generated. This data is supplemented by a continual flow of data regarding processing progress, weather service information and many other kinds. The ability to sort this information according to relevance, and then connect the relevant data with the business data of the respective order to ensure a quicker and more efficient processing of that order—all of this turns the mounds of data pertaining to the things into smart data.

Therefore, the connection of end devices is the first significant step that any IoT solution must include. This step is the spark for a fusion of the real thing and its data, of the real and digital world, so to speak. Connectors that make this step possible must fulfill important requirements.

First of all, they must be capable of understanding the language of the device, its digital dialect, and translate it into a report, without any loss of information, that can be implemented for the corresponding evaluation and employment of the data, such as in the form of a signal that switches a drive on and off.

Secondly, the integration of the device must ensure that program steps can be executed via the network directly in that device, such as to trigger a signal, possibly in connection with the data of other things networked with that device. Or, the other way around, data from the things can be used to make management decisions, such as in our data farming example, where information might be collected from the field which could affect the deployment of an additional harvesting machine.

The connector also has the task of guaranteeing a smart connection. Should the network be interrupted, the connector has to repair data flow and update the data. In addition, the connection must meet the highest security demands. Nobody should have the ability to hack into the connection to enable unauthorized access to data or the manipulation of the data flow. All of these tasks are the responsibility of the connectors.

Once the things are networked and access to their data is enabled, the proper management has to be arranged. Data management in its conventional form would be overtaxed. For the networking of things, an extreme data volume, a large variance of data types and a sudden and extremely fast data flow are not the exception, but the rule. Data management must thus possess limitless storage space, on the one hand, even if the intelligence of the network sorts out the information not required immediately after its collection, thus preventing a data tsunami. On the other hand, the data management system must also allow targeted access within a very short time period, to enable decisions to be made in real time via the end device, if necessary. In addition to the enormous storage capacity, which would wisely include the assistance of cloud technology, data management should also be infinitely scalable, from ad hoc decisions in real time to a thorough data analysis over a longer time period.

The last step that an IoT solution must offer regards the analysis and evaluation of data. Depending on what data are used for what purpose, suitable tools for visualization, calculation and every possible kind of statistical analysis must be available. This includes, for instance, as in the digital farming example, the capability of device data to be linked to data from corporate software, process data and other outline data from the company, as well as with any other data from the internet. Only then can the right decisions be made by product users or a machine drive at the right moment and in real time.

Closing the data chain is, of course, not a one-time event. The availability of data from the networked devices leads to a regular circuit, in which the data—and the networks and people who use them—continually become smarter. Every analysis, every statistical evaluation, every new end node in the network augments the continually growing knowledge about the interrelationships. It will encompass more than the largest and best research group has ever been able to compile.

13.3 IoT Solutions and the SAP Ecosystem

SAP has set the target of supporting its customers to the fullest extent on the way to the Internet of Things, and has given this goal high strategical priority (Fig. 13.1). The IoT solutions should be all that is needed, from the collection of data from a networked device to data management to evaluation and the triggering of a concrete action. At SAP, we have coined a phrase for this: "Close the loop from thing to insight to outcome," that is, the bidirectional closing of the chain from the thing to data analysis to the action. The preconditions are well-suited, as several components of such solutions have already been tested and are in use on a daily basis by hundreds of thousands of customers. Now, they must be expanded to include the networked end devices.

Standard software by SAP is employed for the optimized control of all processes in the company. The Business Suite 4 SAP HANA (SAP S/4HANA) is based on HANA and its in-memory database. The abbreviation HANA stands for **H**igh **P**erformance **An**alytic **A**ppliance, and illustrates that the fundamental technology is available that can be used to generate IoT solutions as described above. Highly scalable, HANA can analyze very large data volumes in an extremely rapid manner. In connection with the solutions for supply chain management (SCM) and enterprise resource management (ERP), the data of things can now be integrated in the processes of enterprises. The SAP Manufacturing Execution System (SAP ME) was able to communicate with machines before the networking of machines via the internet.

SAP makes an open, largely scalable and secure IoT platform (see Fig. 13.2). In the meantime, it is considered beyond our own clientele to be an important example for a reference architecture for Industrie 4.0. It is based on HANA in-memory database technology, in connection with big data technology such as Hadoop and Spark, which was introduced in 2015 as HANA VORA. The HANA Cloud Platform relies on it for the networking of any kinds of data via the cloud.

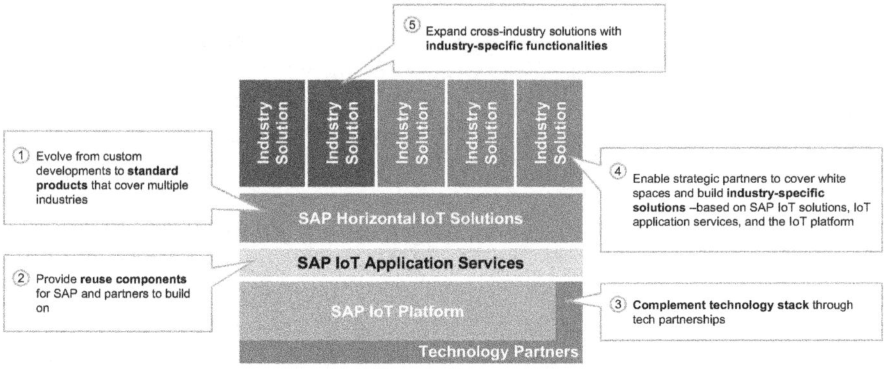

Fig. 13.1 Die Internet of Things strategy of SAP. (© 2016 SAP SE or an SAP affiliate company)

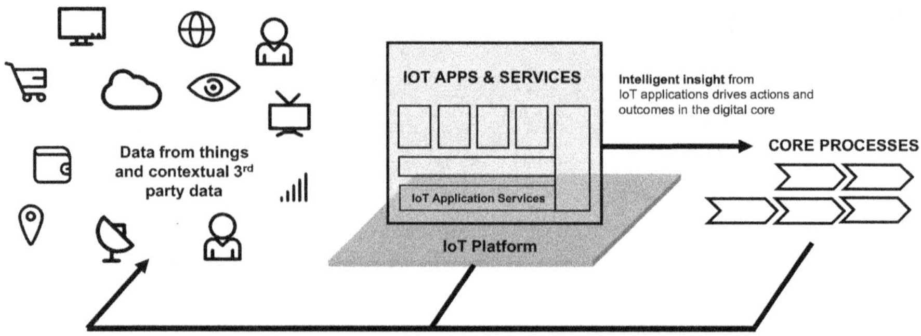

Fig. 13.2 The internet of things suite by SAP and its platform. (© 2016 SAP SE or an SAP affiliate company)

IoT services offer the possibility of integrating end device data, for which standardized services are provided. Via cloud integration, on the other hand, data can be integrated into corporate processes in order to optimize them. The goal of this platform is to offer IoT applications (for which SAP is also setting up a layer of standardized services) that anyone can use to develop applications.

The IoT platform is designed to standardize secure and rapid data flow and enable the integration of all sorts of IoT applications. Openness is so crucial because—similar to the aforementioned Car 2 Car Communication Consortium in traffic—firstly, no single company, no matter what size, is capable of taking all aspects of the Internet of Things into consideration. Secondly, openness is the prerequisite that allows the Internet of Things to develop in the first place, because primarily customers can also turn around and offer their customers applications. The IoT platform is becoming the foundation of an extensive ecosystem that SAP invites all customers and other services providers and developers of IoT applications to join. The networking of things is leading to a networking of the economy.

One good example is the Mindsphere—Siemens Cloud for Industry that was announced at the CeBIT 2015 trade fair. Siemens called it the most important component of its Digital Enterprise Software Suite. And its basis is the SAP HANA Cloud Platform. With the aid of this software, Siemens customers (and, in turn, their customers) can network products and production systems and provide data via the cloud for analysis. Yet, using this cloud, Siemens also targets the optimized use of products and systems, operating surveillance and energy management in real time, invoicing models according to periods of use and all possible scenarios of predictive services.

This industry cloud, based on the SAP IoT platform, will not remain the only one. There will be several others, some with similar goals, and some perhaps with completely different key aspects. Such industry platforms will surely be among the most significant differentiating factors in the competition among industrial enterprises.

13.4 Key Industries and a Sampler of IoT Products

SAP focuses on areas in which, in cooperation with business customers as well as software and services partners, IoT applications can be developed. A few are already available as standard software and can be used for several application scenarios. More are to follow.

Initial topics include production, maintenance, logistics, transportation, vehicles and the integration of smart customers. In addition, several projects can already claim measurable results. With their project Dynamic Maintenance Service, for example, Trenitalia was able to reduce maintenance costs by 8 to 10%. At the high-performance brand Mercedes AMG, which produces highest performance series models in the Mercedes-Benz vehicle range, test drives not able to be concluded successfully can be completed 94% faster, because they can now be aborted in real time if certain parameters are met. The following will present a few solutions in more detail, to illustrate their significance.

13.4.1 Predictive Maintenance and Service

Operators and manufacturers of investment goods, such as machines and systems, generally manage and monitor their products from a considerable distance. If there is a problem it often turns out to be time-consuming and costly to identify the cause. It is even more costly to eliminate the problem, obtain replacement parts and organize a team to conduct repairs. It gets especially expensive when the problem-solving process takes too long or even fails. Then, the system, with its conspicuous consequential costs, will be brought to a standstill or fail to fulfill its necessary functions, perhaps even posing a risk to people.

That is why it has long been a dream for responsible parties to find out about problems punctually, be informed of planned solutions in a quick and inexpensive way, and, finally, be able to organize safe measures that would either avoid a standstill of the machine or system or even prevent the problem from happening in the first place. The Internet of Things can now make this dream a reality. Predictive maintenance is one of the most important fields in which industry is currently working on IoT solutions.

With the SAP Predictive Maintenance and Service Solution, a standard software program has been available since late 2014, based on SAP HANA, that addresses exactly that issue. Remotely via the internet, the data of any combination of systems and devices can be retrieved. Such data indicates operating temperatures, resource consumption, oscillations or vibrations, etc. In short, it delivers information on the "health" of the object of interest. In connection with the historical data of the operation of the respective device, and, if necessary, in connection with comparative data from other devices, as well as with such ambient data as building temperature and climate, capacity utilization and job order planning, it is not only possible to identify emerging problems at an early stage; the information, which has been analyzed and assessed in real time, is now available as operating knowledge and enables real optimization of operations. Service is thus no longer performed by sweepers and firefighters; its high degree of responsibility ensures optimal operation of the system.

For SAP customers, one solution for predictive maintenance and services is a completely natural expansion of corporate software such as Enterprise Asset Management, Customer Service Management or Connected Manufacturing, with which their processes have been supported up to the present. Depending on customer requirements, SAP's predictive maintenance solution can be provided in the cloud as well as implemented on site.

Kaeser Kompressoren, one of the world's largest providers of compressed air systems, currently offers its customers a new degree of quality, based on the predictive maintenance solution which runs on the SAP HANA platform and is precisely tailored to the company's needs. This solution enables the real-time monitoring of parameters such as power consumption, operating condition, security and compressed air quality of a system at the customer's site, always comparing this data to the permissible minimum and maximum values. Via an internet portal, service technicians can analyze this real-time data without having to consult the customer. This naturally speeds up solving any problems and provides for a high degree of reliability and efficiency for the operation of manufacturing systems.

This solution makes Kaeser capable of approaching and completing maintenance tasks at the customer in a predictive way. This improved service results in higher operating reliability and better system runtimes, as well as quicker problem-solving, lower operating risks and shorter innovation cycles, because the knowledge gleaned from the operation of the machines is immediately fed back to development.

Consequently, Kaeser was able to include a new service in its portfolio besides the sales and distribution of compressors: Under the brand name Sigma Air Utility, the manufacturer now also offers compressed air as a service. Customers now no longer need to purchase a compressor. Instead, they receive exactly the amount of compressed air required to do the respective job, and at an extremely high guaranteed availability.

Just how far the value creation chain changes in the course of such IoT solutions can be seen in the work in Kaeser's various corporate divisions, especially in the collaboration between the Design and Compressor Engineering departments and the Service department. For some time now, engineers from Product Design have been spending up to one-fourth of their work time with service specialists, discussing and deciding on the most important demands to development. Service is the area that knows best how well the product works in operation.

13.4.2 Logistics Solutions

In 1950, more than 70% of the world population of 2.5 billion people lived in the country. Since then, population has not only grown to 6.8 billion, but more than half now life in cities. The trend is continuing in this direction. The more industrialization encompasses all countries of Earth, the larger the cities are becoming, and the more difficult it is to organize life in them. Especially all types of traffic are proving to be an increasing problem, for whose solution the limited capacities of available infrastructures, such as roads, railways or waterways, are insufficient. It is becoming increasingly urgent to find new solutions to quickly meet growing demands. That is why, all around in the world, research and pilot projects are being conducted on the so-called smart city, which utilizes the Internet of Things.

One significant component of such solutions involves logistics. How well goods and people can be transported from A to B can no longer be based on the experience of individual traffic participants. So many aspects of traffic circumstances are actually caused by preventable situations, such as searching for a parking space, delivery services failing to get a package to its addressee, avoidable or preventable traffic jams and other conditions that individuals cannot avoid by themselves.

SAP Connected Logistics Software is a new solution for transport and supply chain management. It creates a previously unknown level of transparency in the entire ecosystem of business associates participating in traffic. Connected Logistics provides companies, institutions and individuals with a real-time look at their entire work environment and beyond. Its substantial advantages can be seen using the example of the Hamburger Hafenverwaltung (Hamburg Port Authority, HPA), the largest German port, which must master the loading and unloading of approximately 10,000 ships and nine million containers per year. Sascha Westermann, director of intermodal, operative IT transport management at the HPA, estimates that, by 2025, the port will serve as a trans-shipment center for about 25 million containers annually. And the biggest problem with that, as he describes, is: "We cannot enlarge the port area and need to look for opportunities to use the space we have more efficiently."

With the HPA and business associates T-Systems, SAP is putting together a solution tailored to the Hamburg port for a logistics network that uses the TelematicOne Platform by T-Systems. This solution can be used to collect telematic data of varying sorts in one overview and network it with so-called geofence signals. Geofence signals are generally data from geographic information systems, which pertain to the entry or departure of objects from a defined space. This data can then be linked with the application to create a networked logistics system. For instance, truck drivers can thus receive updated information at any time on accidents or parking possibilities via a connected end device.

If a ship is going to arrive late and the container gate is not open, the driver is informed of available parking spaces. Once the ship has docked, the container gate informs the driver of the shortest path to the gate. The results of this solution for Hamburg are garnering worldwide attention: shorter waiting times, quicker transfer, more efficient route planning and lower fuel costs.

13.4.3 Connected Manufacturing

Industrie 4.0, or the fourth industrial revolution, is seen in Germany as an upheaval that is especially affecting the manufacturing industry: because the networking of people, machines, systems and factories is changing the entire way manufacturing enterprises are organized.

The basis of SAP solutions for Industrie 4.0 is formed by applications which ensure a seamless integration of networked machines into an automated manufacturing system. Manufacturing execution, integration and intelligence applications provide production that holds the right answers ready at the right moment. They are also the link between the factory floor and the management offices. Yet the vision of Industrie 4.0 stretches beyond these realms. It includes the integration of the core functions of a company, from product development to production to the supplier chain and replacement part warehouse. To achieve this, companies will have to link systems engineering with production IT and corporate software. Those who do so are ahead of the competition.

One such visionary enterprise is Harley-Davidson. In one of Harley's new production facilities, every machine is a networked device, and every relevant variable is continuously measured and evaluated. The system components supply performance data that the manufacturing system uses for predictive maintenance, to wholly avoid failure of a machine or tool. The installment of a part into a motorcycle is planned to the tenth of a second, and the system warns factory floor management on the level of individual components if something does not go according to plan. Harley itself measures the temperature, humidity and fan speeds in the building. The continuous evaluation identifies factors that can be used to improve efficiency.

In this new factory, built according to the state of the art and the debate about Industrie 4.0, Harley manufactures 1700 motorcycle variants in one single production line, and every 90s, a motorcycle built to customer specifications rolls off of the conveyor belt; that is 25% more than before. The time required to manufacture a motorcycle has shrunk from 21 days to 6 h.

13.5 Industrie 4.0 as a Political Challenge

The Federal Republic of Germany has made Industrie 4.0 the core of its digital agenda. In Brussels, too, it is a political topic attracting a great deal of attention. SAP sees this as an opportunity to bring topics to the forefront that cannot be solved by industry alone, and is thus also involved on that level in the discussions and activities.

After the representatives of industry, research, the trade associations and both the Federal Ministry for Education and Research and that of Economic Affairs and Energy took over management of the *Plattform Industrie 4.0* in spring of 2015, new communication paths were established on the federal level. In the individual states, the situation varies greatly. Naturally, the places delving into the topic are also the places where industry has an especially great significance for the economy, such as in the states of North-Rhine Westphalia and Baden-Württemberg, in which their own initiatives have appeared in the form of It's OWL and the *Allianz Industrie 4.0*. One great advantage is certainly also that not only industrial associations, but also trade unions, such as the IG Metall, participate in the platform.

SAP sees four core task areas whose basic parameters need to be defined by lawmakers:

1. The promotion of suitable research and innovation activities, such as in the area of standardization
2. The formulation of legal parameters for Industrie 4.0 and the handling of the data generated and used there
3. The promotion of venture capital and tax-related measures
4. Education and advanced training in the digitized economy

The discussion surrounding data security plays a large role in Germany as well as all of Europe. Regarding the Internet of Things, this discussion does not primarily focus on personal data, but technical data that is collected or transmitted by devices and things. In this regard, a detailed debate is necessary; one that will define and design the handling of such industrial internet data. To whom does such data belong? What can be done with it under which circumstances? And how will the protection of personal data be guaranteed if it is a part of industrially-generated information? Here, politics needs to get involved. Especially for data-based business models, lawmakers must make sure to leave enough space for Germany and Europe to realize personal data protection while at the same time ensuring global competitiveness. Regulations that are too strict may lead to Germany falling behind the USA and Asia.

Young start-ups and innovative enterprises also do not have it easy. Many complain about bureaucratic and legislative obstacles that make it difficult for new companies, so important to the economy, to establish solid footing in the Internet of Things and Industrie 4.0. Venture capital that is promoted specifically on the state level could improve this situation.

Once there was a car-scrap bonus in Germany. Now, people are discussing purchase bonuses for electric vehicles. Similar incentive plans for the backbone of digitalization, namely hardware and software, are nowhere to be found. Yet several measures are conceivable, from tax incentives to depreciation allowances. It is positive that the Federal Ministry of Education and Research has decided to put more money into the promotion of small and midsize enterprises. But, on the whole, there is still a lot to be done if Germany as an industrial location is to benefit from its SME industry.

Adjusting education is also necessary. The traditional scholastic and academic paths generate specialists that are excellently qualified for certain tasks in the previous processes of industry. However, we need changes to those educational paths to suit networked, cross-discipline cooperation and systemic approaches.

Improved foundations for understanding the digital world and its important technologies should be laid as early as in elementary and secondary school. Otherwise, Germany will miss out on employing a portion of its youth in successful jobs in industry and the service sector.

Germany also need a greater permeability of its academic departments in order to make multidisciplinary work an element of education, because we once again need generalists in large numbers, who are capable of having on overview of the entire system, with all of its specialist facets. Only such people will be able to take on leadership roles in industry.

Amid all of these questions, the debate today unfortunately focuses too much on preserving inventory and not enough on farsightedness. Too little attention is paid to the opportunities created by digitalization. On the political level, this is more likely to lead to regulatory than to creative measures. The latter, from the perspective of SAP, would be urgent and desirable.

On an international level, as well, such as in dealing with China or the USA, Industrie 4.0 can profit from the active role of the federal government. Several discussions have already taken place on this subject. Especially China is showing a very strong interest in undertaking standardization measures and technical architectures, such as the reference architecture model of *Industrie 4.0* (RAMI40). Regular meetings on the level of working groups have bolstered the impression up to now that the Chinese are interested in long-term, constructive cooperation with German industry and the federal and state governments.

It is time for a comprehensive social debate on the future of the digitized economy and society. The Internet of Things and Industrie 4.0 offers so many positive approaches, so many possibilities to improve work and life, that this debate has the right stuff to increase interest in designing the future on a larger scale.

The Digital Enterprise Takes Shape

14

Anton S. Huber

Abstract

When I wrote my chapter in the first book about Industrie 4.0 about three years ago, the entire situation in this area was characterized by vagueness as to the definition of Industrie 4.0. You could feel a great sense of anxiety and the impression that we were talking about something very significant, perhaps affecting the very existence of some companies, of branches of industry, and even entire national economies, such as in Germany, with a value creation structure characterized by small and midsize enterprises and oriented toward production. In the meanwhile, the fog has lifted a bit, and we think we can make out some sharper outlines. This chapter will attempt to further clarify these outlines here and there, as well as share some impressions I have collected in the area of digitalization in global business. At the 2016 Hanover Trade Fair, it was easy to get the impression that the general anxiety on this topic had diminished considerably. Yet, there were hardly any signs that great progress had been made in defining content. There was, however, to some extent, a conspicuously flexible use of the term 'Industrie 4.0,' overheard when some suppliers described their automation products and systems. If one wanted to make an interim summary about Industrie 4.0 at this point, one would have to admit that, even though not much useful content has been defined, awareness of the quickly progressing digitalization in industry and the resulting expected changes and necessary reactive measures have increased substantially. That fact alone may justify the efforts previously taken.

For pragmatic reasons, because a sufficient definition for Industrie 4.0 had been lacking, in my first chapter of the first book on Industrie 4.0, I concentrated on our own digitalization strategy, which we at Siemens summarize using the term 'digital

A. S. Huber (✉)
Siemens AG, Gleiwitzer Straße 555, 90475, Nuremberg, Germany
E-Mail: Anton.Huber@siemens.com

U. Sendler (ed.), *The Internet of Things*,
https://doi.org/10.1007/978-3-662-54904-9_14

enterprise,' and established its proximity to Industrie 4.0. However, our digitalization strategy began as early as in 2001, with the acquisition of Orsi, a small Italian enterprise which at the time had been focused on the development of MES systems, among other things. digitalization accelerated significantly starting in 2007 with the acquisition of UGS. In this chapter, I will report on the progress we have made in the meantime in the implementation of our digitalization strategy. I will let readers decide what falls under the category of Industrie 4.0 and what does not. I will also relate the observations and developments regarding significant production procedures that particularly rely on digitalization and data consistency.

14.1 Digitalization of Industry

The broad expansion of digital technology use at the end of the 1980s in signal transmission and signal processing led to great changes in its first phase in those companies whose business purpose was the processing and distribution of information in the narrower sense. That is why the effects of this technology were first seen in the entertainment industry, especially obvious in music, film, telecommunications and print media.

In the manufacturing industries, the consequences of progressive digitalization have been showing effects for at least 15 years now, and it is generally expected that, in the coming 10–15 years, it will lead to substantial changes. Some people are even speaking of the fourth industrial revolution in this context. Due to the significance of this topic for the manufacturing industries in Germany, German industrial associations established the initiative *Industrie 4.0*, which is also supported by the federal government. Its goal is to accompany and guide the developments and effects of digitalization in industry and the working world.

Digitalization has long since found its place in companies, in the meantime garnering a high degree of importance. In economic and transactional processes, which are easier to standardize, software support, that is, digitalization, has already progressed greatly and is more systematically pronounced than in the technical value creation processes. Industrial enterprises in recent years have invested many billions of euros in so-called ERP and CRM software, developing, almost unseen by the public eye, into formidable data processing organizations whose information content (data assets) represents a significant portion of the respective corporate value today in many cases. Through the daily work of their many employees, these data assets, and thus the corporate value, are continually growing. This relationship between corporate data and corporate value, which is becoming increasingly apparent, is a significant reason for the rising sensitivity with regard to the safety of this data.

The fault-free processing, storage and increasingly timely provision and distribution of this information in companies themselves, but also between their partners (extended enterprise) is an important prerequisite for a company to prevail in today's economy and succeed in achieving its corporate objective.

Of course, the processing industries still see the transformation process from information and knowledge to physical goods as their core value creation process. Unfortunately, especially in this area, IT and software support is still being used in a very fragmented and haphazard way. This is largely due to the significantly more complex processes and the fact that standardization for these processes, if at all possible, is a great deal more difficult to implement than in economic management processes. Variety in the product creation process is in many cases the highest mode of differentiation among the competition, ensuring advantages over competitors. It is thus understandable that nobody wants to sacrifice this advantage to standardization.

Automobile manufacturers, for instance, despite the fact that, seen from afar, they all only produce one product, namely an automobile, employ a variety of processes in several subsections of product creation which have their justification in competitive advantage. That is why there is no standard process, defined to the smallest detail, for the manufacture of motor vehicles.

It is especially in such differentiating processes that competitive advantage is increasingly being influenced by digitalization, that is, the use of IT and software tools. However, due to the high degree of flexibility required, IT solutions and software tool chains for employment in technical core value creation areas (PLM, SCM) must be designed in a much different way than software used in economic management processes, which allow a large degree of standardization.

At the same time, no matter from what side you approach investment in digitalization of the entire technical workflow in industrial enterprises, you cannot get away without using a platform that ensures joint data management (see Fig. 14.1). Only through such a platform can the enormous production potential be unlocked that is currently on hand in most industrial firms.

Siemens, due to large investments it has made in recent years, has expanded its data management platform Teamcenter, which originally only managed CAD data, into a powerful corporate platform that can manage all technical data, starting from PLM process data right up to production, that is, all data pertaining to the value

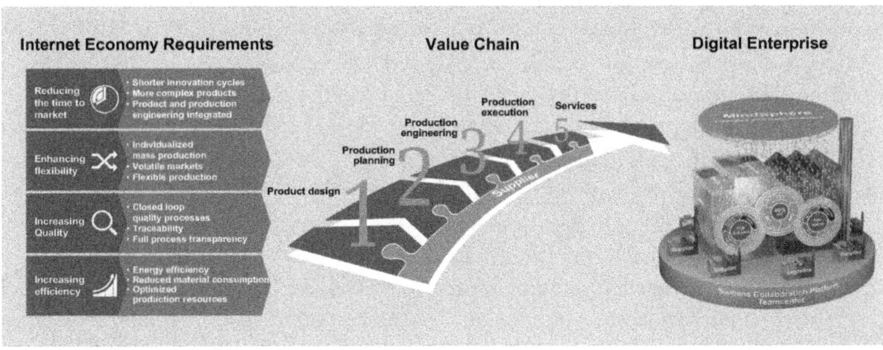

Fig. 14.1 The PLM platform is the backbone without which the entire value creation chain would not be possible. (© Siemens AG 2016)

creation process of an enterprise. Since it was clear right from the beginning that Siemens would never develop all software applications for industrial value creation processes itself, the platform was conceived as an open platform. With the aid of standardized interfaces, customers can connect all of their software applications to the Teamcenter. Thus, the Teamcenter is at the heart of the entire Digital Enterprise Software Suite of Siemens, serving as its common data management platform.

14.2 Digitalization and Standardization

Digitalization of information transfer and processing, however, has made the ubiquitous internet possible, and it in turn has not only led to massive changes in established businesses, but also to completely new business with previously unknown business models, such as Amazon, Facebook and Google, to name a few of the most famous ones. These companies, solely through their existence and business conduct, are contributing to further, momentous changes to the economy and society. Perhaps the most significant changes in this regard are the very high speed of information and the resulting transparency in all areas of life. Both also influence the continuously accelerating economic cycle.

The associated changes are forcing companies to also increasingly accelerate their value creation processes. This can only work if they not only automate their production processes, but also if they continue to automate their information, creation and decision-making processes. The prerequisite needed to achieve this goal is a complete digitalization and seamless linking of all information and knowledge in the company, and especially regarding high value-creation technical processes and areas.

The claim that Amazon, Facebook, Google and other internet companies would not exist, had they first tried to subject their technological base to global standardization and wait before clearing up legal questions with regard to their business models is hard to contest. Interestingly, in addition to the goal of German industry to be the world leaders in the introduction and use of digitalization in production, one of the core elements of the *Industrie 4.0* initiative is precisely about standardization and a guaranteed legal framework.

In the short time in which internet-based enterprises have existed, many of them have already surpassed their economic zenith and are on their way down again, if not already gone. These companies, during their lifetime, did not even notice the blessings of international standardization committees, with their infamous dynamics, let alone profit from them.

As mentioned above, today, new demands for international—or at least European—standards for reference architectures and a guaranteed legal framework is being broadly discussed regarding Industrie 4.0. After lengthy negotiations, such discussions may bear fruit in the distant future, but it is questionable as to whether they will still be relevant to the existing technological, economic and social boundary conditions of today. Only one thing is certain: Any German industry leading digitalization cannot be produced or promoted with such a strategy.

The problems associated with the high speed of innovation naturally cannot be solved by completely renouncing standardization. There are certainly practice-proven technologies in some areas where standardization is worthwhile. However, we must realize that standards do not represent laws which people can be forced to observe. Rather, they sometimes act like dangerous quicksand that buries huge investments within a very short period—as could be observed a short while ago in the communications industry, with the exodus to voice-over IP telephony, which hit Siemens especially hard.

Another problem that cannot be avoided regarding national standards is that they can be used fairly elegantly as a protection of national markets, even when sometimes the wildest of reasons, including "national security interests," are given.

Unfortunately, it is said that leading industrial enterprises cannot wait for the blessings of such renown institutions. Neither can all legal or technical standards for future business be defined in advance—at least not in a competitive environment. As difficult as it may be for some firms, if companies want to improve their competitive position, they must push for the rapid and systematic digitalization of their enterprises. The high innovation rate in digital technologies and global competition will unfortunately cause the state of digitalization to become quickly outdated, such that every target in the digitalization process will be a moving one. The best advice that can be given for digitalization is to be prepared for the continual, rapid development and improvements in IT infrastructure and software. That is why it will not be so advantageous in the future to purchase IT infrastructure and software tools; leasing or renting them would make much more sense.

Industrial enterprises can only maintain their productivity growth and competitive position in the future if they continue to systematically develop and automate their workflows in the specifically technical areas with the aid of continually developed software tools, as has been the practice for years in the realm of production workflows. Due to the high investment rate, the software necessary for these efforts is unfortunately increasingly taking on the character of a consumable with a short shelf life, which is why they require improvements and maintenance regularly and at ever shorter intervals.

14.3 Where Is Digitalization on a Global Level?

As indicated above, digitalization in industry influences the entire value creation chain, and not just production. In the current Industrie 4.0 discussion, however, buzzwords like "autonomous systems," "control in the cloud," "smart robots" and so on, play a dominant role. Yet we cannot forget that the necessary acceleration in industrial value creation cannot be achieved solely with a further increase in the degree of automation in production.

After the takeover of UGS in 2007 and my many customer visits around the world shortly thereafter, I realized that the degree of systematic software use varied greatly from company to company. The early adopters were probably seven years ahead of the middle-ranking industrial enterprises (to which this author considers

Siemens to belong). Not much has changed since then; the gap has not gotten much smaller.

The difference was less about the number and scope of the software tools used than the consequence with which workflows were systematically and consistently connected and supported with software tools. In contrast, in other companies, there were very many different software tools, some even having several different ones for the same task, and similarly, several application islands in which, as a rule, if they even allowed data transfer, it was not automated or consistent. The problems with faulty and untended data cropping up over time as a result are well known.

A really impressive example that lingers in my memory was that of a Japanese manufacturer of digital cameras. This company had already developed its cameras for series production at the time, without actually building even one physical development prototype. Based on Siemens software products, it had established a digital workflow with its own high investments over a period of about seven years. This workflow was based solely on digital mock-ups and simulations (including for vendor parts). With this solution, the period of origin of a new camera was reduced by more than 40%.

If you take into account the position of the German software industry on the world market when evaluating the degree of digitalization of German industry, the starting position is not especially encouraging. The degree of systematic use of software in industrial value creation, however, is particularly worrisome, especially in small and midsize enterprises. In other areas of industry, software is still considered to primarily be a cost factor in need of reduction. The great potential to increase productivity through software often goes unrecognized, and is thus not systematically developed. In contrast to the direct human resources costs in production, the HR costs in the rest of the work processes of a company, especially technical processes, are generally several times higher. The automation of these processes to trigger a necessary increase in productivity is essentially only possible through the use of software. The fact that investments and additional operating costs are necessary and that the resulting gain in productivity cannot be turned into profit at a ratio of 100% still evokes incredulous amazement in many industrial enterprises.

It is probably no surprise that, in an environment like German industry, in which software stores had never really attracted much excitement, no great value was placed on the application of software either. To that extent, we can speak of a very diverse attitude toward software here, which today is having an even more unfavorable effect than it did in the past.

Speaking of excitement, it is remarkable to observe how clearly many Chinese companies recognize the potential of digitalization and, despite relatively low wages and salaries, are systematically and aggressively investing in the software-based support of their technical processes. There is already a large number of Chinese firms which, with respect to digitalization, are among the global leaders, including Haier.

The danger of being left behind in the digitalization process in German industry is less prevalent in the development and provision of hardware and software suitable for Industrie 4.0; rather, it lies in an excessively slow and unsystematic application of available software tools and IT technologies in current value creation processes.

14.4 Integrated Product Development

Since the introduction of the PLC (programmable logic controller), it has been evident that demands to the PLC have steadily risen, and the scope of the PLC code necessary for production sites and machines has reached an enormous degree of complexity.

Around the year 2004, a conviction grew at Siemens that the PLC engineering tools being employed up to that point could only perform complex tasks with difficulty from a technical standpoint, but no longer at costs that were acceptable. This problem, which continued to intensify, led to the definition of a new process step called virtual commissioning. It was designed to test the generated PLC program and its respective hardware environment and make sure it was virtually bug-free before commissioning began on the individual modules of a production system. The consequence was the demand for a comprehensive system simulation, which also took the dynamics of the respective machine into consideration. This meant that the automation logistics of the corresponding machine or machine module would have to have been completed before or concurrent with the development of the machine. Of course, at that early point in time, nobody was thinking about the generation of a PLC code with the aid of a corresponding PLC engineering tool, but more likely about a design tool with which the desired process logistics could easily be graphically depicted. The high-level language code generated by such a tool can subsequently be used to generate the corresponding PLC code with the aid of a compiler. This method has several far-reaching consequences:

1. The generation of a machine's automation logistics is uncoupled from the generation of the PLC code.
2. Automaton logistics is generally indifferent toward any PLC. The customer does not have to make a decision regarding which PLC is to be used for machine automation until a much later time.
3. The development engineer responsible for developing the mechanics creates the process logistics of a machine or production system him- or herself. A software tool is integrated into the mechanics CAD tool for this purpose, with which the engineer can independently graphically generate the process logistics in the machine, without producing a PLC code. The data generated from this procedure also represents the engineer's automation specifications, which are much more complete than any textual specification document.

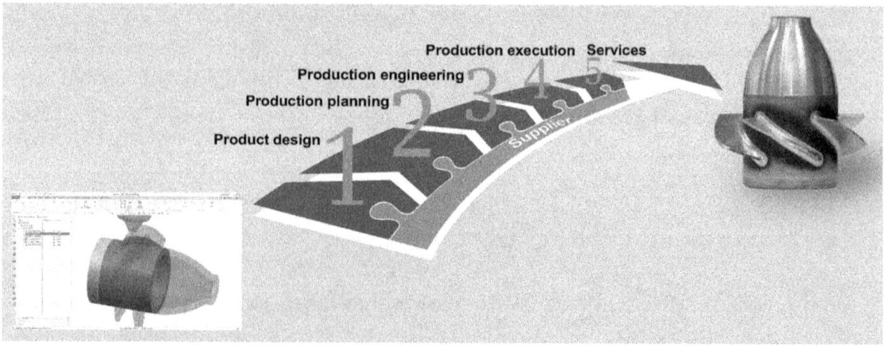

Fig. 14.2 Continuous development from product design to system simulation. (© Siemens AG 2016)

4. The development engineer can virtually operate a model of his or her machine with the generated logistics, and with the help of this simulation, optimize the mechanics and process logistics.
5. The effort required today by modern automation engineers will be reduced by an estimated 70% to 80%.

This notion and ones like it were examined at Siemens in the years 2004 and 2005. In consequence, development of the TIA portal began in the year 2006 and the takeover of the software company UGS took place in May of 2007.

At the 2016 Hanover Trade Fair, Siemens, in the context of its "Digital Enterprise Software Suite," presented a preproduction version of its software tool chain for mechatronics design. In doing so, it implemented exactly the engineering scenario described above of continuous development from product concept to system simulation (see Fig. 14.2). Initial commercial release is planned for the 2017 Hanover Trade Fair.

In retrospect, the development of this tool set was even considerably more complex than first expected. Architecture work for the products NX and Teamcenter proved especially complicated. These products were designed such that they could work well with geometrical objects, for obvious reasons. They possessed no capabilities for contextual management of logical objects as they are employed in automation. After several years of elaborate work, the architectures have been redesigned to also support automation. The genetics of automation engineering is already present today in the CAD Tool NX.

14.5 Digital Connection of Product Development and Production

As can be observed in practical situations, eliminating bottlenecks in a system makes another bottleneck all the more obvious. We also see this here. When the number of products to be manufactured increases based on an accelerated development, then the problems surfacing in the transfer of the product to the production phase and in manufacture run-up are even more disruptive. In addition, the continually evolving individualization granted to customers for their desired products means that the change frequency increases considerably. To control costs, it is vital for all changes to be implemented as quickly and failure-free as possible. Continual software support spanning the entire workflow is essential to achieve this.

In a somewhat more thorough analysis, we find a fundamental problem posing a great barrier to seamless data permeability and consistent data management in practical operations.

As a rule, the workflow plan required for production is generated in the ERP system. Regarding data, it is completely detached from all other software systems used in the PLM area and in production. As a result, the data models do not match. That is why data is fed in from the various sources by hand. It is not hard to imagine that mistakes can happen right in the early phases, and that it is especially difficult to keep the data updated and consistent when the many people involved in the product creation process start making needed changes. This is a process which, especially for the introduction of new products, runs in a continual and diverse manner. Today, there is no software mechanism that automatically ensures that information is made transparent for all participants. Costly errors are inevitable in practical situations.

This problem can be solved easily by not generating the workflow plan detached from the ERP system, but rather—embedded in the PLM system—creating it as a simple add-on. All data required by the ERP system is transferred to it from the PLM system. Consistent data management between the PLM system, workflow and ERP system can thus be provided automatically. This is also the correct process from a work-system point of view, since product and process changes almost always have their origin in the technical areas and can be entered into the PLM system installed right there.

Thus, the workflow plan is generated directly at the source of all product data in the PLM system (parts list, bill of materials, etc.) and from this point on is simply forwarded, without a break in the system. The PLM system makes sure that all changes are always visible to everyone participating in the workflow. All process data required for production and all data relevant for the manufacturing facilities, which are generated elsewhere, can be entered anywhere using the same tool and is then clearly linked to the existing data.

Siemens also made this concept a reality in recent years and presented it to customers and the public and this year's Hanover Trade Fair as a preproduction version under the name "Closed Loop Manufacturing." Using this software system, the work effort and fault frequency in the production implementation of a new product can be drastically reduced. Changes to the product and the production process can also be quickly implemented, and with a high degree of security. With this system, another complex and significant step in the product creation process can be automated and highly accelerated.

14.6 Production-Optimized Products—Design for Manufacturing

For several years now, one of the most important industrial insights has been that, for product development, favorable manufacturability must be ensured right from the start. Production machines, production process and product design are optimized in an iterative process until the production costs become minimal and the product quality optimal. Unfortunately, it is just as common that, due to time constraints, it is impossible for the hardware-supported development processes used in real situations to allow several iteration loops of the product and production process. It is only since the entire value creation chain can be digitized that we have now been able to generate a fairly good digital twin, that is, a complete digital representation. Using the digital twin, parallel product development is now possible, and with the aid of the simulation, an optimization of product and production process is feasible. This results not only in an optimized product and respective production process with regard to cost and quality, but also, in some cases, a significant reduction in development time.

14.7 Additive Manufacturing

In contrast to the removal of material in layers to produce a particular workpiece (done with conventional machine tools), additive manufacturing represents the layered assembly of a workpiece. Although the principle is easy to understand, implementation of this technology extending to industrial use has been delayed for some time, especially due to high technical and material demands. The basic patents for this procedure stem from the second half of the 1980s. Siemens has been working with stereolithography, as this procedure is called, since 1989.

Great advances in materials and the additive procedure in recent years have made this technology market-ready, and is employed today not only for manufacturing prototypes, but also in the series production of highly-resilient parts for gas turbines, airplanes, rocket engines, Formula 1 cars and several other applications. Now, without tremendous risk, it can be said that this production technology will significantly change the industrial manufacturing world more in the coming years than any other process. The production times of workpieces will continue to be reduced, and the quality of the finished parts will steadily improve, with regard to the produced surfaces as well as to stability and elasticity.

Depending on demands to the finished part, this technology is already competitive for industrial series production of up to 10,000 units per year. The new design software with integrated simulation options for product and production make it capable of raising the full potential of this technology. For example, great savings in materials and thus a reduction in weight can be achieved in workpieces manufactured from solid materials with the aid of so-called bionic designs, while maintaining or even improving mechanical wear.

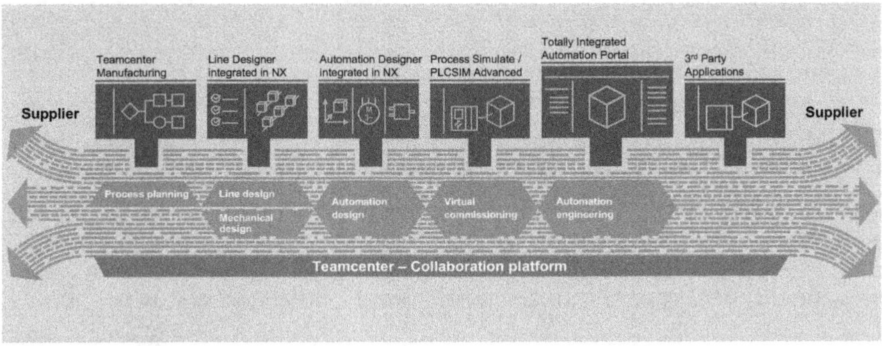

Fig. 14.3 Digital tool landscape for design and production with additive manufacturing. (© Siemens AG 2016)

The flexibility that companies achieve when using this production technology—coupled with a seamless digital tool landscape, from product planning to machine control of the 3D printer—is no less impressive. Mass customization, as it is called, that is, tailoring individual, specific products to their respective customers, will become possible in several areas.

For this purpose, Siemens has already developed a software tool landscape (Fig. 14.3) with which all work steps can be accomplished digitally, from product planning to the generation of the control program for the Sinumerik, the computer which controls the 3D printer. We now literally have a "magic button" that developers can press at will when they want their object to be produced. This technology, which has also reached series-production readiness, was also presented at this year's Hanover Trade Fair.

In the future, 3D printers and the accompanying digital workflow are a technological combination that will not only be necessary in many producing enterprises involved in the internet economy, but in any enterprise hoping to secure its longevity.

14.8 Mass Production with Machine Tools—Mass Machining

The supreme significance of speed in the internet economy, in our case, shortening the time to market, can be seen in the following example:

Up to about ten years ago, mobile phone cases were exclusively produced using a plastic injection molding process. This process is usually chosen for parts that are manufactured in large quantities, because the high tool costs can be set off by the high production lots. Since mobile phones are produced in lots of several hundred million, this procedure is especially suitable.

As suggested above, a corresponding form, or injection mold, has to be manufactured into which the liquid plastic can be injected. The plastic part thus produced is removed from the mold after the plastic cools.

For this process, the production and optimization of the injection mold is extremely time-consuming, sometimes taking several weeks or months, depending on the complexity of the part. Therefore, reacting quickly to market demands or product innovations of competitors is only possible with a relatively long delay. In a very season-driven business like that of mobile phones (such as at Christmastime), the low flexibility described represents a large business risk. The respective manufacturers have thus been looking for a flexible process that requires no die-cut parts. Such a process already existed: milling the case from a metal block with the aid of a machine tool. The advantage was a very high degree of flexibility; it was possible to produce a different case with every run, with virtually no time delay. The disadvantage was that the production of the cases was significantly more expensive. Because of the enormous time competition, however, the more expensive production process prevailed. One consequence of this was the sudden ordering of tens of thousands of machine tools. Siemens was also able to profit greatly from this boom with its CNC machine control system, Sinumerik. Such machines can primarily be seen in China, where they stand by the thousands on large factory floors and produce smart phone cases around the clock, 365 days a year. About ten years ago, nobody would have believed that such simple parts could have been produced in such large numbers with such an expensive process as single milling from a metal block. The needs of internet business have made it necessary to rank the savings in time higher than the higher costs for the part. The internet economy has ensured that conventional industrial assessment standards, previously seen as stable, have suddenly lost their validity. It would be wise to be prepared for many more such surprises in the future.

14.9 Cloud Technology in Industry

To close this chapter, I would like to examine the topic of cloud technology and its significance for industry. Cloud technology is not new. We differentiate between the public and the private cloud. Roughly, the difference can be described as follows: In the public cloud, users do not know where an application is physically running. They also do not know where their data is being physically stored. It could basically be anywhere in the world. In a private cloud, customers can either agree with a provider where their applications and data are to be physically stored, or users can operate their own cloud. The latter case does not represent a service business, because the customer is the owner of the cloud infrastructure.

In addition to the all-too-familiar, existing risks relating to data security on the internet and in IT systems, this issue is becoming more problematic through the use of public cloud technology, especially where data, and not only apps, are stored in the cloud. Of course, a great deal is being done on all fronts to keep a handle on developing problems. However, this also means additional costs, as well as a reduction in transaction speed, which could be especially relevant with regard to industrial automation (control- and regulation-related intervention).

In the meantime, the conviction has spread that the desired degree of security cannot be achieved using technology alone. It has also been observed that, for most IT applications, outside-in security (that is, protection from unauthorized access from outside, such as hacker attacks) is easier to achieve than inside-out security (data theft with the aid of data storage media, the installation of back doors, etc.), because the latter has a much more critically pronounced human component.

Just how convinced cloud providers are of the security of their services can be easily seen in the guarantees cited in the contractual conditions. The user can decide for every use whether he or she wishes to carry the additional risk or not.

First and foremost behind the cloud technology lurks a business principle: Every type of IT service (from IT infrastructure and processing power to storage space, to application software) is made available to any interested party via the internet without these parties having to make any investments, except for perhaps an end device. The services provided are invoiced according to use. This business principle is of particular interest for users, who can switch providers without great effort. The higher the switching costs are, the riskier this technology will be for users. We can assume that every degree of inflexibility in a specific timeframe must be payed in higher prices. A fairly comprehensive study of cloud users for ERP software conducted recently showed no indication of price advantages for this technology in comparison to conventional installations.

For several years, Siemens, as well as other companies, has been offering customers so-called remote services. Data transfer necessary for these services is secured via conventional communication lines. During the recent update of the technological basis at Siemens, the company selected a cloud technology for its own remote service business. The Siemens industry cloud platform "MindSphere" was largely based on SAP technology. It will also soon be available for the platforms of all other known cloud providers. Siemens also makes its platform available to its customers, securing all prerequisites needed for customers to also be able to install their own apps, such as for data analysis. Due to contractual restrictions, Siemens is not authorized to access the data of its customers stored in the cloud. Such access would only be possible on an individual contract basis.

The position of Siemens on the use of industrial data is clear: Customer data is exclusively available to that customer for use—unless there is an individual contract stipulating a different right of use.

Considerable hype has developed in recent years around cloud technology in industry. Especially regarding remote service and additional, completely new business models, expectations are high. Yet insiders know that data transfer is not the big problem in remote service; instead, it is often the equipment of the machines and systems monitoring the service, with their expensive sensors, which represent a relatively high hurdle. That is not about to change with cloud technology.

Just how high expectations to completely new business models are, is a puzzle. Based on the fact alone that industry is primarily a B2B environment, we must assume boundary conditions that have a fairly conservative effect on new business models. Here, too, considerable disillusionment will soon set in, if it is not already doing so.

In summary, we can say that, in the last three years since the first book was published, both digitalization on the whole and Industrie 4.0 have continued to develop in a relatively evolutionary way; to date, there is no sign of revolution in sight.

Industrial Connectivity And Industrial Analytics, Core Components of the Factory of the Future

15

Jan Stefan Michels

Abstract

The following essay provides an overview of the topic of Industrie 4.0 and intelligent technical systems in the realm of production. It starts with the motivation to achieve and employ Industrie 4.0—the challenges facing manufacturing enterprises. Based on that discussion, the major aspects of Industrie 4.0 and intelligent technical systems will be described. The essay closes with concrete approaches for implementation, as well as a few practical examples, spanning infrastructure for digitalization to consistent use of generated data for the optimization of production.

15.1 Industrie 4.0 and Intelligent Technical Systems

Driven by new technologies in microelectronics and software, the dynamics in the development of technical systems are swiftly increasing. This can be seen not only in the private realm, with the many technical "helpers" that we use every day and in smartphones and motor vehicles, where such advances often emerge first, but also in the industrial environment. It is obvious that machines are becoming more and more intelligent and can adapt on their own power to new ambient conditions and requirements. Simultaneously, their range of functions, reliability and efficiency are growing at a brisk pace.

This is especially true for production. Ever since the term Industrie 4.0 was coined in 2011 at the Hanover Trade Fair, research institutes, companies, associations and politics have been scrutinizing ways to specify its potential and achieve

J. S. Michels (✉)
Weidmüller Interface GmbH & Co. KG, Klingenbergstraße 16, 32758 Detmold, Germany
E-Mail: JanStefan.Michels@weidmueller.de

U. Sendler (ed.), *The Internet of Things*,
https://doi.org/10.1007/978-3-662-54904-9_15

technologies and solutions to harvest that potential [1]. The primary understanding of Industrie 4.0 in this context is the utilization of information and communications technologies in manufacturing companies. The term "intelligent technical systems" is also used within the context of production, that is, machines and systems based on the symbiosis of engineering and information technology and which are capable of adapting to the wishes of the user and ambient conditions [2].

However, the term Industrie 4.0 should not be understood too narrowly because, in the end, virtually all corporate areas will be affected by digitalization of production. The German *Plattform Industrie 4.0* thus defines the term as a "new step in the organization and control of the entire value creation chain, spanning the lifecycle of the product, which is increasingly driven primarily by individual customer wishes and the continued increase in market complexity" [3]. This shows that it not only pertains to the systems and technologies on the shop floor, that is, within the factory, but to the complete value creation system, including the product lifecycle and the supply chain.

15.1.1 Megatrends and Drivers for Manufacturing Companies

If we examine the major megatrends (Fig. 15.1) and drivers of global development [4, 5], we basically find just a few influences to which the development dynamics of recent decades can be traced: The term **globalization** represents the increasing social and economic linking of nations. **Demographic change** describes the change in global population numbers and age distribution. The increasing **shortage of resources** as well as **climate change** are rooted in population- and economic growth—most certainly caused by technological development, which, in turn, is the key to counteract this development. Last but not least is the development toward a **global knowledge society**, meaning a growing significance in knowledge as the basis of communal living and cooperation in society and business.

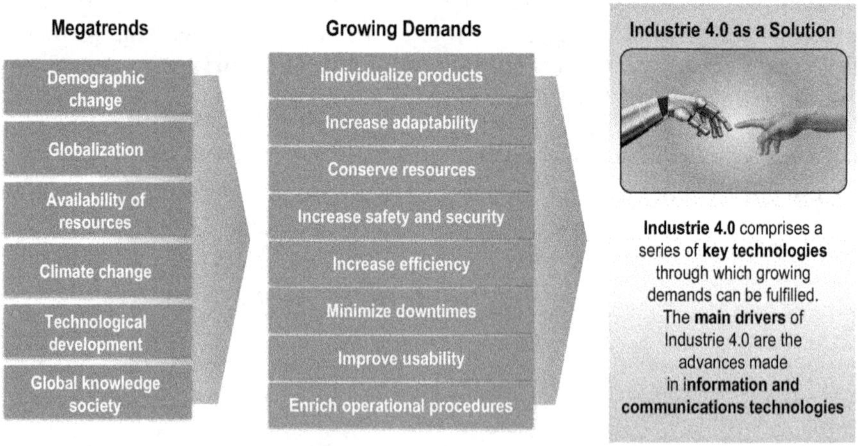

Fig. 15.1 Global megatrends and demands of manufacturing companies. (Weidmüller)

These trends are surely not new, but have been perceptible for decades. Nevertheless, they are a hot topic, because they are driving product innovation and the business models of almost all enterprises. In order to prevail in global competition, they deal with the following challenges:

- **Individualize products:** Nowadays, customers do not want to make what they see as compromises with standard components, but prefer custom solutions for their individual problems. On one hand, this demand is a good opportunity to make your product stand out from the competition, but on the other hand, customers will increasingly expect the availability of such individual products as a matter of course. Even if most of the examples come from the consumer industry, we can clearly see that custom-made solutions are also increasingly in demand for industrial applications.
- **Increase adaptability:** Even if product volume is increasing overall, one consequence of individualization is that the lot size of each specific part and product is decreasing—right down to the proverbial "lot size one." This presents enterprises with the challenge of needing to make their innovation process and supply chain considerably more adaptable and flexible in the future. This not only pertains to flexibility with regard to volatile lot sizes and production jobs, but also to changing customer needs and thus changing products and technologies.
- **Increase efficiency and conserve resources:** In global competition, manufacturing companies are faced with the necessity of continually raising the productivity of their processes and systems. Basically, this concerns the use of all production factors, but especially the use of energy and raw materials. Generally, there is great potential here to improve the efficiency of production. At the same time, demands from the legislative and normative side are on the rise, such that here, too, there is a necessity to handle resources efficiently.
- **Minimize downtimes:** The availability of production systems is a decisive factor in securing a competitive advantage. On one hand, system standstills lead to lost turnover, and on the other hand, they usually bring even more significant costs in their wake—especially when they are unplanned and cause high costs for repair and maintenance. Excellent examples include production processes that must run continually, such as in power generation, steel production and the pharmaceutical industry. Minimizing downtimes is thus also a significant driver for a series of research projects in the areas of condition monitoring and predictive maintenance (see Sect. 15.4).
- **Increase safety and security:** The task here is to make sure that people and machines remain unharmed in production areas, even during unforeseen downtimes. There are several relevant legislative and normative regulations in this regard. Due to technological change, which is being accelerated by the introduction of Industrie 4.0 concepts, among other things, new requirements are emerging for which the corresponding regulations must be worked out, such as for the certification of modular machines and systems. In addition, this point refers to the protection of data, information and intellectual property from the unauthorized access of third parties. Demands to information security are, of

course, nothing new, but have intensified significantly through the increase in networking and digitalization beyond corporate borders [4].
- **Shorten development times:** This refers to time to market, that is, the speed at which a company develops solutions and introduces them to the market. This capability of implementing product innovations quicker than other enterprises is certainly a primary success factor in global competition. The key is to thoroughly understand customer needs and be able to translate them into the corresponding specifications, then achieve them in a suitable product. Naturally, technology management and innovation management play a significant role. However, at the same time, the digitalization of the product creation process offers a considerable potential to decrease time to market [6, 7].
- **Improve usability and enrich operational procedures:** Despite all automation, people still play the main role in monitoring and optimizing production—this is not only true for today, but will continue to be the case in the future [8]. digitalization generally offers the potential of significantly raising transparency about the status of processes and resources, thus forming the basis for a further rise in efficiency and quality. Against this background, the goal is to raise this potential with the aid of new technologies, while increasing ergonomics for employees in production and alleviating them from monotonous and strenuous tasks.

15.1.2 Trends in the Applications

If you project these needs onto the current situation in the realm of machine and systems engineering as well as manufacturing companies, you can clearly see where the potential lies for further evolutionary development. Without wanting to give away the concrete technical approaches detailed below (see Sects. 15.3 and 15.4), the following cites the main points of potential which open up to machine and systems engineers upon consistent employment of Industrie 4.0 concepts and basic technologies [9–11]:

- **Flexibility**, that is, the ability to implement a variety of manufacturing tasks that are already taken into consideration in the development phase. This means that, in the future, machines and systems will be able to produce a much larger spectrum of replacement parts, components and end products. At the core, this is part of the answer to the demand for more adaptability (see Sect. 15.1.1), i.e. flexibility regarding technical requirements as well as temporal and capacity-related requirements.
- **Adaptivity**, the possibility for machines and systems of adapting to changing environmental conditions and targets. In other words, they will be capable of reacting autonomously to environmental or demand-related changes, adapting their functions to those changes and optimizing their operation dynamically according to various targets. This happens autonomously, without the user taking action and beyond application cases anticipated by developers [2].

- **Modularity:** Machines and systems today are generally developed and optimized based on a single purpose. This leads to them being built as monoliths, with only limited capability to meet flexibility and adaptivity needs. That is why, in the future, they should be constructed in a modular fashion, divided into individual, independent functional units. These units have specific tasks in the manufacturing process, and can be more or less combined freely with each other or replaced with other modules. Modularity pertains to all subsections, including mechanics, electrical system, electronics and software, as well as other domains as needed. To enable this, standardized interfaces and an object-oriented procedure are required in the engineering process [12].
- **Decentralization:** Modularization on the machine level is followed by a modularization of the automation technology and thus also machine control. Consequently, the control program is integrated in the software modules, which correspond to the function of the machine modules, and are distributed to various intelligent devices. These devices are not necessarily limited to the currently conventional stored program controls or industrial PCs, because other automation devices, such as drive controls, IO modules or communication infrastructure devices (Ethernet switches and routers) can also be used with them. Today, they are efficient enough to take on individual control or regulation tasks [13].
- **Plug and produce:** Plug and play, known from consumer and office IT, has only been implemented in automation technology to a small degree. However, especially due to modularization and decentralization and to control engineering and commissioning efforts, it has gained considerable significance. The main prerequisites are methods and models for the self-description and self-configuration of automation devices, which are currently the object of research and development [12]. The goal is to have automation devices and machine modules be able to "describe themselves" and parametrize themselves, such that commissioning can be performed automatically and efforts for configuration and parametrization considerably reduced. These principles are not only employed in the initial installation of a system, but also for the expansion or exchange of individual devices. In addition, plug and produce assumes standardized interfaces (mechanic and electrical, and especially regarding protocols, models and semantics).
- **Function integration**, that is, the expansion of a system's functionality to include new features. In this regard, miniaturization and new manufacturing technologies play a large role in bringing mechanics and electronics together. This not only pertains to automation devices themselves, but also their integration into the production equipment and processes, such as the integration of sensors into machine parts and components, or equipping them with communication interfaces.
- **Transparency of status and lifecycle information:** For this, machines continuously send their own status and configuration data as well as process data to the network, meaning throughout all phases of its lifecycle, in a transparent and complete manner. Services can then access this data to realize new applications

and services. The basis for this is provided by simple and inexpensive sensors. The increase in their precision and the availability of these signals and data in the entire network lead to a significant increase in data volume and thus the need for data transfer and storage. The term "big data" refers to this phenomenon [14].

- **Diagnosis of processes and status:** The primary application for the use of this data, which is already becoming evident, is the comprehensive and consistent recording of the status of production processes, machines and systems and the automation technology that drives these processes. This enables processes to be diagnosed and thus deviations in the running operation to be identified and signals to be sent. In addition, this forms the foundation for consistently optimizing manufacturing processes based on such detailed data, which is accessible online [15].
- **Reliability**, generally encompassing availability, reliability, functional security and information protection [2].
- **User friendliness**, so that users can easily, quickly, and comprehensibly interact with these systems. One significant prerequisite is to reduce complexity to the extent needed by users for their particular situations.
- **IT security:** Important aspects of Industrie 4.0 are digitalization and networking, which are also the requirements for achieving the potentials mentioned above. The flip side is the necessity to protect these principally open networks from third-party attacks, not only to protect a company's intellectual property, but also to guarantee functional security and integrity. That is why IT security measures need to be undertaken for future Industrie 4.0 solutions [16].

15.2 From Intelligent Technical Systems to Industrie 4.0

The consequence of these trends and needs is the further development of traditional mechanical and mechatronic solutions into intelligent technical systems, an effort which has been worked on intensively for a few years now. If such systems are networked together and interact with a common goal, so-called cyber-physical systems result [2]. They represent a core component of Industrie 4.0. An additional aspect is the digitalization of business processes, as well as the networking of companies and factories to form value creation networks. The following sections examine these systems in detail, illuminating examples of the potential they offer.

15.2.1 The Digitalization and Networking of Products

Industrie 4.0 and intelligent technical systems have an especially high relevance for production. The essence is the employment of information and communications technologies [1, 17]. This not only refers to the use of these technologies in machines and systems, but also in the development process for new products and their corresponding production systems, also known as the product lifecycle. Industrie 4.0 offers a way to optimize currently operating processes; and yet, it also offers much more: We are talking about the paradigm shift indicated above, which redefines value creation and business models in manufacturing companies [17]. The most important aspects include [9]:

- **Horizontal integration**, that is, the networking of several systems of the production IT along the value creation process within an enterprise as well as beyond corporate borders, to form value creation networks. This is nothing more than companies in the future being more completely networked than they are today—not only economically, but also with regard to information technology.
- **Vertical integration**, which refers to the networking of various levels in automation technology and corporate control, from actuators and sensors to control and supervision levels, to the planning level. The vertical networking and communication between hierarchical levels significantly improves information transparency. This, in turn, is the prerequisite for realizing analysis and monitoring functions as they are discussed in the context of Industrie 4.0., which Sect. 15.4 examines more closely. Based on vertical integration, the self-optimization of significant product resources and processes becomes conceivable, which promises a yet unattained level of flexibility and control of the increasing complexity of production processes. Through vertical integration, production systems can thus be designed to be more flexible and reconfigurable.
- **Consistency of engineering.** This especially refers to how business processes and value creation chains in product and production system creation can be optimized using consistent information models, tools and interfaces. In future, all instances involved in the product creation processes—from product design and production planning to production itself, to service and operation—should be able to access consistent and compatible information and models. This aspect is related to the performance creation process of a manufacturing company, while the first two aspects relate to order processing.

The core functions of this new architecture are

- The **digitalization** of signals and information from the process and systems. This includes equipping workpieces and operating materials, right down to individual devices, with communications interfaces and data models, in order to continually record significant process and status variables and make them transparent. Because simple components and devices are currently not capable of communication, there is significant potential here (see Sect. 15.3.1).
- Their **networking via internet technologies** and the safeguarding of information protection or **IT security**, that is, safe data provision and transfer processes that are protected from unauthorized access by third parties.
- The **continuous analysis** of the status of process and system. The term "industrial analytics" describes the data-driven generation of process models based on statistical methods and machine learning, as well as the continuous comparison of the model with the real process, to identify anomalies, predict errors and thus establish the foundation for **optimization measures** (see Sect. 15.4.2).

These measures pertain to the machines and systems themselves, as well as the production processes which they run.

- The **visualization** of the process status and **feedback into the process** close the control loop and lead the system to its optimal state, which is continually monitored and, when needed, re-optimized.
- These functions are typically mapped in **superordinate IT systems**, such as in web-based or cloud-based platforms. Such platforms are implemented decentrally in many cases, because they are flexible and can adapt to changing needs. However, they can also be used as local IT solutions (such as within a factory or production cell), for instance, to implement critical requirements to reaction times or information protection. The primary range of functions lies in the provision of calculation and storage capacity, as well as a fundamental infrastructure and interfaces for the implementation of desired services. At the same time, these solutions map the required functions for remote access, primarily including authorization maintenance and provision of more secure, encrypted transmission technologies such as VPN (see Sect. 15.4.1).
- The **consistency** of information models and communications technologies along the value creation chain and across corporate levels is targeted at being able to uniformly utilize data and information generated in a value creation system in all process steps and on all levels. Today, there are several monolithic systems, many with proprietary interfaces and information models, that lead to lossy transfer and incomplete transparency. To implement Industrie 4.0 concepts, however, consistent data exchange is a prerequisite, such that urgent action is needed in this regard. In addition to information models and communications technologies themselves, comprehensive semantics are required to secure the uniform interpretation of the information [4].
- The provision of all relevant information over the entire lifecycle of a product or machine in a digital model, the so-called digital twin, or **administration shell**, as the *Plattform Industrie 4.0* calls it [18]. In addition to the ability to communicate, the administration shell is one of the key aspects of the so-called Industrie 4.0 component. The administration shell does not have to be implemented in the component itself, but rather, the relevant information can also be stored in superordinate databases to which a clear link exists. The data stored there pertain to information on the type (material number, parts lists, data sheets), as well as the instance, that is, the concrete components used in an application (such as parameterization, status data and operating times).

While the new architecture dissolves the hierarchy of the established automation pyramid, it does not stand in contradiction to it. The validity of operational information and control systems (such as systems for enterprise resource planning (ERP), the manufacturing execution system (MES), supervisory control and data acquisition (SCADA) as well as process control itself are not called into question, but integrated. In doing so, new solutions may well be discovered, such as distributed control functions. At the same time, the most varied of architectures will be established in the future for the entire IT, of which cloud-based systems will make up a large part. In any case, however, corresponding solutions are necessary which ensure IT security and prevent unauthorized third-party access to data and the IP.

15.2.2 Definitions and Architectures for Industrie 4.0

The fundamental technological concepts of Industrie 4.0 (see also Sect. 15.2) described in the previous section were initially formulated to be abstract from any concrete requirements and specifications for specific use cases, and purposefully describe the breadth of the idea of digitalization and the networking of products. However, to make the matter concrete, prepare real applications for implementation and derive the necessary standards, various architecture models were created in a collaborative effort between companies, research institutes, associations and politics. The most significant of these are briefly described below (Fig. 15.2):

- **RAMI4.0/Reference architecture model for Industrie 4.0:** The RAMI4.0 was developed by the German *Plattform Industrie 4.0* in cooperation with leading enterprises, universities and industrial associations. It delineates the framework which makes up the main aspects of Industrie 4.0 and establishes the relationships between them. Specifically, RAMI4.0 includes the three dimensions of

Fig. 15.2 The main aspects of Industrie 4.0. (Weidmüller)

the (1) **hierarchy** of the workpiece or product, stretching to the proverbial networked world, the (2) **product lifecycle**, from the initial idea to its scrapping, and the (3) **functionality** ("layers"). The last dimension cited primarily refers to the digital representation of a product or machine, and structures it in individual functional layers. The RAMI4.0 serves to put the complex and manifold world of Industrie 4.0 into order, so that a common basis can be created for implementation projects and the necessary standardization can be prepared [19].
- **Industrie 4.0 component:** It links a real object from the production environment, such as a workpiece or machinery component, with an abstract model, such as a digital specification or a functional model. This virtual model is known as the **administration shell**. For instance, the Industrie 4.0 component 'IO system' not only includes the real hardware, based on electromechanics, electronics and software, it also encompasses 3D CAD models for system engineering, functional specifications for the selection process and business data for the offer generation process and commissioning. Furthermore, Industrie 4.0 components not only model general type specifications, but also information on the concrete employment of an individual instance. This means a product lifecycle can be individually traced. In addition, Industrie 4.0 components are capable of communication to a minimal extent, to be able to exchange relevant information [18, 20].
- **IIRA/Industrial Internet Reference Architecture:** The North American equivalent to the German *Plattform Industrie 4.0* is the Industrial Internet Consortium. This association of enterprises and research institutions in the environment of the Internet of Things has developed an architecture which was publicized under the name Industrial Internet Reference Architecture. The IIRA includes the three dimensions (1) **key characteristics** (safety, security, resilience), (2) **viewpoints** (business, usage, functional and implementation) and (3) **systems concerns** (in the sense of development goals). These dimensions constitute a concrete system in the environment of Industrie 4.0, such that, analogous to RAMI4.0, the development tasks can be derived, with a view to a concrete product development as well as with a view to standardization or technology development activities [21].

These three reference architectures surely do not solve concrete development tasks of a company; instead, they structure the development process and thus support a target-oriented approach, under consideration of all relevant aspects. They simultaneously serve to form a framework for a specific application field, which maps all relevant aspects and establishes a relationship between them. Within this framework, existing standards can be allocated, missing standards derived and, especially, interfaces between the individual solution components of Industrie 4.0 can be identified and development requirements derived from them. Thus, these reference architectures contribute greatly to strategic technology development and standardization, and help set the course for a synchronized and efficient implementation of Industrie 4.0 solutions.

15.2.3 Areas of Application for Industrie 4.0

Even if the concept of Industrie 4.0 certainly does not address any fundamentally new challenges and is partly based on technologies which are already available today, it forms the foundation for a paradigm change in production and automation. This opens up the potential for innovation in the areas of components, solutions and business models which we cannot yet imagine today. Nevertheless, there are currently already pilot applications that can certainly demonstrate the potential of Industrie 4.0. A few such approaches will be briefly mentioned here, which do not represent a complete list. The following section will examine them in more detail.

The digitalization of the process and status data of an industrial system creates the basis for generating a precise model. Using such models, anomalies can be identified and a **forecast for the status of processes and the system** can be derived, with which a time-related projection of faults and malfunctions is possible. This enables the system operator to react even before these undesired states occur, to secure the availability of the systems and the stability of the processes [15, 22].

The use of technologies for the **self-optimization of production processes** goes even further: It allows changes to be detected in the process with the aid of intelligent sensors. The causes for such changes may be related to the raw materials, or in the machine or tool itself. On this basis, the machine control can use self-optimization methods to autonomously derive measures and initiate them to return the process to its original state or even reach a new optimum [23].

A further example from the context of energy management is **energy-efficient process optimization**: Here, a manufacturing process is extensively equipped with sensors, and the resulting sensor signals are digitized. These signals are evaluated using intelligent algorithms—the term industrial analytics is used for this process—and linked to further information, such as the current energy price. This offers the possibility of optimizing the process with regard to cost and increasing its energy efficiency. Furthermore, the energy behavior of the production system can be predicted in such a way that peaks in energy consumption can be identified, and the operator can reduce or switch off processes in order to prevent load peaks [24].

The step toward production networks is based on the shift to decentral production units or manufacturing modules. To avoid the need for servicing, which highly-qualified employees would have to perform on site—**remote maintenance** solutions are of great significance. As a rule, web-based services are used which, on the one hand, realize a continuous data and information exchange, and on the other hand, also offer a safe and flexible infrastructure.

The final application example is the **digitalization of the engineering** of production systems. Whereas the development, realization and lifecycle management of machines and systems, in many cases, are hindered today by heterogenous information models and IT systems, Industrie 4.0 concepts lay the groundwork for relevant data and models to be used and interpreted autonomously and continuously, that is, without interface loss. This is based on standardized information models, for which technologies such as OPC-UA [25] or eCl@ss [26] are significant components. In addition, it requires comprehensive semantics describing how these models and the respective data are to be interpreted. The goal must be the capability for extensive self-description, which covers all phases of the life-cycle and thus all types and instances of a product which takes into account the requirements of all engineering disciplines and offers access to all relevant systems via the corresponding implementation.

15.3 The Infrastructure for Industrie 4.0

As we have seen in Sect. 15.2.1, digitalization of products is at the core of Industrie 4.0. It is the prerequisite for horizontal and vertical integration, and thus the foundation for the potential addressed. In addition, it plays an important role in the implementation of new manufacturing structures characterized by modularization and decentralization. Yet, where do we stand regarding the infrastructure for digitalization in future production, especially with regard to the availability and accessibility of relevant data and information in a manufacturing operation? What further consequences will there be on infrastructure that can we already identify today?

15.3.1 Data Consistency and Information Transparency

In most cases, we find two different worlds regarding data consistency and transparency: office IT and production IT. Due to their differing origins, they are based on different technologies and architectures which today are difficult to integrate. For example, machine control is the node at which all sensor data come together, but which only makes that data available to the systems on a higher level after deliberate programming. What is more, the systems on various levels work with different interfaces, protocols and information models, such that they are hardly permeable. In many instances, this is also due to the use of proprietary interfaces which work within the realm of one manufacturer, but can only be made transparent to systems of other makers with considerable programming effort.

Consistency can be achieved if the systems on the various planning levels of a company use uniform protocols and information models which also allow degrees of freedom for the specific requirements of any system. For this purpose, service-oriented architectures and cloud-based solutions are also being increasingly employed in the realm of automation. They allow components and systems to exchange information transparently across all levels, provided of course, that they use uniform interfaces and information models and that this information can also be interpreted by the corresponding semantics.

Ethernet has established itself as a foundation for network infrastructure. It has also been further developed and will continue to evolve for the specific needs of production. Specific protocols have been added, depending on purpose and specifications. Approaches to merge them in a consistent way include technologies such as OPC UA [25], MQTT [3] and MTConnect [27], which have already established themselves as quasi-standards in specific applications. In addition to Ethernet, however, there are further potentials for other communications technologies for special applications, such as radio-based procedures for remote or mobile machines or subordinate communications systems such as IO-Link for the networking of simple and inexpensive devices.

Yet, in any case, an important prerequisite is that all relevant components are capable of communication, so that they can be integrated into the overall system. According to the Industrie 4.0 components mentioned in Sect. 15.2.2, passive communication capability is the minimum. However, if we are talking about automation devices, such as sensors or interface modules, active communication is needed. This means that, for instance, traditional, analog signal transducers are expanded with the addition of an Ethernet interface, via which process and status variables of the transducer itself as well as the connected devices can be transmitted to the superordinate systems. They can thus be integrated vertically into the overall system, and the signal path of the classic automation equipment from the sensor to the control unit is not affected by this process.

With all of the openness and permeability of office IT and production IT, steps must be taken to ensure that unauthorized access from outside is not possible. Attacks by third parties leading to the loss of data or intellectual property or causing malfunctions in the production run cannot be ruled out completely. However, employing the corresponding technologies and encryption procedures or certificate-based authentication supplies the prerequisites for adequate IT security. These technologies are partially integrated in the established standards of automation, but some must be implemented using dedicated solutions, such as security routers.

15.3.2 Industrial Connectivity for Future Production Structures

Horizontal and vertical integration, as well as the transformation in the way production facilities will be structured in the future, have a considerable impact on the infrastructure of industrial automation. The distribution of communication, in addition to the necessary electrical energy, from sensor and control signals and possibly other subsections (such as pneumatics and compressed air), represent a significant share of the costs, but are also linked to high installation expenditures. That is why electrical connection technology—industrial connectivity—is a decisive factor in the implementation of Industrie 4.0 [11].

Comprehensive digitalization first requires that numerous sensors are installed in the system and in the process. Along with the increasing modularization of production facilities, this leads to a considerably higher number of interfaces for which the corresponding connection technology is required. Compared to the currently used components, there is a significant potential for innovation to increase the ease of handling and durability, so that they will withstand the rough conditions of production.

That is why connectors with tool-free installation will play a major role. At the same time, hybrid and application-specific solutions for energy, signals and data have the potential to reduce the number of interfaces, lower costs and increase flexibility.

Even if radio technology can profit from digitalization and a gain in usage, we can assume that in the future the major portion of signals and data will be transmitted in a line-based manner, that is, with cables and connectors. Nevertheless, there is a great potential for innovative transmission technologies, such as the contactless transmission of energy, signals and data. It offers the advantage of durability and wear-free operation, even under high environmental demands and frequent operation. Connectivity based on contactless technologies supports the modularity of future systems and ensures their flexibility and availability. Further potential lies in the integration of sensors: The monitoring of connectors contributes greatly to the availability of production systems. Furthermore, status information can also be gained. In addition, components which, to date, have not been able to be monitored can be upgraded retroactively to serve as Industrie 4.0 components (see Sect. 15.2.2), which can then be integrated into automated systems.

15.3.3 Integrated Solutions for the Infrastructure of Industrie 4.0

On the next-highest abstraction level above the individual components—on the level of infrastructure for energy, signals and data—there is even more potential. Integrated solutions (see Sect. 15.3), such as the infrastructure box created for the research factory "Smart Factory KL", enable modular machines to be supplied in a simple and flexible manner and to be integrated into the infrastructure. The infrastructure box represents a modular and flexible, expandable solution for the distribution of energy, signals and data, as well as safety and security, which also collects relevant infrastructure status variables, such as energy consumption, and makes them available for evaluation. It thus supports the so-called 'plug and produce' procedure, meaning quick and simple commissioning—not only for the connector technology itself, but also for its embedding in superordinate IT systems. Technologies such as OPC-UA allow data and information to be distributed without having to implement additional, complex middleware [28] (Fig. 15.3).

To meet the demands of a secure and reliable infrastructure in modular production facilities, one can also implement new topologies: While today's infrastructure is generally realized as a line with individual branches, modular solutions require tree or circular structures. The consistent continued development stems from structuring the system as a network, offering not only safety in cases of faults or malfunctions, but also the added benefit of "routing" energy, much like data packets, meaning data is able to be distributed through the network according to corresponding optimization criteria. Last but not least, industrial connectivity is complemented by the digital model which, serving as an administration shell of an Industrie 4.0 component [18], encompasses all information pertaining to that component and its specific use. There is potential in optimizing the engineering, as well as in supporting commissioning and replacement on site.

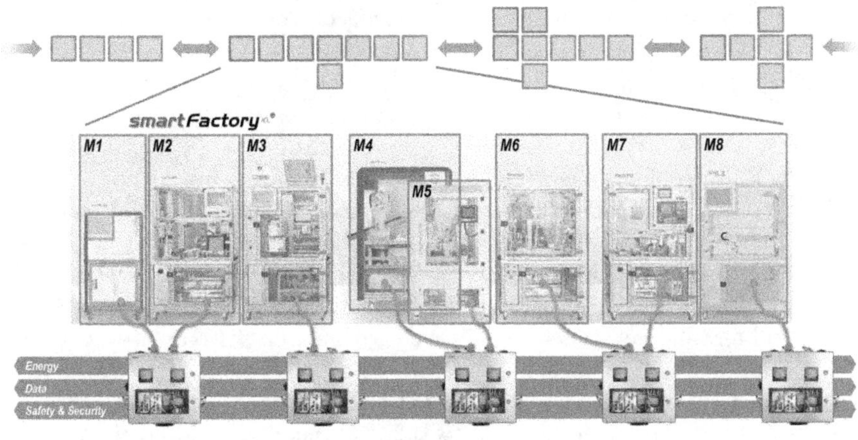

Fig. 15.3 Integrated solution for the infrastructure of modular and flexible production facilities. (Weidmüller)

15.4 Data-Based Optimization of Availability and Productivity

If we turn once again to the needs of manufacturing companies (see Sect. 15.1.1), we see that the main topics by far are availability and productivity. Here, the use of the data, made possible by digitalization, plays a major role. It creates a degree of transparency previously unknown, and thus also meets the requirement of being able to contribute greatly to optimization, based on this precision and updated description of the status of machines and processes. The first step is remote maintenance. Analytics and self-optimization build consistently on digitalization, offering the potential to take companies to a new level of value creation.

15.4.1 Remote Maintenance

Three primary aspects of Industrie 4.0 include modularization of machines and systems, their decentralization as well as their transformation into value creation networks, in which manufacturing companies will work in the future. Simultaneously, the demands to availability and productivity are increasing, whereas digitalization and networking are not making automation technology any easier, but rather more complex. To nevertheless offer fast and professional service with such structures, and be capable of reacting quickly if something should go wrong, remote maintenance, meaning the direct access to the configuration, parameterization and programming of a machine, is gaining in importance.

The term 'remote maintenance' refers to using a networked interface to gain direct access to the user interface of a corresponding machine from a distance, in order to receive all status variables and messages, as well as perform actions to the current configuration of the machine, if needed. Consequently, these machines can also be operated and monitored from a distance just as effectively as if the service technician were on site. The advantages lie in the speed—diagnosis and maintenance become immediately possible, as long as they can be performed without direct access to the hardware of the machine—and in the money not spent on needing a service technician on site, thus saving human resource and travel costs.

Remote maintenance solutions are based on the infrastructure for digitalization and networking, as they are described above in Sect. 15.3. The main components include I/O systems and communication-capable interface modules for the collection of important process and status variables, as well as the network infrastructure, including Ethernet switches and routers, which, on the one hand, enable the digitalization and communication of information, and on the other hand, ensure information protection during access and transmission of data. However, at the core are solutions for remote access, which is generally achieved through web-based technologies. They form the basis for data and information management, as well as the automated monitoring of the system state and the necessary status and warning messages. In addition, the configuration and user management, as well as IT security, with the corresponding encryption methods and a certificate-based authentication, are prerequisite to being able to safely operate remote maintenance solutions.

Lastly, let us consider that classic remote maintenance solutions based on status data and diagnostic information are being increasingly augmented by modern interaction technologies. One example is the use of augmented reality to make it easier for service personnel to perform their tasks and to provide concrete tips and instructions for problem solving. In addition, remote maintenance solutions can also be used for direct communication from machine to machine, to be able to ensure secure networking over long distances.

15.4.2 Industrial Analytics

The term "big data" has been a buzzword for some time now. It stands for the processing of large data volumes with the aid of statistical and mathematical methods. The attribute "big" refers to the three dimensions of data volume, processing velocity and complexity as well as variety [14]. Within the context of Industrie 4.0, we use it to indicate the ability to use data generated by a production process or value creation system to increase productivity [15]. We can also use the term 'industrial analytics' in this context (see Fig. 15.4).

The starting point is data which is generated by sensors and automation devices in a production facility. This data represents process variables, that is, information describing the actual manufacturing process, as well as status variables of the machines and their assemblies and components. Depending on the respective job and target, it is a good idea to also incorporate additional measurement technology, for instance, to be able to identify previously unknown relationships and negative effects. This raw data is digitized and provided to the corresponding database

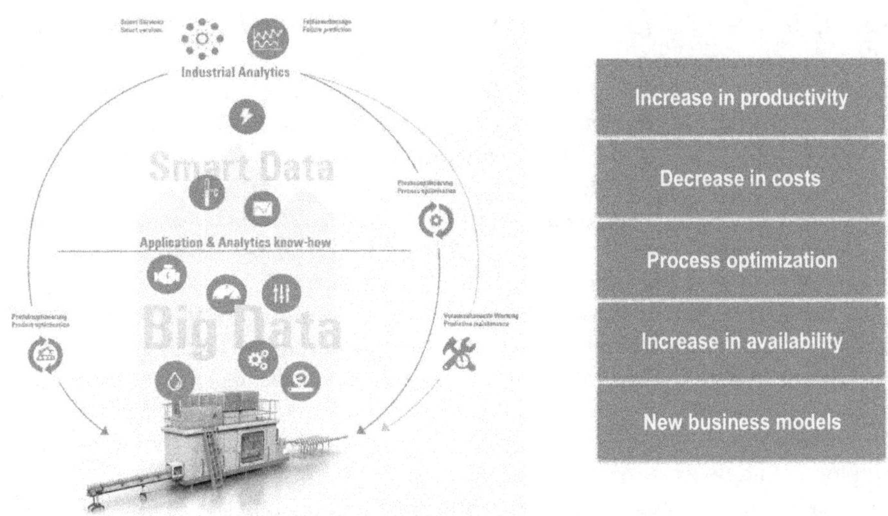

Fig. 15.4 Industrial analytics procedure. (Weidmüller)

systems for processing. In this regard, by the way, the term big data is ambiguous: It can also refer to the number of set measurement points; in typical machines, such as a plastic injection molding machine, they can easily add up to 200 or more signals. The spectrum ranges from simple, binary switches to sensors with a high signal and demand interval. Nevertheless, the data volume remains controllable for typical automation devices, because the volume of raw data for a manufacturing machine with various binary and analog sensors generally lies in a range from tens to a few hundred megabytes for a period of about one week. From today's standpoint, the upper end of the spectrum for data volume in production is certainly image processing systems and other complex measuring instruments, which continually generate a considerable data volume [29].

In the next step, the truly significant data must be extracted from the raw data. Of course, this step is very dependent upon the respective task and optimization criteria. Things like statistical procedures, filter systems and classification mechanisms or pattern recognition procedures are employed for this purpose. This foundation is used to generate a model of the technical systems corresponding to the target. There are several different procedures from the environment of machine learning available which can be used. The primary goal is to identify the relevant connections and dependencies in the course of individual signals and in the correlation of various signals. In addition, there are other dedicated algorithms, such as ones which can extract the relevant statuses of a machine or process from a given data amount or identify the behavioral patterns in a set of comparable processes or products [15].

The models generated in this way are compared with the actual data during the running time of the process. Deviations indicate anomalies, that is, effects that deviate from the desired behavior. Whether these deviations will actually lead to a malfunction or initially have no negative effects needs to be evaluated in each case. Such an evaluation leads, on the one hand, to a decision about whether the process can continue to run or whether intervention, such as maintenance or optimization measures will be taken. On the other hand, this information is fed back into the model to further develop and specify it. The objective is to obtain natural models that can run autonomously and can derive the necessary action options without additional outside support. For this process, advanced analytics methods are being increasingly employed that work predictively and thus, based on the data being collected at the time, can make a prediction about the future behavior of the process. Such technologies enable error detection even before the error has occurred, thus giving operators the capability of minimizing malfunction downtime and ensuring the optimal availability of their processes. A visualization of the results of the analytics aids operators on site in interpreting those results and implementing the corresponding measures [22].

In principle, the steps of building a model and generating a prediction should be achievable solely based on the extracted data. However, practical situations have shown that the key to the success of industrial analytics projects lies in the close cooperation of the data scientists—those specialists for algorithms, who mainly work in a data-oriented manner—with the engineers—those specializing in the process and the operating materials, who are familiar with known modes of action and, in many cases, work in an experience-based way. The danger of working on a purely data-related basis lies in the proverbial "hearing the grass grow," while the danger in an exclusively engineering-based viewpoint is "not seeing the forest for the trees." The potential of integrating both approaches is gaining and considering new knowledge without negating extensive experience-based knowledge.

Alternative architectures are possible for the implementation of an analytics solution. First, there are the process-related components, which collect and digitize process and status variables. They must be capable of communication, in order to be able to feed the collected signals into the network. Such components can, for example, include so-called remote I/O systems or communication-capable signal transducers, as well as industrial control units. All relevant data must be put into a common data model to prepare it for analysis. The question as to where the data is stored and processed depends on the required storage space, calculating capacity, processing speed and access possibilities. The spectrum ranges from cloud-based solutions to industrial PCs or embedded devices that are installed on premise, that is, directly in the process. Cloud-based solutions are characterized by virtually unlimited storage and calculating capacity, yet due to their reaction time behavior, are generally not real-time-capable. Automation devices possess comparably little storage and calculating capacity, but, due to their on-premise installation and resulting shortest reaction times, are suitable for process control. Against this background, the typical storage- and calculation-intensive phase of modelling is usually accomplished in cloud-based solutions, while the execution of the process runtime model can also be implemented on premise, due to the considerably lower demands to storage and calculation [22].

15.4.3 Self-Optimization in Production

Closely related to industrial analytics is the self-optimization of production systems and processes. While analytics focuses on the recognition of patterns and cause-effect correlations in large data sets and on predicting system behavior, the goal of self-optimization is to adapt system behavior during run time to changing environmental conditions and, especially, changing targets. Both, however, are based on the digitalization of the production process and the comprehensive collection of process and status data.

Self-optimization overlays the technical system and process and the relevant signals and information with multi-layer information processing. These layers are characterized by extensive adaption possibilities, as well as interconnections of various proximities to the technical process and thus various reaction speeds, similar to the layer model of cognition science for behavior control. Process control is found on the lowest level, which reacts in hard real time but can only be varied between different configurations and parameterizations. At the highest level, so-called cognitive operators are used to optimize the system according to various targets, thus having the ability to intervene extensively in the system configuration and system behavior. Examples include the optimization of system behavior in accordance with security or with energy efficiency, which may be relative at various times during operation and must be prioritized accordingly, in order to ensure functional capability [2].

One example for the use of self-optimization in production is for industrial forming processes, in which the behavior of the operating resources (such as machine dynamics, speed, temperature and wear) as well as external influencing variables (for instance, the stability and geometry of the semi-finished products and influences from upstream process steps) can significantly affect the quality of the articles being produced. The use of self-optimization techniques enables the employment of various regulator configurations, depending on operating conditions and the basic parameters of production (such as specifications from disposition and synchronization with upstream and downstream process steps), as well as the ability to switch on or off certain tools and specifically calibrate these options to match particular situations and targets [23, 30].

A second example is the energy-efficient process optimization of plastic injection molding, an energy-intensive process, due to the necessary thermodynamics and the high dynamics of the operating materials themselves. Linking process control with a superordinate optimization procedure according to energy conservation criteria enables the optimal operating point between productivity, quality and energy efficiency to be achieved, based on respectively current basic parameters. At the same time, this serves as an example for the use of vertical integration, because, to implement energy-efficient process optimization, energy costs in real time must be available, which, for instance, can be achieved through the integration of data from the EPEX energy exchange [15].

In addition to the potential of self-optimization, both examples also demonstrate the benefits of vertical and horizontal integration (see Sect. 15.2.1). These practical examples also provide solutions for the issues mentioned in Sect. 15.1.2 regarding the trends and potentials in mechanical and systems engineering, especially adaptivity, flexibility and diagnosis.

15.4.4 Cyber-Physical Production Systems

If we project the characteristics of self-optimizing systems onto a production network consisting of various machines, systems and production plants, we receive a concrete example for a cyber-physical production system, also known as CPPS. In comparison with an intelligent technical system, which reacts independently to environmental influences and can implement the relevant optimal state at any time, a CPPS can connect several such sub-systems that are connected with each other—some over great distances—and communicate and cooperate with each other, to form a superordinate system. Sect. 15.5 shows the technical concepts developed and being further expanded by the leading-edge cluster it's OWL (Intelligent Technical Systems OstWestfalenLippe) [2] (Fig. 15.5).

To refer back to the examples mentioned in Sect. 15.4.3, a CPPS would, for instance, be created if data from upstream process steps are integrated in the determination of the optimal process parameters of a particular production resource. In this way, for example, a manufacturer of steel tape can collect information on the geometry, alloying and stability of the semi-finished product in his or her processes and provide this information to the operator of the forming process, who can then set the optimum values. A further example is the possibility of obtaining the overall energy consumption of all operating equipment in a factory and predict any threatening, costly load peaks, which could then be prevented by a targeted reduction in the speeds of individual machines, under consideration of the current order situation, production jobs already started and the capabilities of individual pieces of equipment.

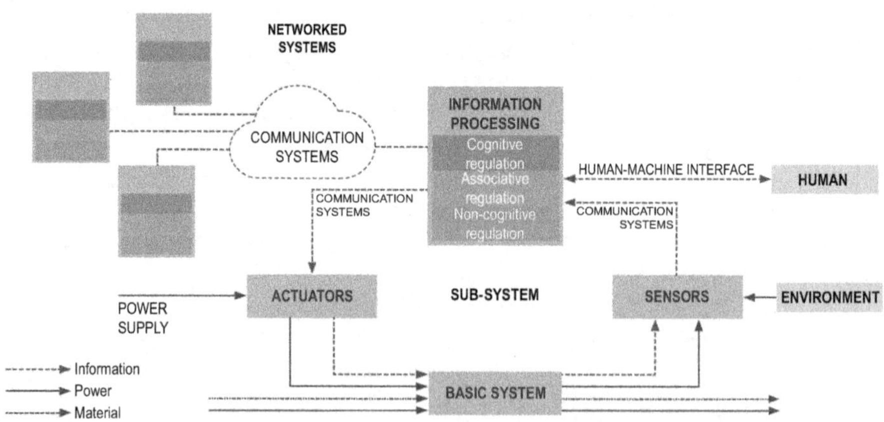

Fig. 15.5 The technical concepts of leading-edge cluster it's OWL for intelligent technical systems. (Gausemeier et al. [2]; it's OWL)

15.5 The Factory of the Future Requires More Than New Technologies

The previous sections, especially the examples described, illustrate that the concept of Industrie 4.0 offers concrete potential for manufacturing companies: because it will only be a matter of time before technologies that are new to manufacturing but meet existing needs will be introduced to the manufacturing process—thus the question is when, not if. This is not only true for the concepts and examples described in Sects. 15.3 and 15.4. Beyond those usages, there are several other potential uses for information and communications technologies in production, including, for instance, the digitalization of engineering, the support of production-related tasks using virtual methods or the generation of new business models for manufacturing companies and their suppliers.

The **digitalization of engineering** means the use of consistent and comprehensive models and interfaces to increase the efficiency and quality of the development and construction processes for production plants. In addition to standardized information models, its foundation is formed by comprehensive semantics, in order to ensure clear interpretation of the information mapped in the models. Virtual reality and augmented reality offer manufacturing enterprises the potential to support people in their process steps by providing them with information. This enhances their activities and enables them to perform unfamiliar steps simply and safely.

The concept of Industrie 4.0 and the expansion of the existing technology portfolio to include digitalization also puts manufacturing companies and their suppliers in the position of being able to **expand their business models**. Where, for the most part, the sale of a physical product and servicing throughout the product lifecycle are the current business focus, the ability to take an acute look at the status of processes and systems opens up opportunities for new services and business models. Examples include the optimization of manufacturing processes, operator models for production resources, benchmarking or the flexibilization of the supply chain, for which digitalization is a prerequisite in any case. However, we can also be sure that we currently lack the imagination to completely forecast the new opportunities that will be created by Industrie 4.0.

On the other hand, it is important to meet the prerequisites. Several approaches have been cited for the development of concrete, new technologies, and even more can be found in other essays in this book. Yet, in addition to technological development itself, **standardization** is also a significant component, as it is needed to ensure comprehensive applicability and investment security. International demands must be taken into consideration, to avoid one-time solutions and technological dead ends.

Among these prerequisites, however, is the methodology by which such systems are to be developed. The term "**systems engineering**" describes the framework of procedural models, methods and tools that can be employed for the development of today's products. Yet along the way to intelligent technical systems, further action is needed [31]. The same is true for the legal framework: The new technical concepts upon which Industrie 4.0 are based also require new legal and normative approaches, so as not to stall its implementation. Last but not least, the path to Industrie 4.0 must also include the support of industrial associations, trade unions and politics, in order to establish the necessary investment-friendly framework and create the right incentives. These efforts will make the concept for the factory of the future—Industrie 4.0—a comprehensive social challenge, yet one which creates a varied and promising spectrum of new opportunities.

References

Primary references

1. Kagermann, H., Lukas, W.-D., & Wahlster, W. (2011). Industrie 4.0: Mit dem Internet der Dinge auf dem Weg zur 4. Industriellen Revolution. *VDI Nachrichten,* 2011(13).
2. Gausemeier, J., Dumitrescu, R., Jasperneite, J., Kühn, A., & Trsek, H. (2015). Auf dem Weg zu Industrie 4.0: Lösungen aus dem Spitzencluster it's OWL. http://www.its-owl.de/fileadmin/PDF/Informationsmaterialien/2016-Auf_dem_Weg_zu_Industrie_4.0_Loesungen_aus_dem_Spitzencluster.pdf. Accessed 12 May 2016.
3. MQTT.org. (2014). MQTT Version 3.1.1 OASIS Standard. http://docs.oasis-open.org/mqtt/mqtt/v3.1.1/os/mqtt-v3.1.1-os.html. Accessed 12 May 2016.
4. Plattform Industrie 4.0. (2016). Aspekte der Forschungsroadmap in den Anwendungsszenarien. Result paper of the AG2 of the Plattform Industrie 4.0. http://www.plattform-i40.de/I40/Redaktion/DE/Downloads/Publikation/anwendungsszenarien-auf-forschungsroadmap.html. Accessed 12 May 2016.
5. Roland Berger Strategy Consultants. (2015). Trend Compendium 2030. http://www.rolandberger.com/gallery/trend-compendium/tc2030/. Accessed 12 May 2016.
6. Gausemeier, J., & Plass, C. (2014). *Zukunftsorientierte Unternehmensgestaltung. Strategie, Geschäftsprozesse und IT-Systeme für die Produktion von morgen.* Munich: Hanser.
7. Sendler, U. (2009). *Das PLM-Kompendium. Referenzbuch des Produkt-Lebenszyklus-Managements.* Berlin: Springer.
8. Plattform Industrie 4.0. (2016). Arbeit, Aus- und Weiterbildung in den Anwendungsszenarien. Discussion paper of the AG4 of the Plattform Industrie 4.0. http://www.plattform-i40.de/I40/Redaktion/DE/Downloads/Publikation/anwendungsszenarien-fuer-arbeit-aus-und-weiterbildung.html. Accessed 12 May 2016.
9. Köhler, P., Six, B., & Michels, J. S. (2015). Industrie 4.0: Ein Überblick. In C. Köhler-Schute (ed.), *Industrie 4.0: Ein praxisorientierter Ansatz.* Berlin: KS-Energy.
10. Plattform Industrie 4.0. (2015). Industrie 4.0 – White Paper R&E topics. http://www.plattform-i40.de/industrie-40-whitepaper-fue-themen-stand-7-april-2015-0. Accessed 12 May 2016.
11. Zentralverband Elektrotechnik- und Elektronikindustrie ZVEI e.V. (2015). *Elektrische Verbindungstechnik für Industrie 4.0? – Herausforderungen an die elektrische Verbindungstechnik durch den Einzug von "Industrie 4.0"-Konzepten.* Frankfurt: ZVEI.
12. Heymann, S., Jasperneite, J., Schröck, S., & Fay, A. (2015). *Beschreibung von modularisierten Produktionsanlagen in Industrie 4.0.* Transcript of the Congress Automation 2015, Baden-Baden, June 11–12.

13. Hempen, U., Albers, T., Kreft, S., Holm, T., Obst, M., Fay, A., & Urbas, L. (2015). *Dezentrale Intelligenz für modulare Anlagen.* Congress Automation 2015, Baden-Baden, June 11–12.
14. Reichert, R. (2014). *Big Data: Analysen zum digitalen Wandel von Wissen, Macht und Ökonomie.* Bielefeld: transcript.
15. Maier, A., & Niggemann, O. (2015). *On the learning of timing behavior for anomaly detection in cyber-physical production systems.* International Workshop on the Principles of Diagnosis (DX), Paris.
16. Plattform Industrie 4.0. (2016). Security in RAMI4.0. Leitfaden der AG Sicherheit der Plattform Industrie 4.0. http://www.plattform-i40.de/I40/Redaktion/DE/Downloads/Publikation/security-rami40.html. Accessed 12 May 2016.
17. Plattform Industrie 4.0. (2015). Umsetzungsstrategie Industrie 4.0. Result Report of the Plattform Industrie 4.0. http://www.plattform-i40.de/umsetzungsstrategie-industrie-40-0. Accessed 12 May 2016.
18. Plattform Industrie 4.0. (2016). Struktur der Verwaltungsschale. Fortentwicklung des Referenzmodells für die Industrie 4.0-Komponente. Result paper of the AG1 of the Plattform Industrie 4.0. http://www.plattform-i40.de/I40/Redaktion/DE/Downloads/Publikation/struktur-der-verwaltungsschale.html. Accessed 12 May 2016.
19. DIN SPEC 91345:2016-04. (2016). Reference Architecture Model Industrie 4.0 (RAMI4.0).
20. Verein Deutscher Ingenieure e.V. (2014). *Statusreport Industrie 4.0 Gegenstände, Entitäten, Komponenten.* Berlin.
21. Industrial Internet Consortium. (2016). The Industrial Internet Reference Architecture Report. http://www.iiconsortium.org/IIRA.htm. Accessed 12 May 2016.
22. Gatica, P. C. (2016). Produktivitätssprung in der Kunststofffertigung durch den Einsatz von Advanced Analytics. VDMA event "Mehrwert in Produktion und Service durch Big Data Ansätze," ("Added Value in Production and Service through Big Data Approaches"), Frankfurt, April 6.
23. Damerow, U., Borzykh, M., Tabakajew, D., Schaermann, W., Hesse, M., Homberg, W., et al. (2015). Intelligente Biegeverfahren. Entwicklung selbstkorrigierender Fertigungsprozesse in der Umformtechnik. *wt Werkstattstechnik online, 2015*(6), 427–432.
24. Strohbach, M., & Toll, C. von. (2016). Fallbeispiel Energy Management in der Produktionswirtschaft – Einsparungspotential mit datenorientierter Analyse und Big Data Technologien. bitkom Big Data Summit, Hanau, February 16, 2016.
25. OPC Foundation. (2016). OPC Unified Architecture Specification. https://opcfoundation.org/developer-tools/specifications-unified-architecture. Accessed 12 May 2016.
26. eCl@ss e.V, Classification and Product Description. (2016). eCl@ss Technical Standards. http://wiki.eclass.eu/wiki/Category:Rules_and_standards. Accessed 12 May 2016.
27. MTConnect Institute. (2015). MTConnect Standard Version 1.3.1. http://www.mtconnect.org/standard. Accessed 12 May 2016.
28. Jacob, H. (2015). Smarte Fabrik ohne Kopfzerbrechen. *A&D,* 4(2015). Munich: Publish Industry.
29. Gaukstern, T. (2016). *Umsetzung von Predictive Maintenance in der Produktion – Herausforderungen und Lösungen am Beispiel einer Spritzgussmaschine.* VDMA Congress "Predictive Maintenance 4.0," Frankfurt, February 23.
30. Verein Deutscher Ingenieure e.V. (2014). *Statusreport Industrie 4.0 CPS-basierte Automation.* Berlin.
31. Gausemeier, J., Dumitrescu, R., Steffen, D., Czaja, A., Wiederkehr, O., & Tschirner, C. (2013). *Systems Engineering in der industriellen Praxis.* Paderborn: Heinz Nixdorf Institute, University of Paderborn: Department of Product Creation.

Further reading

32. Dumitrescu, R., Gausemeier, J., Kühn, A., Luckey, M., Plass, C., Schneider, M., & Westermann, T. (2016). Auf dem Weg zur Industrie 4.0: Erfolgsfaktor Referenzarchitektur. http://www.its-owl.de/fileadmin/PDF/Informationsmaterialien/2015-Auf_dem_Weg_zu_Industrie_4.0_Erfolgsfaktor_Referenzarchitektur.pdf. Accessed 12 May 2016.
33. Gausemeier, J., Lanza, G., & Lindemann, U. (2012). *Produkte und Produktionssysteme integrativ konzipieren. Modellbildung und Analyse in der frühen Phase der Produktentstehung.* Munich: Hanser.
34. Michels, J. S., Gatica, P. C., & Köster, M. (2015). *Anomalien und Ineffizienzen in Produktionsanlagen erkennen.* Automatisierungstechnische Praxis.
35. Plattform Industrie 4.0. (2016). Technischer Überblick: Sichere unternehmensübergreifende Kommunikation. http://www.plattform-i40.de/I40/Redaktion/DE/Downloads/Publikation/sichere-unternehmensuebergreifende-kommunikation.htmlZugegriffen. Accessed 12 May 2016.